Certificate of Cloud Security Knowledge (CCSK v5) Official Study Guide
In-Depth Guidance and Practice

Graham Thompson

Certificate of Cloud Security Knowledge (CCSK v5) Official Study Guide
by Graham Thompson

Copyright © 2025 Graham Thompson. All rights reserved.

Printed in the United States of America.

Published by O'Reilly Media, Inc., 141 Stony Circle, Suite 195, Santa Rosa, CA 95401.

O'Reilly books may be purchased for educational, business, or sales promotional use. Online editions are also available for most titles (*http://oreilly.com*). For more information, contact our corporate/institutional sales department: 800-998-9938 or *corporate@oreilly.com*.

Acquisitions Editor: Megan Laddusaw
Development Editor: Sara Hunter
Production Editor: Jonathon Owen
Copyeditor: Audrey Doyle
Proofreader: Krsta Technology Solutions

Indexer: nSight, Inc.
Cover Designer: Susan Brown
Cover Illustrator: Karen Montgomery
Interior Designer: David Futato
Interior Illustrator: Kate Dullea

August 2025:   First Edition

Revision History for the First Edition
2025-08-18:   First Release

See *http://oreilly.com/catalog/errata.csp?isbn=9781098173418* for release details.

The O'Reilly logo is a registered trademark of O'Reilly Media, Inc. *Certificate of Cloud Security Knowledge (CCSK v5) Official Study Guide*, the cover image, and related trade dress are trademarks of O'Reilly Media, Inc.

The views expressed in this work are those of the author and do not represent the publisher's views. While the publisher and the author have used good faith efforts to ensure that the information and instructions contained in this work are accurate, the publisher and the author disclaim all responsibility for errors or omissions, including without limitation responsibility for damages resulting from the use of or reliance on this work. Use of the information and instructions contained in this work is at your own risk. If any code samples or other technology this work contains or describes is subject to open source licenses or the intellectual property rights of others, it is your responsibility to ensure that your use thereof complies with such licenses and/or rights.

978-1-098-17341-8

[LSI]

Table of Contents

Preface.. xi

1. **Cloud Computing Concepts and Architectures**.................................... 1
    Defining Cloud Computing   4
        Resource Pools   4
        Tools   4
        Two Definitions of Cloud Computing   5
    Logical Model of the Cloud   6
        Infostructure   6
        Applistructure   6
        Metastructure   7
        Infrastructure   8
    Cloud Computing Models   9
        Essential Characteristics   9
        Cloud Service Models   11
        Cloud Deployment Models   17
    Cloud Security Responsibilities, Frameworks, and Process Models   20
        Shared Security Responsibility Model   20
        Cloud Security Frameworks and Patterns   21
    Summary   24

2. **Principles of Cloud and IT Governance**.. 25
    Corporate Governance   26
    IT Governance   27
    Cloud Governance Changes and Challenges   29
    Effective Cloud Governance   30
        1. Establish a Governance Hierarchy   30
        2. Leverage Cloud-Specific Security Frameworks   30

3. Define Cloud Security Policies	31
4. Set Control Objectives and Specify Control Specifications	31
5. Define Roles and Responsibilities	31
6. Establish a Cloud Center of Excellence or Similar Model	31
7. Conduct Requirements and Information Gathering	31
8. Manage Risks	32
9. Classify Data and Assets	32
10. Comply with Legal and Regulatory Requirements	32
11. Maintain a Cloud Registry	32
Cloud Center of Excellence	34
Key Components of a CCoE	35
Benefits of a CCoE	36
Structuring IT Security Governance	36
Frameworks	37
Policies	37
Control Objectives	40
Control Specifications and Implementation Guidance	40
Thinking All the Way Through the Governance Stack	43
Foundational Governance Principles and Guidelines	44
Determining Risk Tolerance	44
Classifying Data and Assets	45
Identifying Regulatory and Legal Requirements	46
Cloud Security Alliance Tools	46
Cloud Controls Matrix	46
Security, Trust, Assurance, and Risk Registry	48
Summary	48
3. Navigating Risk, Audit, and Compliance.	**51**
Basics of Risk Management	51
Understanding the Risk Management Process	54
Step 0: Determining Risk Tolerance	55
Step 1: Risk Identification	55
Step 2: Risk Assessment (or Risk Analysis)	55
Step 3: Risk Treatment	56
Step 4: Risk Monitoring	57
Step 5: Risk Communication and Reporting	58
Assessing Cloud Services	58
Step 1: Assess the Business Request	59
Step 2: Review CSP Documentation	59
Step 3: Review External Sources	64
Step 4: Map to Compliance Requirements	64
Step 5: Map to Data Classification	65

	Step 6: Define Required and Compensating Controls	66
	Step 7: Obtain Final Approval	66
Governance, Risk Management, and Compliance Tools	66
	Where Compliance Requirements Come From	67
	Artifacts of Compliance	68
	Jurisdictions	68
	Data Localization Laws	72
	Compliance in the Cloud	73
Summary	74

4. Guide to Cloud Organization Management.. 75
Organizational Hierarchy Models 75
   Definitions 76
   Organizational Structures 76
   Organizational Capabilities Within a Cloud Service Provider 79
   Building a Hierarchy Within a Provider 80
   Managing Organization-Level Security Within a Provider 81
Considerations for Hybrid and Multicloud Deployments 85
   Organizational Management for Hybrid Cloud Security 86
   Organizational Management for Multicloud Security 89
   Tooling and Staffing for IaaS/PaaS Multicloud 90
   Organizational Management for SaaS Hybrid and Multicloud 91
Summary 94

5. Identity and Access Management.. 97
How IAM Is Different in the Cloud 97
Fundamental Terms for Understanding IAM 98
   Persona 100
   Attribute 100
   Entitlement 100
   Entitlement Matrix 100
   Role 100
   Attribute-Based Access Control 101
   Policy-Based Access Control 101
   Authoritative Source 103
   Federated Identity Management 103
   Identity Provider 103
   Relying Party 103
   Assertion 104
Federated Identity Management 104
   Common Federation Standards 104
   How Federation Works 105

Managing Users and Identities for Cloud Computing	108
Strong Authentication and Authorization	110
Authorization	110
Authentication	111
Privileged User Management	112
Privileged Identity Management	112
Privileged Access Management	113
Summary	113

6. Detecting Threats in the Cloud 115

Cloud Monitoring	115
Logs and Events	117
Posture Management	119
Cloud Telemetry Sources	119
Management Plane Logs	119
Service Logs	120
Resource Logs	121
Cloud Native Security Tools	121
Cloud Security Posture Management	122
SaaS Security Posture Management	122
Cloud Workload Protection Platform	122
Data Security Posture Management	123
Application Security Posture Management	123
Cloud Infrastructure Entitlement Management	123
Cloud Detection and Response	124
SIEM and SOAR: The Detective and the Robot Guard	124
Security Information and Event Management	124
Security Orchestration, Automation, and Response	127
Collection Architectures	128
Log Storage and Retention	128
Cascading Log Architecture	129
AI for Security Monitoring	130
Summary	130

7. Infrastructure and Networking 133

Cloud Infrastructure Security	133
Cloud Customer Security Techniques	134
CSP Infrastructure Security Responsibilities	135
Infrastructure Resilience	136
Single-Region Resiliency	137
Multiregion Resiliency	138
Multiprovider Resiliency	138

	Cloud Network Fundamentals	139
	Common SDN-Based Components	142
	Cloud Connectivity	144
	Cloud Network Security and Secure Architectures	145
	Preventive Controls	145
	Detective Security Controls	146
	Infrastructure as Code	147
	Zero Trust for Cloud Infrastructure and Networks	148
	Software-Defined Perimeter	149
	Zero Trust Network Access	150
	Secure Access Service Edge	150
	Summary	152
8.	**Cloud Workload Security**	**153**
	Securing Virtual Machines	153
	Virtual Machine Challenges and Mitigations	155
	Creating Secure VM Images with Factories	155
	Recommended Tools and Best Practices for VMs	157
	The Vulnerability Management Lifecycle	158
	Snapshots, Public Exposures, and Exfiltration	159
	Securing Containers	160
	Container Image Creation	160
	Container Networking	162
	Container Orchestration and Management Systems	163
	Container Orchestration Security	166
	Secure Artifact Repositories	166
	Runtime Protection for Containers	167
	Securing Serverless and Function as a Service	168
	FaaS Security Issues	169
	IAM for Serverless Computing	169
	Securing AI Workloads	170
	Large Language Model Assets	170
	Top Nine Large Language Model System Threats	171
	AI Risk Mitigation and Shared Responsibilities	173
	Data Security for AI	174
	Model Security	174
	Infrastructure Security	174
	Supply Chain Security	175
	Summary	175
9.	**Keeping Data Safe in the Cloud**	**177**
	Data Structures	177

Storage Security Primer	178
Cloud Storage Types	178
Object Storage	178
Volume Storage	181
Database Storage	181
Other Types of Storage	182
Data Security Tools and Techniques	183
Data Classification	183
Identity and Access Management	185
Access Policies	186
Data Loss Prevention	186
Cloud Data Encryption at Rest	186
Encryption and Key Management	187
Key Management Service	187
Hardware Security Module	187
Encryption Key Options	187
Encryption Implementation Options	189
Symmetric Versus Asymmetric Encryption	191
Data Encryption Recommendations	195
Data Security Posture Management	196
Summary	196

10. Building Secure Applications. 199

Secure Development Lifecycle	200
Stages of the CSA DevSecOps SDLC	201
Threat Modeling	204
Risk Assessment Matrix	206
Testing: Predeployment	207
Testing: Post Deployment	209
Architecture's Role in Secure Cloud Applications	210
The Impact of the Cloud on Architecture-Level Security	211
Architectural Resilience	211
IAM and Application Security	212
Secrets Management	212
Secrets Management Workflow	213
DevOps and DevSecOps	213
The DevOps/DevSecOps Lifecycle	214
CI/CD Pipelines	215
Web Application Firewalls and API Gateways	217
Agent-Based Deployment	218
Cloud Native Provider Services	218
Third-Party Marketplace Solutions	218

WAF and DDoS Protection as a Service	219
Summary	219

11. Incident Response: From Detection to Recovery........................... 221
Incident Response	222
Incident Response Lifecycle	222
Phase 1: Preparation	223
Phase 2: Detection and Analysis	223
Phase 3: Containment, Eradication, and Recovery	224
Phase 4: Post-Incident Analysis	224
How the Preparation Phase Changes in Cloud Environments	225
Training for Cloud Incident Responders	226
How Detection and Analysis Change in Cloud Environments	228
Impact of the Cloud on Incident Analysis	228
Cloud System Forensics	229
Forensics Blast Zones	232
Cloud Forensics: Container and Serverless Considerations	233
Containment, Eradication, and Recovery	234
Containment	234
Eradication	235
Recovery	236
Post-Incident Analysis	236
Summary	237

12. Deep Dive into Zero Trust and AI... 239
Zero Trust	239
Zero Trust Principles	241
Zero Trust Technical Objectives	241
Protective Framework	241
Simplified User Experience	242
Reduced Attack Surface	243
Reduced Complexity	244
Continuous Authentication	244
Improved Incident Containment and Management	245
Principle of Least Privilege	245
Zero Trust Business Objectives	246
Reduce Risk	246
Improve Compliance	246
Demonstrate Commitment to Cybersecurity	246
Core Logical Zero Trust Components	247
Zero Trust Security Frameworks	248
Software-Defined Perimeter	248

Zero Trust Network Access	248
Zero Trust Pillars	249
Zero Trust Maturity Model Levels	250
Zero Trust Design and Implementation	252
Step 1: Define the Protect Surface	252
Step 2: Map the Transaction Flows	253
Step 3: Build a Zero Trust Architecture	253
Step 4: Create a Zero Trust Policy	254
Step 5: Monitor and Maintain the Environment	254
Zero Trust and Cloud Security	255
Artificial Intelligence	256
Characteristics of AI Workloads	256
How AI Intersects with Cloud Security	256
Summary	258

13. Preparing for Your CCSK Exam 259

Studying for the CCSK Exam	259
Exam Details	260
Signing Up for the CCSK Exam	261
Exam Tips	261
Using ChatGPT as a Study Tool	263
About Generative AI Large Language Models	263
The Importance of Projects	265
Uploading Files	265
Downloading Files	265
Introduction to Prompt Engineering	266
Components of a Good Prompt	267
Creating Study Tools	269
Generating Pretest Questions	269
Creating Flashcards	270
Playing Games	272
Study Plans	272
ChatGPT Annoyances	272
Final Exam-Day Thoughts	273

Index 275

Preface

"The beautiful thing about learning is nobody can take it away from you."
—B.B. King

Cloud computing has fundamentally reshaped how organizations build, secure, and scale their digital infrastructure. With this transformation comes a new set of risks, responsibilities, and security approaches that professionals must understand to protect cloud environments effectively. The Certificate of Cloud Security Knowledge (CCSK), now in its fifth version, was developed by the Cloud Security Alliance (CSA) to help professionals and organizations with a framework for building cloud security implementations. The CCSK is one of the most widely recognized vendor-agnostic certifications in cloud security. It offers a strong foundation in best practices for governance, cloud provider assessment, cloud security architecture, and the technical aspects of securing cloud environments.

This study guide was created to support your preparation for the CCSK exam. It follows the structure of the official CSA study guide and goes deeper into key subjects that all security professionals should be well versed in. No matter if you are a recent graduate, work in the IT field, perform a compliance role, or seek to round out your cloud knowledge as a seasoned cybersecurity professional, this book will serve you well in obtaining your CCSK certification. The following is a list of the knowledge areas covered in this book:

- Cloud computing concepts and architectures
- Cloud governance
- Risk, audit, and compliance
- Organization management
- Identity and access management
- Security monitoring
- Infrastructure and networking

- Cloud workload security
- Data security
- Application security
- Incident response and resilience
- Related technologies and strategies

Each chapter explains core concepts clearly, connects theory to real-world scenarios, and includes review questions to reinforce key takeaways. Whether you're studying independently or in a group setting, this guide is designed to keep you focused on what matters most for the exam—and more importantly, for advancing your career.

Who This Book Is For

I wrote this book for people who want to get ahead and are considering obtaining certification in the field of cloud security. If you are reading this, you are already interested in the security field. Although my top priority in writing this book was to help you pass the CCSK exam, another objective I had during its creation was to set you up for success in obtaining other security certifications. I obviously can't address everything in the field of security in a single book, but I can honestly say I believe the content in this book fills in the assumed knowledge of the CSA material and expands on important material beyond just the exam.

My goal in writing this book was to make the content approachable, comprehensive, and real. I threw away the thesaurus in favor of creating a reader-friendly approach. I wrote this book in the same way that I teach the official CCSK training course. My goal is to teach you, not to sound like a professor. Throughout the chapters, I try to share real-world stories from my years of experience working with large, regulated companies in a variety of industries. I believe these experiences happened so that I could pass these stories on to you to assist with your learning.

I hope you find this study guide useful not only for passing the exam, but also for helping you become a more effective and confident cloud security professional.

Conventions Used in This Book

The following typographical conventions are used in this book:

Italic
: Indicates new terms, URLs, email addresses, filenames, and file extensions.

`Constant width`
: Used for program listings, as well as within paragraphs to refer to program elements such as variable or function names, databases, data types, environment variables, statements, and keywords.

`Constant width bold`
: Shows commands or other text that should be typed literally by the user.

`Constant width italic`
: Shows text that should be replaced with user-supplied values or by values determined by context.

This element signifies a tip or suggestion.

This element signifies a general note.

This element indicates a warning or caution.

O'Reilly Online Learning

For more than 40 years, *O'Reilly Media* has provided technology and business training, knowledge, and insight to help companies succeed.

Our unique network of experts and innovators share their knowledge and expertise through books, articles, and our online learning platform. O'Reilly's online learning platform gives you on-demand access to live training courses, in-depth learning paths, interactive coding environments, and a vast collection of text and video from O'Reilly and 200+ other publishers. For more information, visit *https://oreilly.com*.

How to Contact Us

Please address comments and questions concerning this book to the publisher:

O'Reilly Media, Inc.
141 Stony Circle, Suite 195
Santa Rosa, CA 95401
800-889-8969 (in the United States or Canada)
707-827-7019 (international or local)
707-829-0104 (fax)
support@oreilly.com
https://oreilly.com/about/contact.html

We have a web page for this book, where we list errata and any additional information. You can access this page at *https://oreil.ly/ccsk-v5*.

For news and information about our books and courses, visit *https://oreilly.com*.

Find us on LinkedIn: *https://linkedin.com/company/oreilly-media*.

Watch us on YouTube: *https://youtube.com/oreillymedia*.

Acknowledgments

Thanks to the team at O'Reilly for their support during the creation of this book. Sara, you are a rockstar with the patience of a saint! Megan, I can't thank you enough for this incredible opportunity. It is truly an honor to call myself an animal author.

As always, I want to thank my wife for putting up with me. I love you, Princess. You have given me everything I never knew I wanted. To my four sons, I am so proud of the men you have become. I couldn't ask for more as a father. I love you all.

CHAPTER 1
Cloud Computing Concepts and Architectures

Well begun is half done.
—Aristotle

This chapter serves to set you on a solid footing for what is about to come in the rest of this book. To pass the Certificate of Cloud Security Knowledge (CCSK) exam, you need to fundamentally understand the similarities and differences that cloud computing has with what I call *traditional IT*.

Traditional IT is what companies have been doing for decades: physical datacenters, physical servers, physical networking, and physical drives. In contrast, everything in the cloud is virtual. Well, there are, of course, the physical components just mentioned, but those are procured (sometimes even created) and managed by the provider in a datacenter it runs.

To the cloud service customer (CSC), everything in the cloud is virtual. Some people may argue that the cloud is just running your servers in someone else's datacenter and that traditional IT and cloud computing aren't that different. Some people also say the world is flat. Rest assured, it is a very different world once you start looking into some of the finer points, especially when it comes to security.

Cloud computing can offer organizations significant agility, resiliency, security, and economic benefits if done properly. However, to realize these benefits, it is essential to properly understand and adopt cloud models, ensuring that cloud architectures and practices align with the features and capabilities of cloud platforms.

From an application perspective, simply migrating an existing application or asset to a cloud service provider (CSP) without any changes, known as *forklifting* or *lift-and-shift*, often fails to deliver the expected agility, resiliency, and security, and can even increase costs.

From a security perspective, it is critical to appreciate that security in the cloud is a shared responsibility. I know, you've probably heard this so often that it has started to lose its importance, but it cannot be overstated. Dismissing this key aspect of the cloud can lead companies to a false sense of security. "The provider does everything for me!" is a dangerous and untrue assumption. Do you think your cloud provider does backups for you? It may, or it may not.

In one real-life example, 140 customers of the European cloud provider OVHcloud launched a class action lawsuit for more than €10 million because they assumed OVHcloud backed up their data. When a fire destroyed a datacenter that was hosting their data, they lost everything. OVHcloud stated in its documentation that clients were responsible for backing up their own data, but who's got time to read those pesky documents, right? We'll see more about the documents you should read prior to using a CSP in Chapter 3.

Now, let's imagine the following scenario. Larry, a salesperson at Driveline Solutions (no, not *you*, Larry), is caught stealing customer information from the company's cloud-based customer relationship management (CRM) vendor and selling this information to the competition. Larry is subsequently fired. Six months later, you realize Larry is still stealing client information from the CRM software. What happened? Nobody at Driveline Solutions removed Larry's access to the CRM software when he was terminated. Identity and access management is always the customer's responsibility. After all, how can you expect the CRM vendor to know Larry was fired? We'll see more about the shared responsibility model of the cloud later in this chapter.

Now consider that you were hired to manage cloud access for a business that is using 50 software-as-a-service (SaaS) applications. This means you have to manage 50 different identity stores. That's a very tall task, if not frankly impossible to do at scale. I'll talk about a way to manage identities with federated identity management (FIM) in Chapter 5.

Put simply, if you don't understand the shared responsibility model or the answer to the question "who does what," you'll never be able to properly secure your usage of the cloud. It's that important.

Table 1-1 highlights some examples of cloud breaches. I added them to show what can happen when the cloud customer doesn't understand the shared responsibility model and fails to secure their usage of cloud services.

Table 1-1. Cloud breaches

Customer	Cloud provider	Year	Individuals impacted	Breach information
Shanghai Police	Alibaba Cloud	2022	~1 billion	Unsecured database exposed personal information of approximately 1 billion Chinese citizens for over a year
Verifications.io	Google Cloud	2019	763 million	Unsecured database exposed email addresses and other personal details of over 763 million users
Facebook	Amazon Web Services (AWS)	2019	540 million	Over 540 million user records exposed by third-party developers in publicly accessible AWS Simple Storage Service (S3) buckets
Microsoft (Customer Support)	Azure	2019	250 million	Misconfigured security rules exposed customer support records of 250 million users
Capital One	AWS	2019	100 million	Misconfigured web application firewall allowed access to over 100 million customer records
Uber	AWS	2016	57 million	Attackers accessed AWS S3 buckets using compromised credentials, exposing data of 57 million users and drivers
Cognyte	AWS	2021	5 billion records	Unsecured AWS Elasticsearch database exposed 5 billion records indexed by a search engine
Prestige Software	AWS	2020	Unknown (millions)	Misconfigured S3 bucket exposed millions of records from travel booking platforms
Verizon	AWS	2017	14 million	Third-party vendor misconfigured AWS S3 bucket, exposing data of 14 million customers
FedEx	AWS	2017	Multiple	Unprotected AWS S3 bucket exposed scanned documents including passports and driver's licenses

With that introduction to the cloud out of the way, let's discuss the concepts of cloud security as presented by the Cloud Security Alliance (CSA) and what you'll be tested on as part of the CCSK exam.

Exam Note

You'll be seeing quite a few references to standards by NIST, ISO/IEC, and other organizations in this book. You don't need to start studying these documents. The CCSK exam is about cloud security according to the CSA; it's not about NIST standards. The exam is open book, so if you're facing a question about a Special Publication number, for example (the number, not the content within), you can quickly look it up with a Ctrl-F in the CSA's "Certificate of Cloud Security Knowledge Official Study Guide." This document covers everything from the CCSK study guide (and then some!).

Defining Cloud Computing

As mentioned in the introduction, cloud computing is built by the CSP. CSCs get access to a seemingly endless supply of resources they can procure in an instant. But what do they use to do that? The answer is pools and tools.

Resource Pools

Let's start with pools. There are three different types of pools of resources: compute, network, and storage. The pools are virtualized, for the most part, with limited exceptions that I'll talk about later in this chapter.

This section provides a very high-level view of the capabilities these pools supply. There are many offerings that will be covered throughout the book. For now, I'm keeping it as straightforward as possible.

The virtualization for compute is much like you may imagine. There are hypervisors that allow a physical machine (called the *host*) to run multiple virtual machines (VMs) that are called *instances* (as opposed to *guests* in traditional IT). The hypervisor used (e.g., VMware, Xen, KVM) is not really the CSC's concern.

From a network pool perspective, the CSP has many IP addresses that can be dynamically assigned and released on demand. The network pool goes deeper than just IP addresses, but I think you get the general idea. The pools allow for something to be allocated and then released when it is no longer used by the customer.

Finally, possibly the easiest pool to think of is the storage pool. Think of your typical storage area network (SAN). The SAN may have hundreds of terabytes of storage that is sliced up based on a customer's requirement; essentially, every user gets a networked "home" drive available to them.

Tools

Now, on to the tools part. Quite simply, the tools I'm referring to are the abstraction, automation, and orchestration capabilities of the cloud. Everything, from the initial request of an instance (again, basically a guest VM) through to the billing on a pay-per-use basis, is abstracted, automated, and orchestrated.

Abstraction

Abstraction simply hides (abstracts) the complexity behind what I call the "magic curtain." Providers are very good at masking complexity and presenting a very familiar way for customers to build and configure things. Take building a cloud server, for example. All you have to do as the customer is select the amount of processor power (vCPUs), memory, and storage you want. Most cloud providers offer a wide range of what someone once called "T-shirt sizes." Want a server instance with one CPU and

1 GiB of RAM? Just click a box. Want an instance with 448 CPUs and 24 TiB of RAM? Just click a box. Of course, the provider may limit such large and costly instances based on manual review and approval, but at the end of it, it's as simple as clicking a box. The abstraction hides all the complexity away from you. This abstraction is a leading feature that makes the cloud an on-demand self-service consumption model.

In traditional server virtualization, the hypervisor is responsible for abstracting the hardware away from the guest VM, which we call an *instance* in cloudspeak. It both segregates the instance from other instances on the same physical server and isolates its resources from other resources. This isolation aspect is critical because, without it, there's no such thing as security in the cloud. This is an example of how the pools we discussed earlier are built.

Automation

Barring special circumstances that may require a manual review (such as the scenario in the preceding section), everything in a cloud provider environment is fully automated using APIs. Quite simply, if there isn't automation, you don't have a cloud system, as it won't meet the essential characteristics of the cloud (covered later in this chapter).

Orchestration

Turning our attention now to orchestration, think of a conductor of an orchestra. The conductor manages musicians to create the music you listen to when you are at a performance. In a way, the conductor is managing the workflow of the music. This is what cloud controllers do. They manage the individual components to process a complex workflow, from the initial request for resources, to the billing, and ultimately to the customer no longer using the resources. This results in a fully functional, automated system for customers to adopt and adapt to meet their needs.

Two Definitions of Cloud Computing

These foundational aspects of the cloud allow for the following definition of cloud computing from the National Institute of Standards and Technology (NIST) Special Publication 800-145:

> Cloud computing is a model for enabling ubiquitous, convenient, on-demand network access to a shared pool of configurable computing resources (e.g., networks, servers, storage, applications, and services) that can be rapidly provisioned and released with minimal management effort or service provider interaction.

Another organization, called the International Organization for Standardization (ISO), defines cloud computing in its ISO/IEC 22123 (which replaced ISO 17788 and the broader 17789 documents in February 2023) as follows:

> A paradigm for enabling network access to a scalable and elastic pool of shareable physical or virtual resources with self-service provisioning and administration on-demand.

You may have noticed I referred to ISO as "ISO/IEC." This is because ISO works with another organization, called the International Electrotechnical Commission (IEC), as a joint technical committee for the ISO standards that involve technology. So, when you see ISO, ISO/IEC, or JTC 1, they all essentially mean the same thing.

Notice the similarities? They both say pretty much the same thing. Remember that the CSA bases its definition of "cloud" on NIST 800-145 and ISO/IEC 22123.

Logical Model of the Cloud

Now let's dive into a logical model of the cloud, which divides the cloud into four distinct layers. Examining the cloud in this way helps delineate the differences between traditional IT and cloud services. The biggest change between traditional IT and cloud services that impacts security lies in the metastructure. These layers are shown in Figure 1-1 and are covered in the sections that follow.

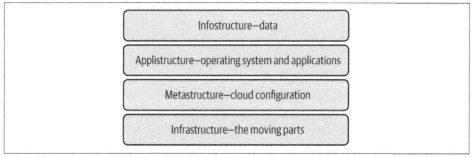

Figure 1-1. Logical layers of the cloud

Infostructure

Infostructure is where the information and data reside. This could be file storage, databases—whatever. Security in this layer doesn't really change; how you secure data may change based on the service being used to store it, but the principles of data security remain the same.

Applistructure

Applications and all of the services used to build and support them reside in the applistructure. Your applications could be running on a Microsoft or Linux server of your own, or they could be running in a wide variety of new technologies such as containers, microservices, or serverless compute (I cover these technologies in Chapter 8 when I address cloud workload security). If you take an image of a running system and migrate it into the cloud, nothing changes from a security perspective. In this scenario, operating systems will always need patches and application security still applies as it always has. As you start to build cloud native applications to take advantage of the new technologies the cloud offers, your security is likely to change dramatically.

Metastructure

The metastructure is the game-changing aspect of the cloud. In this layer, you configure and manage a cloud deployment of any type. The single biggest thing you need to understand immediately about the difference between the cloud and traditional IT is the metastructure. It is within the metastructure layer that you build the virtual tools required for a virtual world (the cloud).

The metastructure is also where you "adopt and adapt" provider controls to secure your environment. Controls such as security groups (virtual firewalls) are built by the CSP and made available to customers. Customers then have to define and apply their own firewall rules to limit network access to a server instance.

You'll perform configuration in the management plane through a graphical user interface (GUI), through a command-line interface (CLI), or programmatically through an application programming interface (API), depending on what the provider offers to interact with its infrastructure.

Application Programming Interfaces

Although numerous APIs exist, the two most commonly used and most relevant for cloud services at this time are Representational State Transfer (REST) and Simple Object Access Protocol (SOAP). REST APIs use standard HTTP calls (GET, PUT, POST, DELETE) and are widely used in web and mobile applications due to their lightweight nature and ease of integration. From a security perspective, REST is reliant on other security services. For example, to encrypt data in transit, REST would rely on TLS for this task. As for SOAP APIs, these use XML for messaging and have security built-in (via support for WS-Security standards). Although considered by many as a "legacy" standard, SOAP is still often used when security is paramount, such as high-value internal transactions.

Of note, other APIs such as gRPC (developed by Google) and GraphQL (developed by Facebook) are growing in popularity but are not widely supported like REST APIs.

Right now, I'd like to call out the need for virtual tools for a virtual world. Want to add a new user for SaaS? You do it here. Want to set up a zero trust network in infrastructure as a service (IaaS)? This is the place to do it. If your team knows nothing about the metastructure, it knows nothing about securely configuring, managing, or responding to incidents in the cloud.

Make no mistake: you are in charge of configuring and managing this layer. Configuration and management mistakes in this layer are why so many companies have been burned in the past when using cloud services (and will likely continue to be burned for the rest of time).

The following sidebar discusses an example from a project I was on that clearly summarizes the importance of understanding metastructure security.

From the Trenches: Metastructure Logging

I was assigned to an IaaS assessment project for a company with over $1 billion in revenues. The IaaS implementation was built by a global consulting company with billions of dollars in revenue. In other words, this wasn't exactly a mom-and-pop shop with a cloud infrastructure built by the next-door neighbor's kid.

During this project, I asked the company's security director to show me the metastructure logs. These are needed to see who was logging in to the cloud console, what they were doing (to meet compliance requirements), and so on. Kind of important, don't you think? The director tried to access them and realized he didn't have permission. I asked if his team would have access, and he said that if he didn't have access, nobody on the security team had access to the logs. So we agreed he would get this fixed, and we rescheduled for the next week.

During the next meeting, the director said he was given access to the logs. When I took a look at them, however, the logs were empty. This global, multibillion-dollar company never turned on logging in the metastructure. It had logging enabled at the applistructure layer but not at the metastructure layer. No logging, no alerts, no compliance. (As a side note, this is what assessments are for, which I discuss in Chapter 3. They catch mistakes like this.)

Infrastructure

The server, networking, and storage pools exist at the infrastructure layer. Security at this layer involves properly securing the physical world. Do you run a private cloud that you own? If you do, then you own this layer. Have a public cloud? If so, this layer is owned and operated by someone else. In other words, it's the provider's world, and you're just working in it.

To that end, let's now look at the cloud computing model that the CSA uses as a foundation of cloud services.

Cloud Computing Models

In "The NIST Definition of Cloud Computing (SP 800-145)," NIST provides a widely accepted framework that defines the core elements of cloud computing. This document describes cloud services as having five essential characteristics, three service models, and four deployment models. The CSA builds on this foundational document to frame the discussion of the cloud to promote effective security strategies in the cloud. Figure 1-2 shows the different essential characteristics, service models, and deployment models.

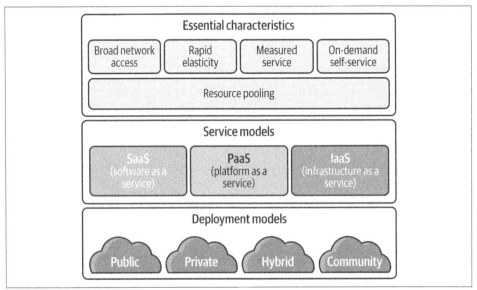

Figure 1-2. Essential characteristics, service models, and deployment models

Essential Characteristics

The essential characteristics of NIST's cloud framework lay out what the customer should expect from their cloud provider. All of these characteristics should be offered by the provider. Simply put, if you don't get these from the provider, you're not getting a cloud service; you're getting cloudwashed. *Cloudwashing* is a term used to describe companies that try to present their service as a cloud offering, but aside from marketing, there is no cloud capability.

There are five essential characteristics you need to know about, and one additional characteristic defined by some as "essential." Confusing, I know! I discuss them all in the following sections.

On-demand self-service

The on-demand self-service characteristic gives you the ability to provision resources on your own, without human intervention at the provider's side. Put another way, if your provider tells you that your ticket for a new server instance is very important and it will act on it in 48 to 72 hours, you're being cloudwashed. In Chapter 6, you'll see how this self-service characteristic can be used to automate security response capability using APIs through the implementation of event-driven security.

On-demand self-service is the source of *Shadow IT*. This is simply employees sourcing their own cloud solutions to perform their work. More on this in the upcoming discussion of SaaS.

Broad network access

Cloud computing is also characterized by availability over a network (such as the internet). There is no special requirement for direct physical connectivity or provider-supplied network connectivity. For example, you could manage an entire IaaS implementation via the browser on your cell phone. (I highly recommend not doing this, but you could if you really want to ruin your eyesight!)

Broad network access is also a major change for security. You no longer have a perimeter that that your company has spent years of effort and money building. As a result, you need to place new security controls in the cloud to secure the workloads themselves as well as secure your access to the cloud service.

Resource pooling

Resources (compute, network, storage) are the most fundamental characteristics of the cloud. Resources are pooled and consumers are granted access. A consumer's access to the pools is tightly isolated from that of other consumers, typically based on policies at the provider's side. NIST 800-145 specifically calls out multitenancy as being an aspect of this essential characteristic. More on this in a few moments.

Rapid elasticity

This characteristic is the most powerful aspect of the cloud. It enables consumers to scale resources based on demand, often automatically (note that access can be manual and scaling still applies). Scaling can occur in a couple of different ways. *Scaling up* generally refers to using more powerful servers (such as a four-CPU configuration as opposed to two), whereas *scaling out* refers to adding more servers (e.g., adding servers to a web farm to service requests).

Depending on the application and architecture, you want to make sure your provider supports scaling either up or out to meet demand. In addition to having the ability to add capacity when demand increases, you need to be able to *scale down* when demand drops. This aspect is critical, because you don't want to scale up to respond to a temporary increase in demand and then stay there in perpetuity and be surprised when the provider's bill is suddenly three times what it was the month before!

Measured service

The measured service characteristic makes the cloud a pay-as-you-go model of computing: you're simply charged for what you use. Another term often used to describe measured service is *utility computing*, which is akin to how you consume electricity or water from a utility. In the past, companies would build factories beside a body of water to generate their own power. Eventually, governments built a shared power system that companies used instead.

Multitenancy

Multitenancy means being used by multiple customers (called *tenants*). NIST, ISO/IEC, and the CSA each look at multitenancy in a slightly different way:

NIST 800-145
    Multitenancy is addressed as part of the resource pooling essential characteristic.

ISO/IEC 22123 (replaces ISO/IEC 17788)
    Multitenancy is its own essential characteristic of the cloud.

CSA
    Multitenancy is built into cloud computing and is a natural part of how it works.

Exam Note

Be prepared to have a question that may test you on knowing that, unlike NIST, ISO/IEC specifically calls out multitenancy as a separate essential characteristic.

Cloud Service Models

Despite what marketers would have you believe, there are only three cloud service models you need to know about. These are IaaS, platform as a service (PaaS), and SaaS. These are often referred to as the *SPI stack*. The CSA unsurprisingly calls all the other made-up "X as a service" offerings *XaaS*.

Think of these service models as being built on top of each other, as shown in Figure 1-3. At the base, you have IaaS. PaaS is a platform built on top of IaaS, and then finally, you have SaaS at the top.

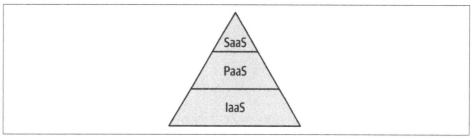

Figure 1-3. Cloud service models

Infrastructure as a service

IaaS is the underlying foundation that consists of the physical facilities and infrastructure hardware. The hardware itself may be customized, proprietary, or standard off the shelf, but it's still hardware, like you'll find in any datacenter. The difference, however, is in the resource pooling, abstraction, automation, and orchestration.

Abstraction is usually based on virtualization of servers, networks, and/or storage. It is this abstraction that allows for the pools of resources to be created (e.g., a group of hypervisors all working together). The orchestration enables a controller to request resources from the pools of resources, and all this is automated through the use of APIs (mostly RESTful APIs).

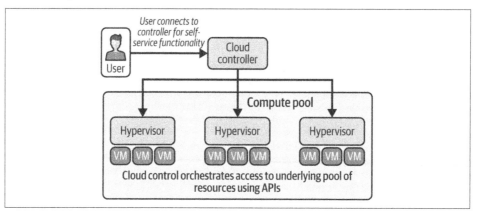

Figure 1-4. Cloud controller orchestration

Let's look at a scenario that ties this all together. Say you want to create an Ubuntu server instance with two CPUs, 12 GB of RAM, 2 TB of storage, and two network cards. Here's what happens behind the scenes at the provider side (shown in Figure 1-4):

- The cloud controller contacts the compute controller to request that a new server with two CPUs and 12 GB of RAM be created.

- The cloud controller contacts the storage controller to allocate 2 TB of storage. This storage is connected to the new server instance through a storage network.
- The cloud controller requests two virtual network interface cards from the network controller.

After all of this is performed, the cloud controller takes the requested Ubuntu server image, copies it to the newly created virtual server, boots it, and configures it. Once this is done (measured in seconds or minutes), the controller makes the connection information available to the consumer.

The IaaS service can usually be accessed via multiple methods—web, CLI, or API. These interfaces are created and made available by the provider for customers to manage their virtual environment, hence the term *cloud management plane* (part of the metastructure logical model covered earlier in this chapter). In fact, the display of a web interface is mainly for human convenience. The provider will take actions performed graphically and convert them to API calls that are then executed.

As a cloud consumer, anything you can do via the web interface (and more) can be done via the API calls that are exposed. More mature cloud implementations by consumers are programmatically driven through accessing APIs. In fact, this programmatically driven virtual infrastructure (referred to as a *software-defined infrastructure*, which is covered in Chapter 7) is something that every cloud consumer should strive for. The less human intervention there is through a web browser, the better, because there will be less human error and a much higher level of agility.

Virtualization and Hypervisors

The best-known form of virtualization is a VM, which is generally synonymous with hypervisor (also called *virtual machine monitor*, or *VMM*) technology. Essentially, the hypervisor acts as the host and allows a single hardware server to host many VMs, which are referred to as *guests*.

The hypervisor is tasked with "tricking" the guest machines into thinking they are directly accessing the underlying hardware, but in reality, they are operating in an isolated virtual environment with their own virtual hardware resources. Put in a more polished way, the hypervisor is an abstraction layer that decouples the physical hardware from the guest operating system.

There are two types of hypervisors of note: Type 1 hypervisors are installed directly onto the physical server (such as VMware ESXi, Xen, or KVM), and Type 2 hypervisors are installed on top of the operating system already running on a server (such as VMware Workstation, VMware Workstation Player, or Oracle VM VirtualBox). I can't imagine any CSP using anything other than a Type 1 hypervisor for virtualized workloads.

Shared Versus Dedicated Workloads

Most workloads are run on multitenant shared server platforms, meaning that different customers run workloads on shared servers. This may seem like a security risk, but the risk is mitigated through the use of *isolation* (this is the key word when it comes to cloud security, by the way). However, if VM isolation were to ever fail, cloud security would be at risk. This risk was highlighted by the Spectre and Meltdown vulnerabilities, which exploited flaws in the underlying CPU hardware that had the potential to break VM isolation on shared physical servers. For those who want to avoid this potential risk, many CSPs also offer isolated servers to customers. (The following are terms used by AWS. Other CSPs call them other names.) There are three main options available to meet this need:

Dedicated instances
Dedicated instances are run on server platforms dedicated to a single customer. They are more expensive than "traditional" shared servers. Many customers opt for these instance types to handle regulated workloads, such as those governed by the Health Insurance Portability and Accountability Act (HIPAA), Payment Card Industry (PCI), and other compliance standards. This instance type can help with compliance with different standards, but it is not strictly required by any regulation or standard at this time.

Dedicated hosts
Like dedicated instances, dedicated hosts are also used by a single customer and are not shared with other customers. The difference is that dedicated hosts allow customers to meet some licensing requirements such as per-core licensing. You can choose the CPUs and memory dedicated to different instances you run on your dedicated host.

Bare metal servers
This instance type also offers a dedicated server platform for customers to consume. The main difference is that there's no virtualization layer. This could be an option if your use case requires direct access to the underlying hardware or enhanced performance by removing the virtualization layer.

Now, you might be thinking, why not just use dedicated or bare metal servers? Cost. Given different providers and instance sizes, I'm not going to attempt to discuss exact pricing, but some calculations I ran had these three options costing more than 10x the cost of shared instances (and that's being conservative).

In all these cases, it is important to remember that you don't avoid all other multitenancy risks. You still have a shared network, shared storage, and third-party administrators.

Platform as a service

Of the three service models, PaaS is the blurriest. According to the CSA's definition, PaaS adds a layer of integration with application development frameworks, middleware capabilities, and functions such as databases, messaging, and queuing. Figure 1-5 demonstrates a PaaS offering built on top of IaaS that creates a shared platform on which applications are run.

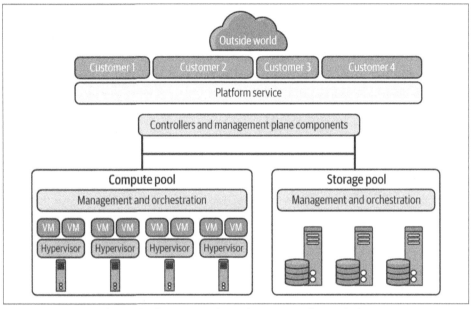

Figure 1-5. PaaS offering built on IaaS (from the CSA guidance doc)

In the PaaS service model, the provider builds the infrastructure (or leverages IaaS from another provider), creates a shared platform that customers will leverage, and may expose security controls it believes customers want control over. The main benefit of using PaaS is that it removes the overhead associated with building and maintaining servers and shifts that responsibility to the provider (the service becomes somewhat of a black box). Customers in turn leverage this multitenant platform that is fully managed by the provider.

You can think of PaaS as a development platform that you can use to gain quick access to an environment to build things on or to leverage for functionality. Take a "database as a service" PaaS offering, for example. Rather than launching an instance, configuring the operating system, and then installing and configuring your chosen SQL software, you simply choose the SQL platform you want and answer a few questions, and your database is available within minutes. This reduction of building and maintenance may lead to PaaS being cheaper to run than IaaS.

The downside to PaaS, as far as security is concerned, is that controls exposed to the customer are restricted compared to those possible in IaaS. Consider this example scenario. A major provider's SQL PaaS offering enforces an eight-character password for the master SQL account. It's embedded within the service and isn't even part of the provider's identity access management (IAM) offering. There's no password complexity enforcement, no rotation, and no way to check whether the password meets policy. This isn't to say PaaS is inherently insecure; it may, in fact, be more secure than a compliant application built in IaaS or in your own datacenter. But compliance isn't security, and vice versa.

Change management is another issue you can run into with the PaaS provider owning and managing the platform. The provider can, and will, change which platforms will be supported and which ones will be deprecated over time. This may arise due to the software becoming end of life (EOL) and no longer supported by the original vendor, or it could be due to a lack of sales at the CSP.

It is on you not only to be advised of these changes, but also to identify potential issues and fix them before your provider makes the change. For example, if you are running application code in a development platform, you may eventually get an email from your vendor announcing the introduction of a change to the platform that will break your application if your code has a dependency on functionality that is being deprecated. In a way, your provider is now dictating part of your change management. The provider may give you weeks, or it may give you months. It's up to your provider, not you, because your provider owns the platform.

Software as a service

The SaaS model can be simply described as "renting a ready-to-use application from a provider." All SaaS applications are inherently multitenant, allowing access through web browsers and mobile apps. Additionally, many SaaS applications support API access, with the type (typically REST or SOAP) and functionalities offered depending on the specific provider. The architecture behind a SaaS application can vary widely, from a single server handling both web and SQL services (posing a single point of failure) to a highly complex system with load balancers, redundant server farms, serverless components, and more. There are no strict rules or regulations governing what a SaaS provider must include in its service architecture.

From a security and due diligence perspective, an important aspect of SaaS services is that the SaaS provider may use a separate provider for IaaS or PaaS purposes. The biggest issue here has to do with salespeople exaggerating the security of their application because it's being run in a different provider network. To be honest, I can't say if this happens because of ignorance or because they have no problem lying to prospective clients to secure the sale.

As you already know, the cloud is a shared responsibility, and the SaaS vendor is just another customer to the IaaS provider. If the application you are consuming has security issues at the applistructure layer (such as privilege escalation), that is 100% on the SaaS vendor. Along the same lines, the SaaS vendor that says its application is PCI or HIPAA compliant because it's being run in a compliant infrastructure is equally guilty of ignorance, or worse. And yes, this happens way more often than it should.

Even though the CSP the SaaS vendor uses may indeed be compliant with a given standard, its application may not be. Let's consider PCI Data Security Standard (DSS) and logging requirements. Requirement 10 in PCI DSS states that applications must perform logging. How does a provider's facilities and platforms being PCI compliant meet this requirement? It obviously doesn't. This is referred to as *compliance inheritance*. Both the CSP and the customer (the SaaS, in this case) must meet compliance requirements for their own portion of the shared responsibility model that is the cloud.

SaaS is also likely to be the leading source of Shadow IT in your company. Due to the self-service capability essential characteristic, obtaining a SaaS app to get work done can be extremely easy to do. There are all kinds of issues with Shadow IT. Who is reviewing the contract? Would you believe there are SaaS vendors out there that have a clause in their contracts (that nobody reads) that states any data uploaded to the SaaS application transfers ownership to the CSP? You should, because there are. Who is managing access to the application and data within? These are just two reasons why Shadow IT is a nightmare for companies. We'll discuss discovering cloud services in use (and Shadow IT) when we talk about cloud access service brokers in Chapter 4.

A final note about the SPI stack: not every available category of service fits nicely and cleanly into one of the three tiers. Some may even span tiers. Take Salesforce, for example. Salesforce has a turnkey SaaS application and it has PaaS functionality that allows companies to develop custom applications that leverage the data created and stored via its SaaS application.

Remember, these service models are merely a descriptive tool that gives you an idea of what the provider is offering regarding the responsibility shift associated with the offering. It is by no means a rigid framework. Generally, IaaS gives customers the most security responsibility, PaaS less so, and finally, SaaS has the CSP with the most (but not all!) responsibility.

Cloud Deployment Models

Both NIST and ISO/IEC outline four cloud deployment models that describe the ownership and consumption of technologies. These deployment models are distinct from service models, allowing for combinations such as a private PaaS or IaaS. For the CCSK exam, it is crucial to remember the importance of the trust level among tenants sharing the service, and the governance capability of each deployment model.

Public cloud

This model is straightforward. Anyone in the world with a credit card (stolen or not) can sign up to use the service. The infrastructure is owned and managed by a third party and is located off premises, typically in datacenters geographically dispersed from your location.

Private cloud

A private cloud is designed exclusively for a single organization. This can mean the infrastructure may be owned and managed by the organization itself or by a third-party provider, and it can be located on premises or off premises. The flexibility lies in who manages it and where it is physically located. For instance, your internal team can set up and maintain a private cloud within your own datacenter, or you can engage a private cloud supplier to do so in its facilities. The critical aspect is that only authorized personnel from within your organization can access the cloud, ensuring controlled and secure access.

Private clouds often cater to organizations with specific security, compliance, and governance requirements, providing enhanced control over data and applications. They are particularly beneficial for industries like finance, healthcare, and government, where regulatory compliance and data sensitivity are paramount. Essentially, a private cloud is characterized by controller software that automates and orchestrates access to a pool of resources, providing a tailored cloud environment for your organization's needs.

It should also be noted that a private cloud is also multitenant. An example of a tenant in a private cloud would be the groups in your company. Take HR and Finance groups, for example. These are two separate tenants as far as the private cloud is concerned, because the HR group shouldn't have the same access to Finance's resources, and vice versa. This means they have different security boundaries. The difference is that other private cloud tenants are known and trusted.

Community cloud

A community cloud is generally built for multiple trusted organizations with similar concerns (such as a risk profile). The community cloud is much like a private cloud in that it can be built and managed by your company, or it can be outsourced. The co-tenants are also contractually bound. The key difference between a private cloud and a community cloud is that the financial risk is shared across multiple contractually trusted organizations in the community cloud.

Hybrid cloud

This one is unique in that it has two meanings. According to NIST, the definition of a hybrid cloud is two or more unique cloud deployment models (e.g., public and private clouds) that are bound together by standardized or proprietary technology. This enables data and application portability.

The other "industry-accepted" definition is the use of a public cloud and your own datacenter. In other words, you don't need to have the automated and orchestrated private cloud for your implementation to be considered a hybrid cloud.

The biggest advantage of a hybrid cloud is the ability to "keep your public data public and your private data private." This model allows you to have complete control (read: governance) over your sensitive data and take advantage of a public cloud for non-sensitive workloads.

From a more technical perspective, a hybrid cloud also allows for *cloud bursting*. This is a model in which an application primarily runs in a private cloud (or an on-premises datacenter) and "bursts" into a public cloud when the demand for computing capacity spikes. This allows an organization to handle peak loads without overprovisioning resources in its private infrastructure.

The NFL and the Premier League are perfect examples of how cloud bursting can be used. Both leagues play the majority of their games on the weekend. I think it's fair to assume their websites are not generally too busy in the offseason or on a random Tuesday when there are no games scheduled. However, on the weekend, they both have substantial demand spikes. By implementing a hybrid cloud with cloud bursting, they can have their public-facing websites' supply of resources burst in the public cloud to meet demand. I won't get into the architecture of this, because every provider does this differently, but implementation generally consists of dynamic provisioning of servers (often called an *autoscaling service* by providers), dynamic routing, and a load balancer to distribute workloads across the servers in the autoscaling group of web servers. Once traffic drops after the games are over, the autoscaling service can reduce the number of servers to reduce costs. This is an example of the power of rapid elasticity in action.

Bonus: Multicloud

This isn't a deployment model per se, but it's a strategy or approach worth mentioning here all the same. A multicloud model is exactly what you probably assume. It uses multiple public cloud services from different CSPs. This typically happens when a customer uses multiple IaaS providers (such as AWS and Microsoft Azure). The degree of integration between the two is not the main concern. It's having to secure multiple environments that may offer similar services, but can be very different in terms of functionality and configuration, which makes building and maintaining equally secure environments challenging. Your organization will need subject matter experts (SMEs) for each environment. In other words, multicloud equals multistaff.

Cloud Security Responsibilities, Frameworks, and Process Models

Now that we have covered the essential characteristics, service models, and deployment models of the cloud, let's get into the critical aspect of the shared security responsibility model (SSRM) and some frameworks that your organization can leverage to build secure cloud environments.

Shared Security Responsibility Model

Although I already covered shared responsibility earlier in the chapter, it is worth reemphasizing. It's important to remember that the CSP has the responsibility to secure the cloud, while customers retain the responsibility of securing their use of cloud services.

Effective cloud security requires understanding the division of responsibility in cloud environments. Knowing who is responsible is crucial; allow CSCs to fill control gaps or consider alternative CSPs. You could generalize and say that CSCs have the most security responsibility in IaaS and the least in SaaS. Although this is true, it is always best to understand the responsibilities for both the customer and the provider in every cloud service being considered, before signing any contract.

To ensure a clear allocation of security responsibilities in the cloud, the CSA recommends that CSPs document security controls and CSC features, and design and implement them properly. Often, such a document is called a *shared security responsibility matrix*. See Figure 1-6 for an example matrix from Microsoft.

CSCs should create a roles-and-responsibilities matrix to track security responsibilities and ensure compliance alignment. This is a really important point that I will discuss in further depth in Chapter 3. If you don't directly allocate responsibility to an individual or group, it will fall through the cracks, creating a risk and security issue.

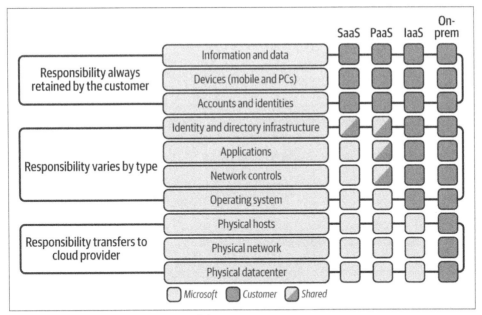

Figure 1-6. Shared security responsibility matrix

Cloud Security Frameworks and Patterns

When it comes to implementing cloud security, you don't have to go it alone. There are numerous frameworks by different organizations that you can leverage to implement your own cloud security controls.

You might be asking what the difference is between frameworks and patterns. Good question! *Frameworks* are comprehensive and cover a wide range of security domains, while *patterns* are specific solutions for particular problems. Together, they help ensure comprehensive and effective security practices.

For example, a framework may state that you require authentication of all users, providing a high-level directive. A pattern, on the other hand, will tell the architect how to implement that authentication, offering specific methods and techniques. Essentially, the framework outlines what needs to be done, while the pattern details how to do it.

I like to refer to these as "the shoulders of giants to stand on." There is a short list of frameworks and patterns you can use to securely build cloud systems and benefit from the defensibility they deliver. What do I mean by defensibility? Let's say your system is breached. What sounds better when the CEO demands answers?

- A bad response might be: "I dunno, boss. We did what we thought was a good idea."
- A good response might be: "We followed an industry-leading framework used by enterprises and governments around the world."

I'd say the first answer would likely result in a "resume-generating event," while the second answer would give the CEO the ability to defend the company from angry stakeholders and you the ability to keep your job.

Frequently discussed frameworks

Here are brief descriptions of several frameworks that will be covered further in Chapter 3:

CCM
 The Cloud Controls Matrix is a controls framework that lists cloud security controls and maps them to multiple security and compliance standards. The CCM can also be used to document security responsibilities.

CAIQ
 The Consensus Assessments Initiative Questionnaire is a standard template for CSPs to give straightforward yes or no answers to questions created to address the controls found in the CCM.

ISO/IEC 27001
 This is an internationally recognized standard for information security management. It provides a systematic approach to managing sensitive company information so that it remains secure. It includes people, processes, and IT systems by applying a risk management process.

ISO/IEC 27002
 This offers guidelines and general principles for initiating, implementing, maintaining, and improving information security management within an organization. It serves as a reference for selecting security controls within the process of

implementing an Information Security Management System (ISMS) based on ISO/IEC 27001.

ISO/IEC 27017
This offers guidelines for information security controls applicable to the provision and use of cloud services, extending ISO/IEC 27002 with cloud-specific guidance.

ISO/IEC 27018
This focuses on the protection of personal data in public clouds, providing guidelines for implementing measures to protect personal data.

NIST SP 800-53
This framework is a catalog of security and privacy controls for federal information systems and organizations, including cloud environments.

On top of these frameworks, major CSPs (such as Amazon, Microsoft, and Google) offer cloud architecture best practices through initiatives like the Well-Architected Framework, which helps customers design secure, high-performing, and resilient cloud workloads.

Cloud security process model

While the implementation details, necessary controls, specific processes, and various reference architectures and design models vary greatly depending on the specific cloud implementation, there is a relatively straightforward, eight-step, high-level process for managing cloud security:

- Identify necessary security and compliance requirements and any existing controls.
- Select the CSP, service, and deployment models.
- Define the architecture.
- Assess the security controls.
- Identify control gaps.
- Design and implement controls to fill the gaps.
- Assess the effectiveness of the controls.
- Manage changes over time.

These steps, and much more, are covered throughout the rest of the book.

Summary

This chapter reviewed the foundational information upon which the rest of the book will build. For the CCSK exam, you must be completely clear on the logical model and, more importantly, the metastructure layer where you will configure and manage a new virtual world through the management plane. Other topics you can expect to be tested on include the following:

- Understand the differences between cloud computing and traditional infrastructure—mainly automation, orchestration, and pools of resources.
- Be able to explain how the essential characteristics of cloud computing impact cloud security.
- Understand the shared responsibility model in which the CSP has security responsibility for the cloud and the CSC has security responsibility for its use of the cloud.
- Understand how and why the shared responsibility model of the cloud is impacted by the service model in use.
- Understand the importance of the CSC allocating roles and responsibilities to address security.
- Know the definitions of cloud computing, such as service and deployment models and their associated attributes, inside out.
- Know how to use the CSA CCM to assess and document cloud project security and compliance requirements and controls, as well as who is responsible for each.
- Know how the CSA CAIQ can be used to evaluate and compare cloud providers via the CSP answering questions based on the CCM controls.
- Use a cloud security process model to select providers, design architectures, identify control gaps, and implement security and compliance controls.

Assuming you're still with me, let's move on to the next chapter and discuss cloud governance. By the way, the next two chapters will mostly be focused on the business aspect of cloud security. We'll get more into the technical side starting with Chapter 4.

CHAPTER 2
Principles of Cloud and IT Governance

As a leader, you set the tone for your entire team. Communicate your vision.
—Colin Powell

This quotation from Colin Powell describes the need for governance throughout an organization. Everything about how a company is run (corporate governance), how its IT system is procured and run (IT governance), and how cloud services are procured and secured all comes back to good governance.

In Chapter 1, you saw some examples of what I call "cloud disasters." These came about as a result of companies not paying attention to their portion of the SSRM.

What can help address these issues? Proper governance, which is the topic of this chapter. Governance sets the tone. Without it, you have a Wild West on your hands. Without directive controls, called *policies*, communicated to everyone, people aren't instructed on what is expected of them in building or managing cloud services. I'll talk about policies later in this chapter, but for now, these are simply being referred to as *directive controls*. Policies direct people in what is expected of them and the systems they build.

So, what exactly is governance anyway? Well, it has many different definitions, but let's start with the definition from the *Oxford English Dictionary*:

> The action or fact of governing a nation, a person, an activity, one's desires, etc.: direction, rule; regulation.

OK. So basically, governance means running something.

Corporate Governance

Now let's dive a bit deeper into what corporate governance is. Let's go with what the Information Systems Audit and Control Association, now called ISACA, has to say on the subject of governance in its latest (2019) version of Control Objectives for Information and Related Technologies (COBIT), since it is an authoritative source on the issue:

> Governance ensures that stakeholder needs, conditions and options are evaluated to determine balanced, agreed-on enterprise objectives to be achieved; setting direction through prioritization and decision making; and monitoring performance and compliance against agreed-on direction and objectives.

When talking about corporate governance, ISACA helped add some detail to the traditional definition of the word *governance*. Corporate governance means running a company to meet big-picture objectives while also monitoring compliance with these objectives.

Figure 2-1 is a visual depiction of the structure of corporate governance.

Figure 2-1. Corporate governance

The responsibilities of each domain are as follows:

Board of directors and committees
: Provide strategic oversight, set objectives, and ensure that executive management aligns with shareholder and stakeholder interests. Committees (e.g., audit, risk) specialize in specific governance areas.

Values and ethics
: Define the organization's ethical standards and cultural expectations. Promote integrity, transparency, and responsible decision making across all levels of the enterprise.

Policies and regulatory framework
: Establish internal policies and ensure compliance with external laws and regulations. Provide a structured approach to governance and operational control. Of note, this is known as a *directive control*. It directs individuals on what they must do to support governance. I'll cover the different control types and categories in Chapter 3.

Risk management
: Identifies, assesses, and mitigates risks that could impact the organization's goals and sustainability. Enables informed decision making and resilience.

Accountability
: Ensures that individuals and groups are held responsible for their actions and decisions. Encourages ownership, performance tracking, and ethical conduct.

Monitoring and internal control
: Implement processes to evaluate performance and ensure adherence to policies. Help detect deviations, enforce controls, and support continuous improvement.

IT Governance

Now let's move on to IT governance. Here is how Gartner, a leading global research and advisory firm, defines IT governance in its official IT glossary:

> IT governance (ITG) is defined as the processes that ensure the effective and efficient use of IT in enabling an organization to achieve its goals.

The latest version of the COBIT Core Model includes 40 governance and management objectives for establishing IT governance that are organized into five domains. Figure 2-2 shows a high-level view of these domains. You won't be tested on these as part of the CCSK exam, but knowing the aspects of IT governance isn't a bad thing.

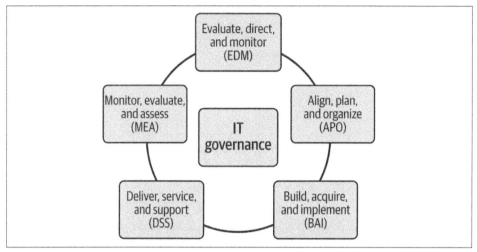

Figure 2-2. High-level view of the COBIT Core Model

Here is a synopsis of each of the five domains in the COBIT Core Model:

Evaluate, direct, and monitor (EDM)
　Focuses on governance objectives, ensuring that stakeholder needs are evaluated, direction is set, and performance is monitored

Align, plan, and organize (APO)
　Covers management objectives related to strategy, enterprise architecture, and resource management

Build, acquire, and implement (BAI)
　Addresses the definition, acquisition, and implementation of IT solutions and their integration into business processes

Deliver, service, and support (DSS)
　Encompasses operational delivery and support of IT services, including security and continuity

Monitor, evaluate, and assess (MEA)
　Focuses on performance monitoring, internal control, and regulatory compliance

Now that you have a high-level understanding of corporate and IT governance, let's move on to the next section to understand the specifics of how the cloud changes IT governance.

Cloud Governance Changes and Challenges

Cloud computing introduces many complexities into an organization's governance approach. Although some considerations may vary depending on the specific type of cloud service being deployed (e.g., SaaS, IaaS, or PaaS), several key considerations generally apply to most cloud services.

Unless you're talking about an internal private cloud, cloud adoption will likely result in a loss of direct control over the IT infrastructure, necessitating the adoption of a new governance framework and processes. Cloud services and data often span multiple jurisdictions, requiring organizations to comply with a broader array of laws and regulations, especially those related to privacy. Visibility and transparency into some cloud services (e.g., PaaS and SaaS) can be challenging, which complicates governance.

It is critical to know that while an organization can outsource some responsibility (authority over actions) for governance, it can never outsource liability. The organization retains accountability (liability for actions or lack of actions) if anything goes wrong. This is the law, folks. It's right up there with "ignorance is not a defense." You can never outsource accountability!

This principle holds true with or without the cloud and is crucial to remember when navigating cloud computing's shared responsibility models. The bottom line is that if you use a service that is breached and your customer data is disclosed, your customers will sue you. You can't point your finger at the CSP and say it's the CSP's fault. You may be right, but you still chose to use that CSP in the first place.

Data ownership rights, classification, and privacy controls may not be immediately clear and therefore require careful examination. Most cloud providers offer standardized services that cannot be customized to meet specific customer requirements. This is due to the sheer volume of customers, making it impossible for providers to cater to individual needs regarding contracts, service level agreements (SLAs), and security controls.

Different cloud providers demonstrate varying levels of maturity and offer a variety of services, licenses, and models. This variability complicates the adoption of a one-size-fits-all cloud policy. Furthermore, cloud services are often built on a chain of providers, adding complexity to governance activities. For instance, a SaaS provider might run on the infrastructure of an IaaS provider.

The use of different shared responsibility models, which depend on the supplier and technology stack, requires a clear allocation of controls and responsibilities between the CSP and the customer. The shared responsibility model can involve multiple parties, including cloud platform integrators, software development companies, DevOps teams, and other stakeholders. Hybrid cloud models further complicate governance due to the complexities of defining clear boundaries between provider and customer responsibilities.

Cloud customers must rely more on compliance and assessment activities than on direct testing, depending on their layer of responsibility. For example, in an IaaS model, the customer remains responsible for security testing applications. Primarily, customers must rely on third-party security assessment reports and certifications from the CSP and understand their shared responsibilities to ensure total compliance coverage. I'll address these third-party assessments and audits in Chapter 3.

CSP offerings may change rapidly, which must be accounted for in governance models. Utilizing cloud services may also require additional skills that may not currently be present within the organization, such as cloud auditing and security skills, and familiarity with cloud-oriented security tools like cloud security posture management (CSPM) or Secure Access Service Edge (SASE). These technologies will be covered later in the book.

To navigate these complexities, organizations must operationalize their governance frameworks to effectively manage their cloud services. Identifying governance gaps and addressing them is crucial for ensuring robust cloud governance and maintaining compliance.

Effective Cloud Governance

Effective cloud governance requires the implementation of a strong framework and policies for secure, compliant, and efficient management of cloud resources. In this section, we will discuss 11 things that various CSA publications say an organization adopting cloud computing should do.

1. Establish a Governance Hierarchy

Establishing a governance hierarchy involves creating a structured framework that defines the levels of authority and decision making within the organization's cloud governance model. This hierarchy ensures clear lines of accountability, facilitates efficient decision making, and promotes adherence to cloud policies and standards. It helps in managing complex cloud environments by delineating roles and responsibilities at various levels.

2. Leverage Cloud-Specific Security Frameworks

Leveraging cloud-specific security frameworks involves adopting established guidelines and best practices designed to secure cloud environments. Frameworks like the CSA CCM (available on the CSA website with a free account) or the AWS/Azure/GCP Well-Architected Frameworks (available on their respective websites) provide comprehensive security controls and measures tailored for cloud services.

Using these frameworks helps organizations implement robust security strategies that address the unique challenges of cloud computing.

3. Define Cloud Security Policies

Defining cloud security policies entails creating formalized rules and procedures that govern how cloud resources and data are protected. These policies cover aspects like access control, data encryption, incident response, and compliance requirements. Clear security policies ensure that all cloud activities adhere to organizational standards and regulatory obligations, reducing the risk of data breaches and security incidents.

4. Set Control Objectives and Specify Control Specifications

Setting control objectives and specifying control specifications involves defining the desired outcomes for security and compliance measures in the cloud and detailing the specific controls needed to achieve these objectives. *Control objectives* provide a high-level view of what needs to be secured, while *control specifications* outline the exact technical and procedural measures to be implemented. This process ensures that security controls are effectively aligned with organizational goals and risk management strategies.

5. Define Roles and Responsibilities

Defining roles and responsibilities involves clearly specifying the duties and expectations for each team member involved in cloud operations. This ensures that every task, from security management to data governance, has a designated owner, promoting accountability and preventing overlaps or gaps in responsibilities. Clear role definitions help streamline workflows and improve coordination among different teams.

6. Establish a Cloud Center of Excellence or Similar Model

Establishing a Cloud Center of Excellence (CCoE), which I'll discuss later in the chapter, involves creating a dedicated team or governance model that focuses on implementing cloud best practices, optimizing cloud usage, and driving innovation. The CCoE serves as a centralized body for cloud strategy, standards, and policies, ensuring that cloud initiatives align with organizational goals and regulatory requirements. It promotes consistent and efficient cloud adoption across the organization.

7. Conduct Requirements and Information Gathering

Conducting requirements and information gathering is the process of identifying and documenting the technical, security, and business needs for cloud adoption. This involves engaging stakeholders to understand their requirements, analyzing existing systems, and gathering relevant data to inform cloud strategy and decision making. It ensures that the cloud solutions implemented meet the organization's specific needs and objectives.

8. Manage Risks

Managing risks in a cloud environment involves identifying, assessing, and mitigating potential threats that could impact the organization's cloud operations. This includes evaluating security vulnerabilities, compliance risks, and operational challenges. By implementing risk management strategies, such as regular security assessments and robust incident response plans, organizations can minimize the impact of risks and ensure business continuity.

9. Classify Data and Assets

Classifying data and assets involves categorizing information and resources based on their sensitivity, value, and criticality to the organization. This classification helps determine the appropriate security controls and access restrictions needed to protect data and assets. It ensures that sensitive information is adequately safeguarded while optimizing resource management and compliance with data protection regulations.

10. Comply with Legal and Regulatory Requirements

Complying with legal and regulatory requirements entails ensuring that cloud operations adhere to relevant laws, regulations, and industry standards. This includes data protection regulations such as the European Union's (EU) General Data Protection Regulation (GDPR), industry-specific standards like HIPAA, and contractual obligations. Organizations must implement compliance policies, conduct regular audits, and stay updated on regulatory changes to avoid legal penalties and maintain trust with stakeholders.

11. Maintain a Cloud Registry

Maintaining a cloud registry involves keeping an up-to-date inventory of all cloud resources, services, and configurations used by the organization. This registry provides visibility into cloud usage, helps track changes, and supports compliance and security monitoring. It ensures that cloud resources are managed efficiently and that potential issues are identified and addressed promptly. The registry can have the following components:

CSP

Document each account/subscription (you'll see in Chapter 4 how many organizations use unique accounts/subscriptions for different workloads to limit the blast radius, especially in IaaS) for each CSP used (SaaS, PaaS, and IaaS). This information helps in understanding the underlying infrastructure and services utilized.

Tracking ID
Assign a unique identifier to each cloud environment to facilitate tracking and management. This ID will appear in logs and other monitoring tools, providing a precise reference point for each environment.

Descriptive name
Provide a meaningful name that accurately describes the purpose or nature of each cloud environment. This makes it easier to identify and understand the role of each environment within the organization.

Compliance classification
Categorize each environment based on regulatory and compliance needs, such as PCI DSS, HIPAA, GDPR, and so on. Proper classification ensures that the appropriate security measures and controls are applied to meet compliance requirements.

Risk classification
Assess and label the risk level of each environment to align with the organization's risk management strategy. This helps prioritize resources and efforts for risk mitigation and ensures that the appropriate level of security controls is implemented.

Environment classification
Distinguish between different types of environments, such as development, staging, and production. This classification helps manage and govern each environment based on its specific requirements. This again comes back to the potential of having multiple accounts/subscriptions in IaaS providers.

Owner
Identify the business owner responsible for each cloud environment. This ensures accountability, responsibility, and clear lines of communication for decision making and resource allocation.

Technical contact
Designate a point of contact for technical issues and operational management of each environment. This helps streamline communication and ensures prompt resolution of any technical challenges.

CSP contacts
Include contact information for customer support and account management at the CSP. This information is essential for addressing any service-related issues and maintaining a healthy relationship with the provider.

I'm telling you from experience that if you walk into a client site to assess cloud usage and the client doesn't have an authoritative list available of the cloud services it currently uses, you are in for a nightmare. You will likely spend the next several weeks, even months, trying to track down all the cloud services used by the company.

Cloud Center of Excellence

I'm going to go out on a limb here and say that well-governed companies are likely to have a centralized function that manages all aspects of onboarding and cloud services management used by the organization. The general term the industry has adopted for this function is *Cloud Center of Excellence* or *CCoE*.

The CCoE is a centralized team or governance model within an organization dedicated to implementing cloud best practices, optimizing cloud usage, and driving innovation. The CCoE serves as a central authority for cloud strategy, standards, and policies, ensuring that cloud initiatives align with organizational goals and regulatory requirements. It promotes consistent, secure, and efficient cloud adoption across the organization.

To ensure the success of a CCoE, it is crucial to secure executive sponsorship and support. This, of course, must be done for every project, but it is particularly critical for the CCoE to be well positioned and be the sole function for adoption of any cloud service.

This involves engaging top executives and key stakeholders to obtain their commitment and backing for the CCoE initiative. Without executive buy-in, it can be challenging to secure the necessary funding and resources. Adequate allocation of resources is essential to support the CCoE's activities and ensure that it can operate effectively.

 If the CCoE is not used as the sole authoritative function for procuring and maintaining cloud services, it isn't worth the effort. If you have one, your cloud usage policies must state that the CCoE is the only means to procure any cloud services across the organization. If you don't have this policy, leadership needs to create one.

Key Components of a CCoE

Following is a quick list of the various responsibilities that should be assigned to the CCoE:

Cloud strategy
　　Defining the organization's cloud strategy, including goals, objectives, and road maps, to ensure alignment with business objectives

Architecture and design
　　Establishing cloud architecture standards, patterns, and best practices to guide the design and deployment of cloud solutions

Operations and management
　　Overseeing cloud operations, including cost management, performance monitoring, resource optimization, and incident response, to maintain efficient cloud environments

Security and compliance
　　Implementing and enforcing robust security policies, compliance requirements, and risk management practices to protect cloud resources and data

Training and enablement
　　Providing continuous training, resources, and support to develop and enhance cloud skills across the organization, fostering a knowledgeable workforce

Vendor management
　　Managing relationships with CSPs and vendors, including contract negotiations, SLAs, and performance reviews

Governance and policy enforcement
　　Ensuring adherence to cloud governance frameworks and policies, including defining roles and responsibilities and establishing accountability mechanisms

Innovation and best practices
　　Promoting the adoption of innovative cloud technologies and practices, encouraging experimentation and the implementation of cutting-edge solutions

Performance metrics and monitoring
　　Defining and tracking key performance indicators (KPIs) and metrics to measure the effectiveness and efficiency of cloud initiatives

Benefits of a CCoE

The benefits of a CCoE are plentiful. As you can determine from the following list, the CCoE ensures maximum value of cloud services to the organization:

Standardization
  Ensures consistent application of cloud best practices and standards across the organization, reducing variability and enhancing quality

Operational efficiency
  Improves operational efficiency by optimizing cloud resource usage, reducing costs, and enhancing performance

Innovation
  Encourages innovation by leveraging the latest cloud technologies and services, fostering a culture of experimentation and continuous improvement

Security and compliance
  Enhances security and ensures compliance with regulatory requirements through robust policies and proactive risk management

Knowledge sharing
  Promotes knowledge sharing, collaboration, and cross-functional teamwork, fostering a culture of continuous learning and improvement

Accountability and governance
  Establishes clear roles, responsibilities, and accountability, ensuring effective governance and policy enforcement

Scalability and agility
  Supports the organization's ability to scale and adapt to changing business needs and technological advancements efficiently

Structuring IT Security Governance

An IT security governance hierarchy is a structured approach that ensures comprehensive and effective management of an organization's IT security practices. I'll discuss the components in more detail in a bit, but for now, Figure 2-3 shows the hierarchical relationship between frameworks, policies, control objectives, and control specifications and guidelines.

The sections that follow break down the four components of the hierarchy with discussions and examples. Don't worry about the contents of the examples. They're just examples, and they won't be on the exam—promise! You will, however, need to know what the components are and how they are related.

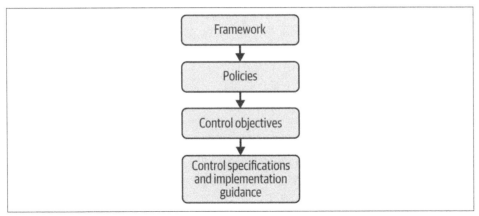

Figure 2-3. Cloud security governance hierarchy

Frameworks

This governance hierarchy begins with a cloud security framework, which provides the overarching principles and guidelines for managing cloud security. Common cloud-focused frameworks include the CSA CCM, ISO/IEC 27017, and Cloud Security Maturity Model (CSMM) by IANS in association with the CSA. These frameworks establish the foundation for the organization's cloud security posture and ensure alignment with industry standards and regulatory requirements.

I want to add an honorable mention to the NIST Framework for Improving Critical Infrastructure Cybersecurity, or simply the NIST Cybersecurity Framework (CSF). Although not cloud specific, it is a framework that is followed by many organizations, especially medium-sized organizations.

Frameworks are essentially the shoulders of a giant to stand on, upon which you can base your cloud security decisions, and they can be tailored to suit an organization's priorities. They aren't extremely prescriptive, meaning they don't tell you what controls you need and how they need to be configured. Take the CCM entry for the DSP-04 control specification, for example:

> Classify data according to its type and sensitivity level.

It doesn't aim to tell you how to do this. It just says it should be done. The bottom line is that frameworks help guide your security decisions; they don't instruct you on how you must achieve the goal.

Policies

Following the framework, policies are developed to direct specific security requirements and rules that the organization must follow. This is why policies are considered a directive control. These policies cover various domains, such as data classification, access control, data protection, incident response, and compliance. They provide a clear mandate on what must be done to secure the organization's information assets.

The following is an example of a policy that could be created to address the control specification DSP-04 from the CCM framework discussed in the previous section. Again, this is not information you need to know for the exam, but it is important to know the format and scope of a policy statement in general.

Purpose

The purpose of this policy is to ensure that all organizational data is classified according to its type and sensitivity level to protect it appropriately and comply with legal, regulatory, and business requirements.

Scope

This policy applies to all employees, contractors, and third-party partners who handle organizational data across all systems and platforms.

Policy

The following is just an example of a generic policy statement. You don't need to study this entry at all. The goal is to understand that a policy statement will direct staff on their responsibilities and the consequences of not following the policy. If this is related to some form of regulatory requirement, external auditors would perform checks to make sure the policy is being followed.

Data classification. All data must be classified based on its type and sensitivity level. The classification categories include, but are not limited to:

Public
    Data intended for public disclosure

Internal
    Data intended for internal use within the organization

Confidential
    Sensitive data that requires protection due to its nature, including personally identifiable information (PII), financial data, and proprietary business information

Restricted
    Highly sensitive data that requires stringent protection measures, including top-secret business information and highly regulated data

Classification process. Data owners are responsible for classifying data under their control according to the organization's data classification categories. Data classification must be determined based on the potential impact of unauthorized disclosure, modification, or destruction of the data.

Documentation. All classified data must be documented in the organization's data inventory, including the classification level and handling requirements.

Handling requirements. Data must be handled in accordance with its classification level. Specific handling requirements include access controls, encryption, transmission methods, and storage solutions.

Public data can be freely shared and disclosed. Internal data must be shared only within the organization and protected against unauthorized access. Confidential data must be encrypted in transit and at rest and shared only with authorized personnel. Restricted data must have the highest level of protection, including multifactor authentication (MFA) for access and strict monitoring and logging of access and usage.

Review and update. Data classifications must be reviewed and updated regularly, at least annually, or when significant changes occur in the data's nature or use. The review process must involve reassessing the data's sensitivity and ensuring that the classification and handling requirements remain appropriate.

Training and awareness. All employees, contractors, and third-party partners must receive training on data classification and handling procedures to ensure compliance with this policy.

Compliance

Noncompliance with this policy may result in disciplinary action, up to and including termination of employment or contracts, as well as legal action if necessary. Regular audits and monitoring will be conducted to ensure compliance with this policy.

Policy review

This policy will be reviewed annually by the IT Security Governance Committee to ensure its relevance and effectiveness.

Approval

This policy has been approved by the chief information officer (CIO) and the IT Security Governance Committee as of [Date].

Control Objectives

Next in the hierarchy of cloud security governance are control objectives, which define the specific goals that the security controls must achieve to mitigate risks and ensure the effectiveness of the security policies. Control objectives provide measurable targets that guide the implementation and assessment of security controls.

It's important to understand that the control objective is a high-level objective. It states what needs to be achieved, not how to achieve it. That comes later in the control specification, or technical implementation phase.

Let's take a look at an example control objective to meet the policy on data classification control from the CCM framework you reviewed in the previous section.

Objective

To ensure that all organizational data is classified according to its type and sensitivity level in order to safeguard it appropriately and comply with legal, regulatory, and business requirements.

Description

The organization shall implement a data classification scheme that categorizes data based on its sensitivity and importance. This classification will guide the application of appropriate security controls to protect data from unauthorized access, disclosure, modification, or destruction.

Control Specifications and Implementation Guidance

At the bottom of the hierarchy are control specifications and implementation guidance. These are detailed instructions on how to achieve the control objectives. Control specifications provide the technical and procedural steps required to implement the controls, such as specific encryption algorithms to use, configuration settings for security tools, and procedures for conducting security audits. Implementation guidance helps ensure that these controls are applied consistently and effectively across the organization.

Let's look at an example of control specifications and implementation guidance using the data classification example.

Objective

To ensure that all organizational data is classified according to its type and sensitivity level to safeguard it appropriately and comply with legal, regulatory, and business requirements.

Implementation guidance

Here is where we can see that more details are being added. The following steps must be followed to meet the control objective that meets the policy that meets the framework (from a bottom-up approach).

1. Data classification scheme. Develop and implement a standardized data classification scheme.

Implementation guidance:

- Define classification categories (e.g., Public, Internal, Confidential, Restricted).
- Create a classification matrix that includes criteria for each category.
- Document the classification scheme in a formal policy.

2. Responsibility assignment. Assign data owners responsible for data classification.

Implementation guidance:

- Identify and assign data owners for each department or data type.
- Provide training for data owners on classification criteria and processes.
- Establish a clear accountability framework for data classification.

3. Data inventory. Maintain an up-to-date inventory of classified data.

Implementation guidance:

- Develop a centralized database or registry to store data classification information.
- Ensure that the inventory is updated regularly with new data entries and classification changes.
- Conduct periodic audits to verify the accuracy and completeness of the data inventory.

4. Classification process. Establish processes and procedures for classifying data.

Implementation guidance:

- Develop detailed procedures for data classification at the time of data creation, collection, or acquisition.
- Use automated tools where possible to assist in data classification.
- Review classification decisions periodically to ensure that they remain appropriate.

5. Access controls. Implement access controls based on data classification levels.

Implementation guidance:

- Use role-based access control to manage permissions.
- Ensure that access to Confidential and Restricted data is limited to authorized personnel only.
- Implement MFA for accessing sensitive data.

6. Encryption. Encrypt data classified as Confidential or Restricted both in transit and at rest.

Implementation guidance:

- Select strong encryption algorithms and protocols (e.g., AES-256 for data at rest, TLS 1.2+ for data in transit).
- Use encryption tools and services provided by CSPs where applicable.
- Regularly review and update encryption practices to align with industry standards.

7. Transmission security. Use secure transmission methods for sensitive data.

Implementation guidance:

- Ensure that all data transmissions use secure channels (e.g., SSL/TLS, VPN).
- Prohibit the transmission of Confidential or Restricted data over unsecured networks.
- Monitor and log data transmissions to detect and respond to unauthorized access attempts.

8. Storage security. Store sensitive data in secure locations.

Implementation guidance:

- Use secure cloud storage solutions with built-in encryption and access controls.
- Implement physical security measures for on-premises data storage (e.g., locked server rooms).
- Regularly review storage security measures to ensure that they meet classification requirements.

9. Training and awareness. Provide regular training on data classification policies and procedures.

Implementation guidance:

- Develop training materials covering the data classification scheme, procedures, and responsibilities.
- Conduct mandatory training sessions for all employees, contractors, and third-party partners.
- Use quizzes and assessments to ensure understanding and retention of training material.

10. Monitoring and auditing. Implement continuous monitoring and regular auditing of data classification practices.

Implementation guidance:

- Use automated monitoring tools to track data access and classification changes.
- Schedule regular internal audits to review compliance with data classification policies.
- Address any discrepancies or noncompliance issues identified during audits promptly.

11. Policy and procedure review. Review and update data classification policies and procedures regularly.

Implementation guidance:

- Schedule annual reviews of data classification policies and procedures.
- Update policies to reflect changes in data types, regulatory requirements, or organizational processes.
- Communicate policy updates to all relevant stakeholders and ensure that they are implemented.

Success criteria

All data is classified accurately and consistently according to the established classification scheme. Appropriate security controls are applied based on data classification levels. Regular audits show compliance with data classification policies and procedures. Training records indicate that all relevant personnel have received and understood data classification training.

Thinking All the Way Through the Governance Stack

Do you see how the lower you go in this governance stack, the more specific the demands become? Now that you know what you need to do, you can start looking at the tools supplied by the CSP to address these requirements. If the provider doesn't address them, you have to look at implementing your own tools to address your requirements. This is known as a *gap analysis for the cloud*. Determine your needs, assess what the CSP offers, and fill any gaps with your own tools.

Foundational Governance Principles and Guidelines

In addition to the hierarchy of governance that I just went through, there are other key elements that come into play when talking about governance. I cover the risk and compliance aspects of the well-known "GRC" (governance, risk management, and compliance) approach in Chapter 3, but for now, there are other elements to governance that I need to address.

Determining Risk Tolerance

Understanding your organization's risk tolerance is crucial for determining the acceptable level of risk when operating in cloud environments. How are you going to govern an environment when you don't understand your risk tolerance? Does your company want to "move fast and break stuff" like a startup, or is it "old and slow" like a 100-year-old financial services company where risk is a four-letter word? *Risk tolerance* refers to the amount of risk that management is willing to accept as the organization pursues its objectives.

Determining an organization's risk tolerance involves evaluating both qualitative and quantitative factors. *Qualitative* (more subjective) factors include considerations like potential reputational damage, the organization's risk culture, and the legal implications of various risks. *Quantitative* (more objective) factors involve measurable impacts such as financial costs, potential revenue loss, and operational disruptions. Together, these factors provide a comprehensive view of the potential consequences of risk, enabling informed decisions about the acceptable level of risk in the pursuit of organizational objectives. This holistic approach ensures that all relevant aspects are considered, balancing numerical quantitative data with the broader, often less tangible qualitative impacts on the organization.

By assessing risk tolerance, your organization can establish a clear security posture and make informed decisions throughout the cloud adoption journey. The CCoE or cloud team should document and communicate the risks associated with cloud adoption to leadership, ensuring that operations stay within the defined risk tolerance.

Risk is usually defined as a calculation of both the likelihood of an adverse event occurring and its impact. Risk assessments should consistently analyze the likelihood and potential impact of adverse cyber and operational incident scenarios relevant to the organization. This can be achieved using assessment methods such as the more qualitative impact likelihood matrix (a.k.a. risk matrix) or the more quantitative Factor Analysis for Information Risk (FAIR) method. In my personal experience, many organizations use the impact likelihood matrix, as it's generally faster. The downside is if you ask 10 people about the risk rating based on likelihood and impact, you'll likely get 10 different answers. It takes a deeper understanding of an organization's risk tolerance to be done effectively.

Classifying Data and Assets

Earlier in the chapter I used classification as the example, for a reason. Data and asset classification is a critical aspect of all IT governance, especially in the cloud. The cloud doesn't need to be an all-or-nothing scenario. You may take a *cloud-first* approach, in which the cloud is used for all new systems but sensitive data is stored in the local datacenter. How can you do this if you don't classify the data?

Here's a real-life example. A company has data from many customers: 15 petabytes (roughly 15,000 TB) of data, in fact. It determines that its datacenter will reach maximum capacity in a few years. It needs to decide if it should use cloud services to lower the capacity demand of its datacenter, or if it should start the process of building a new one (these things don't just happen on their own; it's a multiyear process, as you can imagine). The company realizes it doesn't have a clear classification system that dictates what data could be moved based on contractual restrictions. Rather than trying to classify 15 PB of data, its solution is to let contracts time out and to replace "no third-party processing" with "no offshore processing" to allow data to be stored and processed in the cloud.

While most organizations won't need to make such a dramatic decision, they do need to classify their data and assets based on their sensitivity, criticality, and the potential impact associated with their loss or compromise. Properly classified data/information will facilitate the appropriate selection of providers and security controls and will ensure compliance with legal, regulatory, and contractual requirements for the protection of data.

You want to keep the classification scheme to a minimum. Common classifications include Public, Internal, Confidential, and Highly Confidential. If you go overboard and create 10 different classifications, it will only result in assets being misclassified. For example, the government of Canada has three classifications for citizen data. These are Protected A (lowest), Protected B, and Protected C (highest). Currently, it only allows Protected A and B data to be stored in a cloud environment. Protected C data must be held in internal datacenters.

Additionally, data location is a consideration with cloud computing because data can be hosted in another jurisdiction, sometimes even without the end user knowing (e.g., backups by a SaaS provider being stored in a different country). Some governments or institutions have limits on data transfers outside their borders, or they require additional controls, such as the GDPR. This is another consideration for the CCoE when evaluating a CSP.

Identifying Regulatory and Legal Requirements

The regulatory landscape your company operates under will have an outsized impact on the governance framework you choose. For example, if you are a US government department, you're likely going to follow controls selected from the NIST 800-53 catalog. If you're a healthcare organization, by law you have to comply with HIPAA regulations. Have personal data of EU citizens? You need to comply with GDPR. These are all examples of regulatory and legal requirements companies may face. These will be major inputs into the governance function, all the way up to the framework used by the organization.

In addition to regulatory and other legal requirements, it is important to determine requirements based on the specific risks identified during the risk assessment phase. I'll cover risk assessment in more depth in the next chapter. Before I get there, though, let's wrap up this chapter with coverage of some of the main tools made available by the CSA.

Cloud Security Alliance Tools

The CSA has many reports and best practice documents available to the public. Of all its publications, the following are ones that you can expect to see on the CCSK exam. You don't need to memorize everything from these publications, but you do need to know what they are. I highly recommend accessing the CSA website and downloading a copy of the CCM and CAIQ as well as looking at the STAR registry, also on the CSA website.

Cloud Controls Matrix

I brought up the CCM earlier in this chapter, but it is worth a further discussion when preparing for the CCSK exam and for real life. I can honestly say that I have worked with the CCM and the CAIQ (which I talk about in the next section) in many environments, ranging from publicly traded Fortune 500 companies to governments around the world. Knowing these CSA tools can be a real game-changer for your career. The current version of the CSA CMM is Version 4 (CCM v4). It is a framework of more than 200 control objectives across 17 control domains, ranging from governance and risk management to operational security and data privacy.

A main benefit of the CCM is its support for cloud governance. It assists organizations in establishing and maintaining a solid cloud governance program that effectively manages and oversees cloud risks. This is valuable in ensuring that cloud deployments are aligned with organizational objectives and comply with relevant regulations.

One of the key strengths of the CCM is its mappings to leading standards such as ISO/IEC 27001/27002, PCI DSS (v3.2.1/v4.0), NIST CSF, and others. The CCM calls this *scope applicability*. By mapping with these established frameworks, the CCM ensures that organizations can achieve compliance across multiple standards and regulations.

The CCM allows for control customization (a.k.a. tailoring), enabling organizations to adapt the security controls to their specific cloud architectures, delivery models (IaaS, PaaS, SaaS), and compliance needs. Although the CCM was originally to be used to assess providers, it can also be used by customers to assess their secure usage of cloud services.

Tailoring should be done based on the risk level of the application. The CCM v4 includes what it calls a "CCM-lite" category. You don't need to, nor should you, treat all CSPs the same. Seeking answers to over 200 controls will take a lot longer than asking 50 questions (for example). I'll discuss this further when we discuss risk in the next chapter.

One issue with the CCM is that the control specifications can be somewhat murky. Take the following control (BCR-08), for example:

> CCM AIS-01: "Establish, document, approve, communicate, apply, evaluate and maintain policies and procedures for application security to provide guidance to the appropriate planning, delivery and support of the organization's application security capabilities. Review and update the policies and procedures at least annually."

This isn't exactly something you can ask as a very clear question that can be answered with a simple yes or no response. Generally, if you ask better questions, you usually get better answers. For that, you need to bring in the CAIQ.

Consensus Assessment Initiative Questionnaire

The CAIQ (the cool kids pronounce it *cake*) asks straightforward questions that can be answered in a yes or no format. Let's use CCM AIS-01 as an example again and look at the CAIQ questions:

CAIQ AIS-01.2
"Are application security policies and procedures reviewed and updated at least annually?"

CAIQ AIS-01.2
"Are application security policies and procedures reviewed and updated at least annually?"

See how straightforward these questions are? Anyone can answer with a simple yes or no. Responses to these CAIQ questions allow you to perform due diligence activities in support of the due care principle. In other words, it allows you to assess providers before you onboard them.

Security, Trust, Assurance, and Risk Registry

The last CSA tool I'll cover here is the Security, Trust, Assurance, and Risk (STAR) registry. The STAR registry is a website hosted by the CSA that holds hundreds of CSP responses to the CAIQ. There are two types of STAR registry entries that you should be aware of.

STAR Level 1 is a self-assessment from the CSP. The CSP answers the CAIQ questions with simple yes or no responses. In many cases, it also gives detailed explanations as to why the answer is a yes or a no. These responses often reveal "subservice organizations" the CSP itself uses. Think of the subservice organization as a CSP that your CSP uses, like running a SaaS in a public IaaS such as AWS, for example.

I do have to note that there is no assessment by the CSA or any party as to the truthfulness of CSP responses. Personally, I think it would be ridiculous for a CSP to submit false information to the world's leading cloud security research organization, but it's always a possibility.

STAR Level 2 entries are submitted by third-party auditors as either STAR attestations or STAR certifications. They are based on prominent certifications (ISO 27001) and standards (System and Organization Controls 2 [SOC 2]). The following explanations of STAR attestation and STAR certification are from the CSA STAR website:

STAR Attestation: For SOC 2

The CSA STAR Attestation is a collaboration between CSA and the AICPA to provide guidelines for CPAs to conduct SOC 2 engagements using criteria from the AICPA (Trust Service Principles, AT 101) and the CSA Cloud Controls Matrix. The STAR Attestation provides for rigorous third-party independent assessments of cloud providers. Attestation listings will expire after one year unless updated.

STAR Certification: For ISO/IEC 27001

The CSA STAR Certification is a rigorous third-party independent assessment of the security of a cloud service provider. This technology-neutral certification leverages the requirements of the ISO/IEC 27001 management system standard together with the CSA Cloud Controls Matrix. Certification certificates follow normal ISO/IEC 27001 protocol and expire after three years unless updated.

There is a C-STAR certification as well, but that is exclusive to the Chinese market and likely will not be part of your CCSK exam or daily work activities.

Summary

In this chapter, I discussed the critical importance of good governance across the entire organization, from corporate governance through to governance of cloud systems. We looked at the governance hierarchy and its associated documents. I also introduced risk tolerance, classification of data, and regulations that feed directly into governance programs. You also saw how the CSA tools can assist your cloud governance initiatives.

For the exam, ensure that you:

- Understand that the technical and operational differences of cloud computing will require new governance approaches to maintain effective security.
- Adapt your organizationalal structure with concepts like the CCoE to improve your ability to govern the procurement and maintenance of cloud environments.
- Collect and understand your foundational requirements, including your risk tolerance, compliance obligations, business needs, and existing cloud usage.
- Starting with a security framework, organize your security policies, control objectives, and control specifications in a clear "governance hierarchy."
- Know that the CCM is a control framework that you can use to assess both the CSP and the CSC.
- Know that the CAIQ asks simple questions to determine if the controls from the CCM are met.
- Know the STAR registry levels. Level 1 includes self-assessments that contain CSPs' answers to the CAIQ questions, and Level 2 includes submissions by external auditors as either STAR attestation (SOC 2) or SOC certification (ISO 27001).

So that's it for this chapter's coverage of governance. In the next chapter, we'll get into the *R* and *C* parts of GRC: risk management and compliance.

CHAPTER 3
Navigating Risk, Audit, and Compliance

> *If you think compliance is expensive, try noncompliance.*
> —Former US Deputy Attorney General Paul McNulty

In today's digital landscape, where organizations increasingly depend on cloud services, effective cloud risk management is essential. This chapter explores the critical importance of understanding cloud risks and offers guidance on establishing a cloud risk profile, evaluating CSPs, maintaining a cloud risk register, and performing risk assessments, threat intelligence, and threat modeling.

Basics of Risk Management

Let's start by defining the key terms that are used in the risk management field and throughout this chapter. I'm going to put these in a list for easy reference:

Risk management
    A structured approach to identifying, assessing, and addressing risks.

Asset
    Something of value to the company.

Attacker
    In the risk field, they call this entity a threat actor.

Target
    The asset the threat actor wants access to.

Attack vector
    A means to gain access to the target.

Vulnerability
: A weakness the threat actor can attack to gain access to the targeted asset.

Threat
: Any circumstance, event, or entity that has potential to cause harm by exploiting a vulnerability.

Risk
: Potential loss or harm.

Putting this all together in a sentence in riskspeak, you would say, "The risk management team is concerned there is a risk that a threat actor could exploit a vulnerability as the attack vector to gain access to the targeted asset."

Although there is a clear distinction between threat and risk in formal risk management, these words are often used interchangeably in practice. This is because they are both often used in real life to mean that bad things can happen. Different organizations may use either term when talking about potential negative events that should be addressed.

Now, to address this risk, there are a couple of other terms you need to understand:

Control
: Something put in place to prevent a risk from being realized. This is known as a *preventive* (some call them *protective*) control.

Countermeasure
: Something done in response to a vulnerability being exploited. This is known as a *reactive control*.

Many people in the industry use these terms interchangeably, but there is a difference between controls and countermeasures. Don't worry about this for the CCSK exam, because the exam uses the terms interchangeably.

Since we're on the subject of controls, I think now is a good time to address control types and control categories:

Control types
: There are three main control types: preventive, detective, and corrective. Three additional control types—deterrent, recovery, and compensating—are used by different frameworks.

Control categories
: These are used to break down the different implementation methods.

Table 3-1 lists the different control types, and Table 3-2 lists the different control categories.

Table 3-1. Control types

Control type	Description	Examples
Preventive	Aims to reduce risk before it is realized	Firewalls, MFA, access controls, encryption, antivirus
Detective	Identifies or alerts on events as they occur or after the fact	IDS/IPS, audit logs, security information and event management (SIEM) alerts, CCTV, file monitoring
Corrective (also known as *reactive*)	Takes action to reduce impact or restore systems after an incident	System restores, patching vulnerabilities, incident response procedures
Deterrent	Discourages potential attackers through fear or caution	Warning signs, policy enforcement, security awareness training
Recovery	Restores capabilities or services after an incident	Backups, disaster recovery plans, failover systems
Compensating	Used as an alternative when the primary control (e.g., patching a web server) isn't feasible	Manual approvals, increased monitoring, placing a control in front of a system where a direct control cannot be applied (e.g., implementing a web application firewall in front of a vulnerable web server that cannot be patched)

Table 3-2. Control categories

Control category	Description	Examples
Administrative (a.k.a. Managerial)	Controls based on policies, procedures, and human behavior	Security policies, training programs, background checks, incident response plans
Technical (a.k.a. Logical)	Controls implemented and enforced through technology	Firewalls, encryption, MFA, access control systems, antivirus
Physical	Controls that physically prevent or detect unauthorized access	Security guards, locked doors, fences, CCTV, biometric readers

Again, you don't need to know these for the CCSK exam itself, but this knowledge is fundamental to discussing and addressing risk and should be known by any security professional, cloud or not.

Eliminating any possibility of a risk being realized is not the goal of risk management. Instead, the goal is to apply controls to lower the risk to a level the organization will accept. This is called *risk mitigation*. What you have after the controls have been lowered to an acceptable level is called *residual risk*.

After all, eliminating all risk to data would require that everyone use pencils and paper to do everything. Even then, you would have the risk of unauthorized physical access to the information held in paper format instead of digital format. Risk always exists with everything. It's about taking steps to mitigate (minimize) the risk to an acceptable level for the organization.

There are numerous organizations that cover the threats and risks to cloud environments. The CSA expects CCSK exam takers to have some degree of familiarity with the different risks posed in a cloud environment. One publication the CSA releases on a periodic basis is a "top threats to cloud computing" report. The CSA comes up with different titles for these reports, but they all list what it considers the top threats to cloud computing. I won't cover each of these, because neither the CCSK study guide nor the CSA guidance documents address them. You can find these on the CSA website, and you can search for "top threats" if you want to take an optional deep dive into each listed threat.

Following is a ranked list of the top threats to cloud computing according to the CSA's "Pandemic 11" 2022 top threats research report:

- Insufficient Identity, Credentials, Access, and Key Management
- Insecure Interfaces and APIs
- Misconfiguration and Inadequate Change Control
- Lack of Cloud Security Architecture and Strategy
- Insecure Software Development
- Unsecured Third-Party Resources
- System Vulnerabilities
- Accidental Cloud Data Disclosure
- Misconfiguration and Exploitation of Serverless and Container Workloads
- Organized Crime/Hackers/Advanced Persistent Threat (APT)
- Cloud Storage Data Exfiltration

Reports like this one are referred to as *cloud threat intelligence*. There are numerous sources of this kind of intelligence, such as the MITRE ATT&CK (Adversarial Tactics, Techniques and Common Knowledge) Cloud Matrix, the ENISA Cloud Threat Landscape Reports, the Verizon Data Breach Investigations Report (DBIR), and others. A quick search of these terms will get you to the reports.

Understanding the Risk Management Process

Building on our earlier coverage of some key terms in the risk management field, let's now discuss the risk management process. There are numerous risk management processes out there that provide frameworks that organizations can adopt to manage risk effectively. Examples of such include the European Network and Information Security Agency (ENISA) Risk Management Process, ISO/IEC 27005, and the NIST Risk Management Framework (RMF). Regardless of the environment used (cloud versus traditional), this process remains constant.

All risk management processes are going to have a high-level approach (it is a framework, after all). Let's look at the five general steps of a risk management process in Figure 3-1.

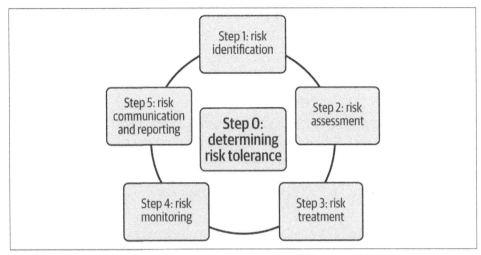

Figure 3-1. Risk management steps

Step 0: Determining Risk Tolerance

I'm labeling this "step 0" because determining risk tolerance (also called *risk appetite*) is performed by the organization leadership as part of an overall risk management strategy in advance of any other risk management activities. It establishes the level of risk the organization is willing to accept while pursuing its objectives and is the key foundation that all risk management activities consider when determining whether a risk is acceptable to the organization. Every organization is going to have a different risk tolerance. For example, a two-person startup would likely have a very high risk tolerance (move fast and break stuff), whereas a 100-year-old bank would likely have a very low risk tolerance. Their risk tolerance will shape how each manages risks.

Step 1: Risk Identification

In this initial step, you identify assets, threats, vulnerabilities, and potential events that could pose risks to the organization. It's important to understand that this is not exclusive to attackers breaching IT systems. It also includes risk arising from natural events such as earthquakes and floods, as well as system failure due to aging hardware.

Step 2: Risk Assessment (or Risk Analysis)

You then perform a risk assessment to assess the likelihood and potential impact of identified risks in order to prioritize risks. This can be done using either qualitative or quantitative methods.

Qualitative assessments are subjective in nature (e.g., low, moderate, high). They take into account both the likelihood of a risk being realized and its impact. Let's consider two examples. In the first, there's a vulnerability that can easily be remotely executed to allow the attacker to access all the data on a server as a powerful system account. In this case, the likelihood of an attack would be high (remote and easy to execute) and the impact would be high (all data at risk).

In the second example, there's a vulnerability that requires physical access to a server, as well as the soldering of a chip to access an encryption key stored in the Trusted Platform Module (TPM). The likelihood of an attack is low but the impact is high. Would the risk assessment for this be high, medium, or low? This is where subjectivity comes into play.

Quantitative assessments use measurable methods. In a scenario where you're trying to determine if a new security appliance should be purchased, you could use quantitative risk assessment. To do this, you need to know the *asset value* (AV) and estimate the percentage of loss based on the type of event. This is called the *exposure factor* (EF). Multiplying these two figures gives you your *single loss expectancy* (SLE).

After this, you need to determine how many times per year you can reasonably expect an event to occur (this could be based on historical actuary tables, for example). This is called the *annual rate of occurrence* (ARO). Finally, now that you know the asset value, the cost of an event, and how many times per year the event may be realized, you can determine the *annual loss expectancy* (ALE). The calculation is as follows:

Quantitative Annual Loss Expectancy formula: $ALE = ARO \times SLE$

As I'm sure you can agree, quantitative risk assessment is generally more time consuming than qualitative risk assessment. In all my years as a cybersecurity professional, I've only ever seen qualitative risk assessment being performed. But the downside to quantitative risk assessment is the degree of subjectivity. Familiarity with the environment will help make more accurate and meaningful rankings for qualitative assessments.

Step 3: Risk Treatment

This step is when you develop strategies to manage risks. Let's talk about some key terms.

Simply stated, *risk mitigation* is when you reduce risk (either the likelihood or the impact of a threat being realized) by applying controls. Control types could be preventive controls to stop an incident, detective controls to identify and detect an incident, and incident and corrective controls to recover from an incident.

As a simple example of risk mitigation, consider the essential characteristic of the cloud in broad network access. As the cloud management console logon page is available to anyone in the world, there is an increased risk of unauthorized access. To lower the likelihood of this risk being realized, an organization may require that MFA be implemented for all access to the cloud management console.

Risk transfer occurs when a decision is made to transfer the risk of something. This is commonly associated with cyber insurance but could also include outsourcing to a CSP. For example, an organization could outsource the risk of hardware failure by using IaaS, where the CSP will be responsible for maintaining the hardware.

Responsibility and accountability are not the same thing. An IT team member may be responsible for patching servers, but the IT manager would be accountable if the team fails to perform its duties properly. You may transfer risk by outsourcing a responsibility to a CSP, but you can never outsource accountability.

Risk avoidance is when you opt out of doing something to avoid incurring risk. This is usually done when it is not possible to mitigate the risk to an acceptable level.

Risk acceptance occurs when you proceed with an activity because the risk is within the organization's risk tolerance. Acceptance is generally only performed after a risk has been mitigated to an acceptable level. The risk that remains is referred to as *residual risk*.

Once the action plan to mitigate is implemented, any residual risks are identified. If these residual risks are considered acceptable (within the risk tolerance), the activity is approved, and residual risks are monitored and will be reevaluated periodically (such as through increased assessment). If the residual risks are not within an organization's risk tolerance, additional controls may be pursued, or the activity may be abandoned.

Step 4: Risk Monitoring

In this step, you continuously monitor risks, as well as the effectiveness of the risk management strategies. This can be done by regularly reviewing the organization's security posture, conducting audits, and updating risk assessments as new threats emerge. Risk monitoring also ensures an organization's ongoing compliance with regulations (e.g., GDPR), standards (e.g., PCI DSS), and laws. From a technical perspective, detective controls such as SIEM; security orchestration, automation, and response (SOAR); and continuous monitoring tools assist in risk monitoring.

Step 5: Risk Communication and Reporting

In this final step, you communicate and report to ensure that all stakeholders (e.g., leadership, regulators) are informed of risks, risk management efforts, and residual risks. This step forms the feedback loop to leadership as to current risk management program success and possible improvements. Communication and reporting will often include documentation and dashboards that report on key risk metrics, incident response activities, and the effectiveness of controls.

The risk communication phase also feeds back to the risk tolerance phase because newly identified risks may change the risk tolerance of the company. For example, a bank I use has a "voiceprint" identification system to verify a caller is truly the customer and not an impersonator. With the new risk of AI being able to copy someone's voice, this would lead the bank to reassess its risk tolerance and potentially replace it with a more secure method. For example, it may introduce a random phrase that a caller must repeat for authentication. This is also an example of how risk can change, and why the feedback loop is essential in continuously addressing risk. These high-level steps form a continuous cycle to help organizations address emerging threats and adapt their risk strategies over time.

Assessing Cloud Services

You must assess potential CSPs before onboarding them. I cannot stress enough how critical this is. For every multibillion-dollar publicly traded CSP, there are 100 CSPs that have a handful of employees and frankly have no clue about governance or risk management. They may have a great technical solution, but how long will it be until they are breached or a critical error is introduced and they lose all customer data? I have seen providers without any business continuity or disaster recovery plans. And don't even get me started about SaaS vendors that claim they are 100% secure because they run everything out of AWS. If a potential SaaS vendor tells you this, politely hang up the phone and never speak with that vendor again. The fact that they don't know about the SSRM tells you everything you need to know about their lack of cloud security knowledge.

To assess cloud services, the CSA recommends the systematic process shown in Figure 3-2 and outlined in the sections that follow.

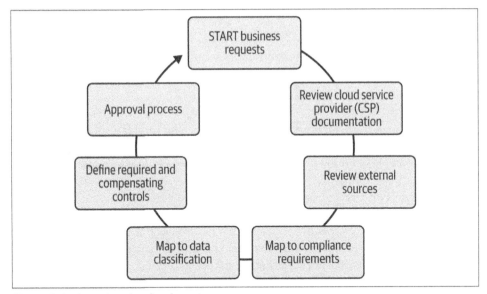

Figure 3-2. Assessing the cloud services process

Step 1: Assess the Business Request

The first step you need to take when assessing a potential cloud service is to ask a critical question: Does the organization even need the cloud service that an employee is requesting, or does the organization already have a similar solution? Why would an organization have five different CRM systems? That just means five different locations where data is stored and needs to be protected (not to mention the cost associated with this). Speaking of data protection, what classification of data will be stored in the system? This will dictate the security controls required and any associated regulations that may need to be addressed.

Step 2: Review CSP Documentation

An organization must understand whether the provider's maturity matches its own. In other words, does the provider have practices in place that an organization would expect? For example, I have seen SaaS providers that don't have any external audits performed and don't even have a disaster recovery capability. Perhaps a startup with two people won't care. But the lack of external audit and disaster recovery plans would be a deal-breaker for more mature organizations.

The CSA advises that you review the following CSP documentation before onboarding.

Security and privacy documentation

Review the CSP's policies for security and privacy as well as data handling practices to ensure that they align with your organization's standards. Providers should be forthcoming with this information.

SLAs and contracts

SLAs outline the performance, uptime commitments, and service availability guaranteed by the CSP. They often include metrics such as response time, resolution time, and the percentage of uptime (e.g., 99.9% uptime). SLAs also define penalties or remedies (e.g., service credits) if these commitments are not met. These are often on a scale of severity. For example, uptime between 95% and 99% may mean a 10% service credit of monthly spend, whereas uptime between 90% and 95% may mean a 20% service credit of monthly spend. Service credits cost the CSP a significant amount of money in unrealized income. A CSP may very well make you provide detailed evidence (e.g., screenshots, logs) of suffering an impact.

The service credit claims process can be very complex depending on the provider. Take, for example, a scenario where your organization spends $10,000 per month on a compute service and $1,000 on an object storage service. The compute service reads and writes to the object storage to deliver service. The object storage suffers an outage and your servers, although running, fail to deliver services as a result. With a commonly used service-specific SLA of 10%, you would be entitled to a $100 service credit because only the object storage was impacted, regardless of it making your service nonfunctional. This is why you need to understand these SLAs before onboarding the provider.

Contracts detail the broader terms of service, including the shared responsibilities, liabilities, data ownership, security obligations, and termination clauses. Contracts typically cover legal aspects like data privacy, compliance requirements, intellectual property rights, and financial terms. Be very diligent when it comes to contract reviews. Some providers are unethical and will put in contract terms that are one-sided.

Take data ownership, for example. There are CSPs out there that state in their contracts that all data uploaded to the system becomes property of the CSP and that you as the client have access to it only while remaining a client. I had this happen to a client. The client got its data back, but the client was a US government agency. Does your company have the same power as the US government to convince the CSP what it did is wrong? Or is your only resort to write a strongly worded tweet? Always have your legal team review the contracts before accepting them.

Terms of service

Understanding the terms of service (ToS) is important to avoid legal or operational surprises post adoption. These may be the only legal contracts between you and the provider.

CSP certifications and audits

There are several certifications and audits that CSPs can obtain and make available to prospective customers to demonstrate a commitment to security. For example, the CSA CAIQ is a series of questions based on the CCM controls framework that can be answered with simple yes or no responses. It provides a comprehensive list of questions that can be used by potential customers to better understand the security and privacy controls in place at a CSP. The issue that may arise is that the completed CAIQ is a self-assessment by the provider with no assessment by a third-party auditor. For that reason, some organizations may insist the CSP have a third party perform an audit to validate security practices and controls under a standard such as the STAR registry program, ISO/IEC 27001 certification, and/or SOC 2 reports. We'll discuss these in the upcoming sections.

Of note regarding the CAIQ is the STAR registry that is hosted by the CSA. The STAR registry has two levels of CSP submissions. Level 1 entries are CSP-supplied responses (self-assessments) to the CAIQ. Level 2 entries (third-party validation) are supplied by independent auditors to represent the CSP's SOC 2 report (called a *STAR level 2 attestation*) and/or its ISO 27001 certification (called a *STAR level 2 certification*). Both level 2 entries incorporate their respective SOC 2 or ISO/IEC 27001 controls audit and an additional audit of cloud controls from the CCM. Organizations seeking stronger guarantees of a CSP's security practices are more likely to favor STAR level 2 entries over STAR level 1 entries due to the additional verification and credibility it provides.

ISO/IEC 27001, ISO/IEC 27017, and SOC 2 are the primary audit standards that many CSPs will use to demonstrate that appropriate security is in place for their cloud services. I'm covering these "pass-through" or "third-party" audits for your understanding of the standards themselves. You won't be tested on the contents of either SOC reports or ISO certifications as part of the CCSK exam, but if you're going to be involved with selecting cloud environments, you should know what these standards are and how they differ. You may very well be presented with the terms *pass-through* and *third-party audit*, though. I'll keep the discussion of each brief.

SOC background. SOC (pronounced *sock*) was developed and is maintained by the Association of International Certified Professional Accountants (AICPA). There are three SOC reports to be aware of:

- SOC 1 is for Internal Controls over Financial Reporting (ICFR).
- SOC 2 is titled "Report on Controls at a Service Organization Relevant to Security, Availability, Processing Integrity, Confidentiality, or Privacy" (AICPA's wording, not mine). The title of the report will be adjusted based on the scope of the report.
- SOC 3 is basically a high-level summary of the SOC 2 report that can be freely distributed (SOC 1 and SOC 2 are only available with a nondisclosure agreement [NDA] in place).

Both the SOC 1 and SOC 2 reports are based on Statements on Standards for Attestation Engagements (SSAE) 18.

There are two types of reports. These report types talk to the depth of assessment. Type 1 is a point-in-time look at control design. Type 2 looks at both the control design and the operating effectiveness of these controls over a period of time.

As a customer, the ideal report you want to see from a CSP is a SOC 2, type 2 report because the auditor tests control effectiveness and not just the design of the controls.

SOC reports address what is known as the Trust Services Criteria (these used to be called *Trust Services Principles*). There are five criteria that the provider can decide to be in scope for the attestation engagement report. The CSP may choose just security (also known as the *Common Criteria*) or all five. It's up to the CSP based on what it believes its customers want. These criteria are:

Security
   The system is protected against unauthorized access, use, or modification. This is mandatory for all SOC engagements.

Availability
   The system is available for operation and use as committed or agreed.

Confidentiality
   Information designated as confidential is protected as committed or agreed.

Processing integrity
   System processing is complete, valid, accurate, timely, and authorized.

Privacy
   A system's collection, use, retention, disclosure, and disposal of personal information is in conformance with privacy notices.

An important note about SOC reports is that they are not a certification. A SOC report is what is called an *attestation engagement report*. A CSP makes an assertion about controls it has in place, and the auditor forms and documents an opinion that appropriate controls are designed (type 1) and, in the case of a type 2 report, the controls operate effectively after performing the tests to validate the CSP's assertion. Any CSP that pays an audit firm for a SOC report will get its SOC report. These cannot be treated as a checkbox exercise. You may see the auditor state a disclaimer or what is known as a *qualified opinion*; for example, "We don't disclose an opinion, because we were not given access to the datacenter in scope." That is from an actual SOC 2 report I read in the past. This disclaimer is as close to a fail as you can get. The CSP still had a SOC 2 report, though.

The final thing I think is important for you to know about SOC reports is the concept of Complementary User Entity Controls (CUECs). I think they're important because they also drive home the concept of the shared responsibility model of the cloud. These CUECs are contained within the SOC report supplied to you by the provider to advise customers that certain controls must be in place by the customer to support the SOC report. Some of the more important items to note that will likely be applicable to all cloud services involve logical security. This includes things customers are responsible for doing, such as establishing administrators, ensuring that accounts in the system are appropriate and checked on a regular basis, and ensuring that accounts are removed once they are no longer required.

ISO/IEC 27000-Series Certification background. While SOC 2 reports are very commonly used to demonstrate a commitment to security by CSPs in North America compared to ISO/IEC certifications, globally, ISO/IEC certifications are very important for many industries. For example, in the latest ISO Survey that lists the number of organizations with ISO/IEC 27001 certification, there are 1,898 organizations with this certification in the United States, 3,630 in the United Kingdom, and 5,599 in Japan. The reason for the difference is that in many jurisdictions, ISO/IEC 27001 certification is required for government contracts and regulated industries.

The purpose of ISO/IEC 27001 certification is to define the requirements for an ISMS. Note that I'm not saying the entire organization, because it all depends on the scope of the ISMS. The scope could be limited by the provider to one group within an organization, and there is no guarantee that any group outside the scope has an appropriate ISMS in place. It is up to the auditor to verify that the scope of the engagement is "fit for purpose." As the customer, you are responsible for determining if the scope of the certification is relevant for your purposes. The scope of the certification can be determined by reviewing the statement of applicability (SoA) that is part of the ISO/IEC certification documentation.

The SoA is a mandatory document that lists all the controls found in ISO/IEC 27001, whether a control is applicable, justification for a control's inclusion or exclusion from the scope, how each applicable control is implemented, and relevant documentation (e.g., policies, procedures, configurations) for systems in scope.

A complete SoA will likely only be available to customers under NDA due to the sensitivity of the information it contains. Without access to the SoA (or at least a clear understanding of its contents), you are lacking the information needed to determine if the controls in place are adequate for your risk and compliance needs.

ISO/IEC 27002 is a companion document that provides implementation guidance and best practices for the controls found in ISO/IEC 27001. ISO/IEC 27002 is not a certification. It supports ISO/IEC 27001. Think of it as a "how-to" guide for setting up an ISMS in accordance with ISO/IEC 27001.

The ISO/IEC 27017 "code of practice" uses the controls from ISO/IEC 27002 and dictates what should be in place for cloud environments. It has guidance that states what both the provider and customer should do for security. While not certification on its own, its controls can be included in the scope of an ISO/IEC 27001 certification audit to demonstrate adherence to cloud security best practices. Many CSPs incorporate 27017 controls into their ISMS as part of a comprehensive cloud security posture. These controls will be referenced in their SoA.

The ISO/IEC 27018 "code of practice" is focused on the protection of personal data in cloud environments (a.k.a. privacy). CSPs that work with privacy-related data would likely have this certification. Like ISO/IEC 27017, CSPs may demonstrate conformity to ISO/IEC 27018 as part of their broader ISO/IEC 27001 certification by including relevant privacy controls in their SoA.

Step 3: Review External Sources

Investigate external reviews, reported vulnerabilities, and any past security and operational incidents involving the CSP to gauge its security posture and response capabilities. The Common Vulnerabilities and Exposures (CVE) database tracks cloud issues. There are also sites that have examples of known security issues with larger providers that have occurred in the past. IT-specific news sites would be another source you can use to research.

Step 4: Map to Compliance Requirements

When selecting a CSP, it is essential to ensure that the CSP policies and/or certifications align with your organization's compliance needs, such as GDPR, HIPAA, or PCI DSS. This ensures that regulatory requirements are met as part of the SSRM.

Let's consider PCI DSS as an example of the concept of compliance inheritance (this concept applies to many other regulations and standards). PCI DSS has 12 requirements that address security controls ranging from logical security through to physical security. We'll use two PCI DSS requirements as an example to demonstrate compliance inheritance:

PCI DSS Requirement 5.3.1
The antimalware solution(s) is kept current via automatic updates.

PCI DSS Requirement 9.2.1
Appropriate facility entry controls are in place to restrict physical access to systems in the CDE (*CDE* stands for *cardholder data environment*).

Assuming your organization has built its own application that works with cardholder data that is run on a VM in an IaaS environment, you would be responsible for ensuring that 5.3.1 is in place by implementing automatic updates for antimalware solutions used on the VMs you are responsible for building and maintaining. The CSP would be responsible for 9.2.1 by implementing appropriate facility entry controls to restrict physical access to the infrastructure where cardholder data is stored.

This will require that the CSP environment meets PCI DSS requirements to be considered "PCI compliant," and your organization's application is also required to meet PCI DSS requirements. Operating a PCI-compliant application in a noncompliant CSP environment would result in your application not passing an audit, which could lead to penalties or fines imposed by payment card brands or acquiring banks.

Step 5: Map to Data Classification

As discussed in Chapter 2, classification of data and systems must be performed to ensure that appropriate controls are in place to protect data to an appropriate level (and potentially to meet regulatory requirements). Not all CSPs need to meet the highest level of classification you have. For example, a CSP hosting nonsensitive data such as cafeteria menus would warrant a low level of classification compared to a CSP hosting highly sensitive data such as a payroll system.

Some CSPs may have different offerings for different classification levels. Take FedRAMP, for example. FedRAMP authorizes cloud products for use within the US government. FedRAMP has four different impact levels that restrict the maximum data classification that can be used in a FedRAMP-authorized cloud service: Low-impact SaaS, Low, Moderate, and High. The number of controls checked ranges from 125 for low-impact offerings to over 420 for high-impact cloud services. In the case of AWS, FedRAMP has the standard commercial AWS offering that can be used for data classified to the "moderate" classification, and its GovCloud offering that can be used for data that is classified as "high." The classification level of the actual service being used by an organization should be added to the cloud register, which is covered later in this chapter.

Step 6: Define Required and Compensating Controls

Before final approval, the risk management team needs to define any required activities such as configuration settings and control implementations that need to be configured within the CSP, and any compensating controls such as third-party tools that are needed to use the service with the designated data classifications.

Step 7: Obtain Final Approval

Once all these steps are taken and the service is properly secured, someone (preferably the CCoE discussed in Chapter 2) needs to provide final approval before the system can be used for production workloads. After approval is granted and roles and responsibilities are assigned to maintain the service, the CSP can be added to the cloud register, ensuring that the organization maintains visibility and control over cloud adoptions.

Governance, Risk Management, and Compliance Tools

Several tools can be used to assist with GRC activities in an organization. The tools can be technical or nontechnical. Examples of technical tools include IAM, SIEM, data loss prevention (DLP), automated auditing tools, and platforms that track compliance metrics. Nontechnical tools include documentation of responsibilities, contracts and legal agreements, cloud registers, risk registries where identified risks and their perceived impacts and mitigation strategies are documented and managed, and written policies and procedures.

Let's look more closely at the cloud register. The cloud register is a centralized repository that tracks and documents approved cloud providers and services within an organization. It specifies the types of classification of data a service is approved for, the associated risk levels based on the data handled, and the assessment frequency. It helps guide decision making for cloud service usage by ensuring that only services that meet security and data protection requirements are used. As a result, this helps organizations meet compliance requirements. Table 3-3 shows an example cloud register.

Table 3-3. Example of a cloud register

Provider	Service	Data types	Risk level	Assessment frequency
ABC	Object storage	Public, Sensitive	Moderate	Annual
ABC	Virtual networks	All	Moderate	Annual
XYZ	CRM SaaS	PII	High	Quarterly

In Chapter 2, I mentioned how important it is to keep track of CSPs in use. This is what the cloud register is all about. It is a GRC tool that can be used to easily track all the different providers and services your organization uses.

Compliance means adherence to the requirements of applicable laws and regulations, sector-specific codes of conduct and codes of practice, standards, and best practices. These requirements will often be a key consideration when an organization creates internal policies and procedures. In the case of laws and regulations, these must be adhered to in order to avoid fines or even restrictions from continuing business operations. Complying with applicable requirements allows organizations to satisfy internal policies and codes of ethics, safely operate in the market, and in some cases gain a competitive advantage by demonstrating compliance with leading standards, which appeals to both regulated enterprises and other organizations that prioritize security and regulatory adherence.

Where Compliance Requirements Come From

Compliance requirements come from many sources, including the following:

- National and international standards and regulations can regulate the processing, storage, and transfer of certain types of data. For example, GDPR has requirements for processing, storing, and transferring data that contains personal information that all organizations offering services to European citizens must follow, regardless of their industry. There are also industry standards, such as PCI, for credit card handling. If you accept payment and/or process credit cards, you must meet this standard. If you don't collect or process payments with credit cards, then this standard doesn't apply.
- Many standards have cloud-specific guidance, such as the PCI DSS Cloud Computing Guidelines, which provides a framework for ensuring compliance with PCI DSS in cloud environments by addressing specific security considerations, roles, and responsibilities in the shared responsibility model between CSPs and customers.
- Contractual obligations can include SLAs, data processing agreements (DPAs), and other terms that impose specific compliance requirements on organizations, particularly in cloud services.
- Internal policies and standards may need updating if they are too specific for on-premises environments. Cloud environments may require adjustments to account for the SSRM, data residency, compliance requirements, and cloud-specific security and access controls. Policies should also include cloud-specific logging, incident response, and IAM considerations.

Compliance is demonstrated through audits and conformity assessments that evaluate the suitability of the system of controls to satisfy the applicable requirements. For regulations, these audits will likely be performed as an external audit (although you should perform an internal audit first to ensure that deficiencies are addressed before the real audit), whereas adherence to internal policy will likely be performed by an internal audit function.

Artifacts of Compliance

Compliance artifacts include the logs, documentation, and other materials needed for audits and compliance; they serve as evidence to support compliance activities. Customers are ultimately responsible for providing the necessary artifacts for their audits. Therefore, they need to understand what the provider offers and create their own artifacts to cover any gaps. For example, they might need to enhance the logging within an application if server logs on a PaaS platform are not accessible.

The following are examples of compliance artifacts:

Audit logs
  Detailed records of events, actions, and changes within the cloud environment.

Activity reporting
  Reports summarizing user activities, access patterns, and system interactions. Activity reports can help identify unauthorized access, track user actions, and ensure that operational practices align with compliance requirements.

System configuration details
  Documentation of system configurations, including network settings, access controls, and security measures.

Change management details
  Records of changes made to the system, including updates, modifications, and patches. These details are critical for ensuring that changes are authorized, tested, and implemented in a manner that maintains the integrity and security of the environment.

Jurisdictions

You must consider more than just countries as being jurisdictions. Even different states and provinces will likely have their own laws and regulations that must be met. Take California as an example. The California Consumer Privacy Act (CCPA) is a privacy law that expands the very definition of what personal information is. In California, much like in the EU with GDPR, anything related to an individual, even an IP address, is considered personal data and must be protected.

In contrast, PII is what many other US states use. In these states, where the definition of PII is typically narrower (e.g., requires direct identifiers, such as a government ID number or driver's license number), an IP address may not be considered PII unless it's combined with other data that can identify an individual. In other words, you need people assigned to determine privacy issues, because it can get tricky.

Sticking with the United States for a moment, oddly enough, there is no blanket privacy law at the federal level. Privacy laws are regulated by the types of private data, such as HIPAA for healthcare-related information, the Gramm-Leach-Bliley Act (GLBA) for financial information, and the Children's Online Privacy Protection Act (COPPA), which regulates the collection and use of personal information of children under age 13 by online services.

Jurisdictions and their treatment of personal data must be a key consideration for business. For example, I worked on an agriculture technology project that was to use satellites and GPS coordinates to have tractors administer nutrients to soil that would support the crop the landowner was growing (e.g., soybeans versus corn). This was to be deployed across North America. The company leadership had the legal team determine if there were any laws or regulations they needed to consider as part of this new business opportunity. The legal team determined that a GPS coordinate was indeed personal data. Why? They concluded that given a GPS coordinate, you can get an address. With the address, you can get the name of the landowner from the county registrar land records. This one decision made them abandon a North American rollout and limited the project rollout to just the United States. I don't know the exact numbers, but I would assume this decision cost the organization millions in deferred revenue.

Exam Note

Jurisdictional issues are a big deal for companies, and the cloud only complicates things. You can expect to be tested on this.

Cloud deployments will most likely span different legal and regulatory jurisdictions. I mean, is it realistic to assume an organization will only use cloud services hosted in its jurisdiction? The complexity of compliance becomes magnified when operations extend across multiple regions, each with its own legal and regulatory frameworks governing data privacy, security, and other critical factors. Let's delve deeper into the factors influencing jurisdictional considerations in the cloud environment.

Cloud providers and cloud consumers operating in multiple regions will face multiple jurisdictions where various laws and regulations apply. This is affected by:

- The location of the cloud provider
- The location of the cloud consumer
- The location where the individual whose data is being stored lives (called the *data subject* in GDPR)

- The location where the data is stored
- The legal jurisdiction of the contract, which may be different from the locations of any stakeholders
- Any treaties or other legal frameworks between those various locations

An example is the requirement to issue a breach notification in the country you are operating in, even if the data was hosted in a different region.

To give you an idea of some of the privacy laws and regulations organizations may face, following are some jurisdictions and the privacy laws that exist.

European Union/European Economic Area's GDPR

This is the privacy law that made organizations take note of the importance of securing privacy-related data. GDPR has various rights that are granted to individuals:

Right to access
   Allows individuals to obtain confirmation of whether their personal data is being collected and to access that data along with related information. This is why you see many websites offer you the ability to download everything they know about you. One example is Google. Try it; you may be surprised how much Google knows about you!

Right to rectification (correction)
   Gives individuals the right to have inaccurate or incomplete personal data corrected without undue delay.

Right to erasure ("right to be forgotten")
   Enables individuals to request the deletion of their personal data when it is no longer necessary, consent is withdrawn, or processing is unlawful.

Right to data portability
   Allows individuals to receive their personal data in a structured, commonly used, and machine-readable format and to transfer it to another controller (we'll cover this role shortly).

Right to object to processing
   Lets individuals object to the processing of their personal data when based on legitimate interests (e.g., business relationship) or direct marketing.

Right to restrict processing
   Permits individuals to limit how their personal data is used.

Right not to be subject to automated decision making
> Protects individuals from decisions made solely by automated means that significantly affect them, including profiling, unless specific safeguards are in place (think of AI systems).

Companies that fail to comply with these requirements face fines from their country's Data Protection Authority. Although this is a European regulation, it applies to companies in different countries, including the United States. This is because of extraterritoriality. By the letter of the law, if a service is available to Europeans, GDPR applies. This is why you now see that essentially every website you go to has a privacy notice. Companies can't really determine if a European is traveling to New York City, for example, and they certainly don't want to restrict themselves from selling to a market that is bigger than the United States, so they abide by GDPR for fear of violating the regulation.

How does it make executives stand up and take notice? GDPR administers huge fines if an organization is found to be noncompliant. Take Meta's US$1.3 billion fine, or Amazon's US$800 million fine (as of this writing, both Meta and Amazon are appealing their fines). Fines of up to 4% of global revenue or €20 million (whichever is higher) will make any organization follow the rules of GDPR, don't you think?

Under GDPR, there are certain roles that you should know about. We won't cover all of them, and these won't come up in the CCSK exam, but they are good to know about all the same:

Data subject
> The person (e.g., customer, employee) whose personal data is being collected.

Data controller
> The party that collects data subject information and is responsible for determining why and how the data is processed. It must ensure that appropriate controls (legal, technical, and organizational) are in place to protect this information.

Data processor
> The party that processes the data. It must ensure that the controls from the data controller remain in place, and it has its own security measures to protect the data it processes on behalf of the data controller.

To bring all this together, if you buy a car part from Driveline Solutions and that company uses a SaaS to process your order, you are the data subject, Driveline Solutions is the data controller, and the SaaS provider is the data processor.

Here's a fun fact regarding GDPR. It seems likely that every organization will eventually face some form of GDPR reprimand and/or penalty in the future. Even the European Commission, which is a main architect and enforcer of GDPR, was issued a reprimand by the European Data Protection Supervisor (EDPS), which is the supervisory authority for monitoring and ensuring data protection compliance for EU government agencies (including the European Commission), for use of a "login with Facebook" registration link for a conference it was hosting. The fact that this link sent user information to Facebook was found to violate rules on international data transfers. GDPR isn't just about computer systems, by the way. It's any form of personal information. Ask the restaurant owner who had a camera pointed at the sidewalk outside their restaurant without proper notice, or the waiter who left a comment card on a table that was seen by another customer. In both situations, GDPR penalties were applied to the business owners.

Brazil's LGPD

Brazil's *LGPD*, which stands for *General Personal Data Protection Law* in English, is inspired by GDPR. Like European law, it also sets a high standard for data protection, emphasizing individuals' rights over their data, requiring consent for data collection and processing, and imposing strict penalties for violations (2% of revenue realized in Brazil, capped at US$10 million per violation). This is an example of how countries around the world will likely follow the lead of the EU in tightening privacy laws in their own countries.

Other countries that either have implemented privacy laws inspired by GDPR or are in process of getting these laws passed include Japan with its Act on Protection of Personal Information (APPI), Australia and New Zealand with their Privacy Acts, Canada with the Consumer Privacy Protection Act, South Korea, and India, among others.

Data Localization Laws

Another key jurisdictional item that multinational organizations must consider is that of data localization laws. In some jurisdictions, such as the EU, there are contracts that must be signed to allow the export of personal data to other jurisdictions. In other jurisdictions, such as China and Russia, all personal data is prohibited from being exported out of the country. Other jurisdictions still may restrict certain types of personal data from being exported; for example, India restricts export of financial data. As mentioned earlier, privacy is a very tricky area for companies and does require dedicated roles to determine responsibilities when multiple jurisdictions are involved, which is very common when the cloud is involved.

Exam Tip

As Ferris Bueller famously said, life moves pretty fast. Although I doubt you will be asked questions regarding country-specific laws (the goal is to understand the principles), know that governments are changing laws all the time. If you ever get a question on the CCSK exam about a law that you know has changed from the time this book or the study guide was written, go with the book answer, not with what you know is the case at the time you take the exam. The testing organization will never contradict its written material. What it will do is remove any associated questions to a subject where things have changed.

Compliance in the Cloud

Although there are many different regulations and laws that organizations must address, they all have several standard requirements.

Secure handling

Access to sensitive data must be tightly controlled, and confidentiality and integrity of data must be maintained when it is processed.

Secure storage

Encryption and other protective measures must be implemented to safeguard data at rest and in transit. Additionally, proper data retention and deletion policies and practices must be in place. Different data types may have different retention and deletion requirements. For example, a bank may have a policy that tax-related data be retained for seven years, whereas data regarding currency transactions may have to be retained for five years.

Due care and due diligence

These two terms are often used interchangeably, but there is a key difference between them. Due care is often a legal requirement, and a lack of due care can lead to civil lawsuits (being sued for negligence if harm results from inadequate due care). In the context of security and risk management, due care is demonstrating to stakeholders that data is protected from threats and vulnerabilities. This is typically achieved by adhering to industry best practices and security standards. It demonstrates that your organization is acting responsibly. Think, for example, about the question, "What would a prudent person do?" This is due care.

Due diligence, on the other hand, is the process of continuously ensuring that due care is being practiced. For example, an organization could practice due care by having certified security professionals secure customer data. It would be practicing due diligence by selecting the appropriate training, ensuring attendance, and keeping track of employee certification status to ensure that this is maintained.

Audit trails

Maintain comprehensive records of data processing activities to demonstrate compliance with regulatory requirements. Audit trails will be a key item that auditors will review when performing audits. Although this domain is focused on GRC, audit trails are also critical for incident response and forensics purposes.

Summary

In this chapter, we discussed everything the CCSK material addresses as part of the risk, audit, and compliance domain.

For the CCSK exam, ensure that you:

- Can define key risk terms (asset, threat, risk, etc.).
- Can explain why you can never completely eliminate risk.
- Know that the CSA does have cloud threat reports (e.g., "Pandemic 11") and that this is a form of risk intelligence.
- Can describe the risk management process (from risk determination to risk communication) and that risk management is a continuous process.
- Recognize that all CSPs must be assessed for risk prior to usage. Remember the steps involved in assessing risk, from the initial business request through to approval.
- Remember that external certifications and pass-through or third-party audits give customers enhanced confidence in the security controls in place within a CSP.
- Can describe the benefit of the cloud register and how it tracks providers and services consumed.
- Understand what drives compliance requirements (laws, regulations, standards, contracts).
- Know what compliance artifacts are and the examples provided.
- Can explain the impact of the cloud and how multiple jurisdictions and privacy rights are a main driver of compliance, with different laws around the world.

In the next chapter, we'll move on to the more technical aspects of the CCSK material, beginning with organization management.

CHAPTER 4
Guide to Cloud Organization Management

Good order is the foundation of all things.
—Edmund Burke

Multiple reports state that in 2024, the "average" company was using more than 300 SaaS applications. However, these numbers can be misleading. So let's be conservative and cut that stated number in half. That leaves us with more than 150 different applications where data is stored and a lot of applications that need to be secured and managed.

Now consider IaaS and PaaS usage. How many applications and systems does an organization run in these service models? Does the organization use multiple clouds where it may have workloads in multiple IaaS providers? This adoption of multiple SaaS, PaaS, and IaaS services, either purposefully to meet business requirements, through mergers and acquisitions, or through the lack of governance, is commonly referred to as *cloud sprawl*.

Securing and managing all these different environments is what this chapter is about. Let's get into it with a view of managing larger IaaS implementations with organizational management approaches. Subsequent sections of this chapter will address common security controls for SaaS, hybrid cloud security, and multicloud environments.

Organizational Hierarchy Models

Before we dive into the core material of this section, I'm going to provide some key definitions. All CSPs offer similar features. This is what the CSA calls *feature parity*. Providers will likely use different names for the same concept. How they are implemented will almost certainly be very different. Organizational hierarchies are an example of this.

Exam Note

Even though we're about to cover different CSPs and products by name, you will not be asked any questions regarding individual CSPs and their own terminology or how items are implemented and configured. Remember, the CCSK exam is vendor agnostic!

Definitions

The following are key terms the CSA uses in its material:

- An *organization* is the highest level of structure within a CSP.
- A *group* represents a collection of deployments.
- A *deployment* refers to an isolated environment within a CSP.

All major IaaS providers offer a way to create an organizational hierarchy. Table 4-1 is an example in action.

Table 4-1. CSP organizational hierarchies

CSP	Organization	Group	Deployment
AWS	Organization	Organizational Unit (OU)	Accounts
Microsoft Azure	Tenant	Management group	Subscription
Google Cloud	Organizations	Folders	Project

Differentiating Accounts

There are AWS accounts, and then there are user accounts. These are not the same thing. This is why you will see me use the term *AWS account* or *deployment account* throughout this chapter. You can think of an AWS account as what is created when you initially sign up for AWS. Then, you would create individual user accounts for your employees that will work with the AWS management console. In this section, I'll mostly be using the terms AWS uses.

Organizational Structures

Utilizing multiple deployments is a strategic approach recommended by the CSA and all the major IaaS providers to reduce the impact of adverse events or breaches, adhering to service limits imposed by CSPs, and facilitating the logical separation of different technology stacks. I know that's a mouthful, so let's break it down a bit. Remember that a deployment is an isolated environment. Utilizing multiple deployments means you are implementing a hard security boundary. Among the many benefits of architecting enterprise cloud adoption with this approach, our primary focus for the CCSK exam is that it creates isolated environments. This isolation limits the extent of a breach as the impact is limited to a single deployment. In turn, this minimizes incident response efforts as fewer systems will be impacted.

This strategy is commonly referred to as *limiting the blast radius*. Let's imagine a scenario where an attacker gains access to an administrative user account with full control of an AWS account. If all applications are in that one AWS account, everything is at risk. However, if you were to create a separate AWS account for every application, the blast radius would be limited to that one application being at risk. This separation that is created by using a *hard security boundary*, such as multiple AWS accounts, is commonly used and highly recommended by CSPs. For example, I've worked in environments with over 70 different AWS accounts where each application was run in a separate AWS account. I also know of organizations that use the same approach with hundreds of separate AWS accounts.

Figure 4-1 shows two different organizational architecture approaches. On the lefthand side, you see a single AWS deployment account with three virtual private clouds (VPCs). These are *soft security boundaries*. If an administrative user account in the IAM system is compromised, all workloads within that single AWS account are at risk. On the righthand side, you see three separate AWS accounts. In the event that an administrative account in the Dev AWS account is compromised, the extent of damage is limited to that single hard security boundary.

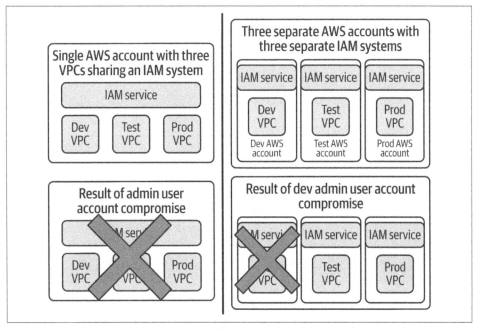

Figure 4-1. Comparing organization architecture approaches

Organizational Hierarchy Models | 77

At this point, I should mention a major difference between AWS, Microsoft, and Google organizational implementations. The way that Microsoft and Google implement their IAM system is different from how AWS implements its system. AWS uses separate IAM systems for different AWS accounts by default. Both Microsoft and Google use more of a logical separation, with a shared IAM system where accounts are centralized and logically scoped (or assigned) to individual deployments. This won't be on the CCSK exam; I just wanted to mention this for those who may be familiar with Microsoft or Google Cloud implementations and may be confused by Figure 4-1.

That said, managing multiple deployment accounts can be challenging. You need to use a structured and hierarchical system to organize cloud resources. This is why CSPs offer tools for customers to manage multiple accounts. We'll cover some of these in the upcoming sections of this chapter.

While it's important to create organizational hierarchy, there are many ways to implement that strategy. Each cloud environment does it differently, and each method comes with its own complexities. As you expand your use of cloud technologies, understanding the structural differences and terminology used by major CSPs like AWS, Azure, and Google Cloud is important. This chapter aims to clarify these concepts and present a standardized approach to discussing and implementing organizational structures in the cloud.

Figure 4-2 is an AWS example of organizational hierarchy and how it limits the blast radius.

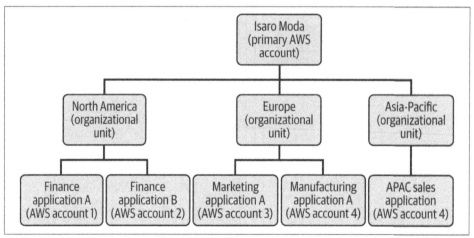

Figure 4-2. Isaro Moda account separation using AWS accounts

Figure 4-2 depicts Isaro Moda Global, a global women's fashion company founded by Isabelle Roy. The company has 1,500 employees in its Montreal headquarters; it also has an office in Milan with 200 employees and a sales office in Singapore with 25 employees. Manufacturing is done by a third party in Turkey. Due to this global presence and the company's need for all 1,725 employees and its third-party manufacturer to have access to systems, it made the decision to adopt cloud services. It built its architecture using a primary AWS account at the top, and three OUs that act as grouping mechanisms under the primary account based on geography. Under these OUs, individual applications run in their own AWS accounts. These act as individual blast zones (we'll cover why I'm calling them *blast zones* later in this chapter).

> The naming AWS uses for AWS organizations is suboptimal. First, an AWS account has nothing to do with user accounts. When you see "AWS account," it's the account you get when you sign up for AWS, not an IAM account. Second, I have no idea why AWS chose to use the term *Organizational Unit*, which is very well known in the Active Directory world. Again, don't worry about this for the exam. I'm just trying to address any confusion you may have.

Aside from implementing a blast radius, setting up an organizational hierarchy opens up great management potential, from managing billing to implementing guardrails through what AWS calls *service control policies* (SCPs), which we will cover later in this chapter.

Organizational Capabilities Within a Cloud Service Provider

There are four main capabilities that organizational management will deliver:

- Groups allow customers to isolate deployments via a customizable hierarchy.
- Policies (e.g., SCPs) act as guardrails that can be applied to a group or individual deployments. These typically enable and disable features, often down to specific API calls or even individual parameters.
- User account centralization and/or federation supports centralized management of an organization's users and their entitlements.
- Each CSP supports its own set of shared security services. These vary greatly, but support for central logging is nearly always available. In many cases, security services deployed in accounts will report up to the primary account, giving complete visibility of all accounts in a central location.

Organizational Hierarchy Models | 79

To maintain consistency over many deployments in an organization, CSPs offer landing zones and account factories:

- A *landing zone* acts as a blueprint for new accounts, subscriptions, or projects. It defines critical configurations such as security controls, governance policies, networking settings, and compliance requirements to ensure that new environments adhere to the organization's standards.

- An *account factory* is the service that automates the creation of new accounts/subscriptions/projects within the landing zone. Note that some CSPs may bundle this functionality with the landing zone service they offer, while others may implement it as a separate functionality. This is another example of CSPs generally offering similar features with different functionalities.

Together, landing zones and account factories simplify cloud management by ensuring consistency, enhancing security, and enforcing governance across all cloud deployments. This approach reduces manual effort, minimizes misconfigurations, and ensures that organizational standards are uniformly applied as new environments are created. Additionally, these can be automated through the use of infrastructure as code (IaC). We'll cover IaC in Chapter 7.

Building a Hierarchy Within a Provider

Customers typically adopt one of three models to define their hierarchy, each with its own advantages and operational implications. The CSA doesn't say one is better than the others. Customers are free to combine elements from different models to best reflect their operational realities:

Business unit and application based
> This model was presented earlier to create those smaller blast-radius areas where every application ran in its own AWS account. It aligns well with business unit–focused IAM hierarchies but may be less efficient for policy management unless cloud features closely align with business units and applications.

Environment based
> In this model, environments (e.g., development, test, production) are set up as the OUs, followed by separate accounts for business units or applications underneath. This model benefits policy management by establishing baseline security and operational policies for different environments, but it may not align well with IAM hierarchies or billing and cost management needs.

Geography based
> This model starts with geographic regions (e.g., North America, Europe, APAC) at the top, followed by business units or environments. It benefits customers that

have international operations with diverse security and regulatory requirements specific to each region.

Managing Organization-Level Security Within a Provider

We have discussed the benefits of implementing organization-wide policies and automating the creation of separate environments for applications to limit an incident's blast radius. One point I want to emphasize is that the application of policies is done at the top of the organization and is enforced throughout all accounts/subscriptions within the organization itself. More importantly, these guardrails cannot be altered at the lower levels. Not only are guardrails applied at the beginning, but they remain consistent.

In the next sections, I expand on some of the benefits of organization-wide policies for some different areas covered by the CSA to prepare you for the CCSK exam. Remember, the exam is vendor agnostic and will not ask questions about details specific to providers, such as terms they use. This is why I'm trying to avoid vendor-specific terms in this book when possible. The main goal is the benefit that top-down governance can deliver.

Identity provider and user/group role mappings

As previously mentioned, the organization represents the highest level of deployment consolidation, and all groups and subaccounts are created and managed on a top-down basis. At this top level, identity management can be centralized to determine who can access and manage subaccounts. These capabilities are defined by an identity provider (e.g., internal Active Directory, identity brokers) and a set of user/group role mappings. This is potentially separate from IAM inside the deployment.

At this highest level, there are two important factors to consider:

- Minimize privileged user access to limit high-level alterations or privilege escalations.
- Restrict who can create subaccounts in the organization, but enable teams to easily create new deployments for their environments (e.g., development, sandbox, production) that match the policies in the team's hierarchy. This is where the landing zones and account factories can accelerate those teams and ensure consistency.

In the organizational hierarchy established by CSPs, technical policies define security controls across deployments. This ensures that even administrators with full control over a specific deployment are subject to organizational restrictions that they cannot modify or delete. The major IaaS providers all offer these. In AWS, these would be called *Service Control Policies* (or *SCPs*) and can be applied at the OU or deployment level. In Microsoft Azure, you would use *Azure Policy* applied at the management groups or subscription level. Google Cloud calls this functionality *Organization Policy Service* and it can be applied at the organization, folder, or project level (consult Table 4-1 if you need a refresher on the levels).

CSP policies can be categorized into three levels based on their scope. Using our AWS-based Isaro Moda example from earlier in this chapter (a section of it is shown in Figure 4-3), let's look at how the CSP policies can be applied at the different levels, as well as some CSA guidance on each deployment level.

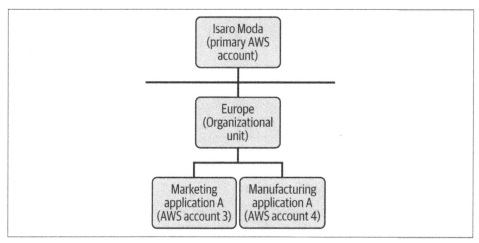

Figure 4-3. Isaro Moda organizational model snippet

Organization-wide policies (top level) are set by the customer and apply to all deployments within the CSC. Due to the difficulty in managing exceptions across such a broad scope, this level typically involves a limited set of foundational policies.

Example: Isaro Moda enforces an organization-wide policy that requires that all users use MFA. This policy ensures that every user in every subaccount uses MFA to perform any action within AWS.

Group-level policies apply to all subaccounts within a specific group. This level is ideal for broad policy enforcement, where policies can accumulate and reinforce each other, especially when subgroups are involved. These combined policies are enforced by the CSP, with deny policies generally taking precedence over policies at lower levels.

Example: Building on the previous example, Isaro Moda is concerned about jurisdictional laws, and GDPR in particular. It wants to ensure that only regions within Europe can be used by any subaccount in the Europe group. To address this, it enforces a policy at the Europe group level that only allows European regions to be used and explicitly denies actions in all other regions outside Europe. As a result, all actions performed in any subaccounts within the Europe group will only be allowed if both of the following apply:

- The user logged in with MFA (based on organization-wide policy).
- The user is performing the action in a European region (based on group-level policy).

Deployment-level policies are tailored for individual accounts, allowing for more specific security configurations. While group-level policies are generally preferred for simpler management, deployment-level policies are essential when deployments require precise and granular security adjustments.

Example: Isaro Moda has two subaccounts within the Europe group—one for a custom marketing application and another for a manufacturing application. A policy in the marketing deployment account mandates that no services other than Elastic Compute Cloud (EC2) and S3 can be used. This policy means users in the marketing deployment account are allowed only if all of the following apply:

- The user logged in with MFA (based on organization-wide policy).
- The user is performing the action in a European region (based on group-level policy).
- The user is using EC2 or S3 services.

For the manufacturing deployment account, there is a concern about data exfiltration to the internet. To address this, a policy stating that no outbound internet gateways can be implemented (which will stop outbound traffic from being able to access the internet) is applied only to this deployment account. This means that users in the manufacturing deployment account are allowed only if all of the following apply:

- The user logged in with MFA (based on organization-wide policy).
- The user is performing the action in a European region (based on group-level policy).
- The user is not using the internet.

Policies can be used in various scenarios, including:

- Enabling and disabling specific services, such as prohibiting the use of an unapproved platform service for deployment. This is beneficial to organizations that do not want new services used until they have been assessed by a third-party auditor (such as what was included in the SOC 2 report that I addressed in Chapter 3).
- Blocking particular API calls to prevent unauthorized or harmful operations.

- Disabling regions to comply with geographic regulatory requirements and maintaining data residency and sovereignty requirements. As we already know, jurisdictions have their own laws and regulations that need to be followed. Additionally, restricting regions can stop a malicious user from launching instances in an unused region, hoping the customer will not notice their activity (such as launching a bitcoin mining VM in the Singapore region).
- Defining conditions such as permitting specific API calls only from authorized network sources/IP addresses. However, this requires both CSP and service-level support, representing one of the more inconsistent capabilities across providers.
- Implementing IAM practices to secure organization-level access and operational tools, including preventing a deployment administrator from restricting access to critical visibility and control accounts (e.g., in the event administrator credentials are compromised).

One final note about these top-down policies: you should have a plan in place to override these restrictions if required to respond to an incident. Take a scenario where an organization restricts the ability to terminate instances across all subaccounts and a server is known to be compromised. The administrator needs to immediately terminate the instance to stop a security breach. This override capability needs to be planned and tested in advance. How this is done is very different across the various platforms. Don't worry about this for the CCSK exam. This is something that should be considered in real life when implementing top-down policies.

Common organizational shared services

Although individual deployments are isolated from one another, customer organizations should aim for consistent policy and risk management across all deployments. The top-down policies we just covered are a great tool for achieving this. However, there are more areas where organizations can centralize security services to better govern cloud environments. In this section, we'll examine several shared services that can help reinforce those policies across deployments.

One of the most crucial shared services for cloud security and governance is consolidated IAM. This provides a unified approach to managing access across deployments and gives the organization a single point of visibility into access control across all resources. While how this is done is different for every provider, the core principle remains the same: user accounts can typically be centralized at the top level, with permissions then delegated to specific subaccounts or resources as needed.

The same approach applies to federated identity management. For example, a federated identity standard such as Security Assertion Markup Language (SAML) can be used to establish a federated identity management trust relationship between the organization's top-level IAM structure and an internal identity provider (e.g., Active Directory Federation Services [ADFS]) or an external identity provider (e.g., Entra [previously called Azure AD], Okta, or other external identity systems). This allows for seamless user authentication and access control across multiple cloud services, while centralizing identity management. You will learn more about federated identity management in Chapter 5.

A final note regarding IAM (for now): as a professional working with cloud services, IAM is the most important aspect of security in the cloud, period. If you get this wrong, you can't get access controls right either. Without these in place, you can't have security. It really is as simple as that. Multiple identity repositories in different accounts will likely lead to overwhelming complexity. And as they say, complexity is the enemy of security.

Centralized logging and security telemetry streamline security monitoring by aggregating logs and data feeds into a single location. The CSA refers to this concept as *cascading log architecture*, where all logs from the cloud environment as well as server and application logs from the various cloud accounts are stored in an account managed by the security team (I'll cover this in detail in Chapter 6). This aids threat detection and response, analysis, and compliance. The logs can feed directly into platforms such as a SIEM system for automated analysis and correlation to aid in threat detection, or a central repository of raw log data, called a *security data lake*, that can be used for deeper analysis and compliance purposes.

Many CSPs offer advanced security services such as threat detection, vulnerability management, configuration management, distributed denial-of-service (DDoS) protection, and more that provide continuous monitoring for malicious activities and unauthorized behaviors, helping to safeguard deployments by identifying threats in real time, enabling quick responses. In many instances, these services can be centrally managed and offer coverage of all deployments. I will discuss this in greater detail in Chapter 6.

Centralized cost management can also be achieved through tagging policies that assign costs to specific applications or business functions, providing greater clarity and control over resource spending. Additionally, centralized billing is also possible where all expenses from subaccounts are rolled up to the top-level account. On top of convenience, this can also lead to volume discounts being realized as all activity is seen as being from the primary or billing account, not from separate accounts.

Lastly, the account factories built with IaC that we covered earlier are also a key functionality to achieve consistent policy and risk management across all deployments.

Considerations for Hybrid and Multicloud Deployments

As I covered in an earlier chapter, there are multiple cloud deployment models that consumers can use to address their business requirements. In addition to the public and private cloud options, there are also community and hybrid options. The hybrid model allows an organization to keep its private data private and its public data public. It also allows for *cloud bursting*, a design pattern enabled with a hybrid cloud architecture. Cloud bursting is used to supply additional capacity when needed, allowing for dynamic scalability. For example, if an organization experiences a dramatic increase in incoming requests to a public-facing web server, new requests can be redirected to a copy of the web server in a public cloud when demand exceeds available internal resources.

Exam Note

Cloud bursting is a major use case for a hybrid cloud. There is a strong possibility that this will be on the CCSK exam.

Multicloud does not mean the same thing as *hybrid cloud*. It is simply using multiple cloud providers. The level of integration between the multiple cloud providers has a strong probability of increasing both the cost and the complexity of your overall cloud usage. This is addressed later in this chapter.

The following sections explore the key considerations for securing hybrid and multicloud environments, focusing on effective organization management, IAM, network security, and the strategic use of security tools.

Organizational Management for Hybrid Cloud Security

Although a hybrid cloud is technically defined by NIST as being two or more cloud deployment models with integration between the two, today's accepted definition is that a hybrid cloud connects the organization's traditional computing facilities with a public cloud provider.

Exam Note

The CCSK exam may test you on both the NIST definition and the fact that you are using two different environments. As I wrote in Chapter 1, a simple way to remember a key benefit of a hybrid cloud is that it lets you keep your public data public and your private data private.

The CSA calls out the following two security items regarding hybrid cloud security. These mainly deal with the integration link between the internal and external environments that comprise the hybrid cloud.

The CSA first lists network security as a critical security consideration when using a hybrid cloud. The network connection that connects the public and private environments could be via a virtual private network (VPN) or via a dedicated private link the

CSP may have available. In either case, the public cloud component should be considered as running in a hostile environment and should not be trusted. As such, all network traffic between the cloud and the datacenter should be treated as potentially hostile and scanned before being accepted. This way, if a cloud component is compromised, the attacker can't have a free pass to move laterally into your organization's private network.

Amazon AWS (Direct Connect), Microsoft Azure (Express Route), and Google Cloud (Interconnect) all offer dedicated private links. They are high-bandwidth, low-latency, private (more secure) connections to a CSP network. These dedicated connections are often only accessible at colocation facilities. Even if they are not using the internet, they should still be treated as potentially hostile networks. Security controls applied on these connections should include encryption, monitoring, and segmentation. Incoming traffic from these dedicated connections from the cloud environment should be inspected prior to accessing an organization's private network. I have been surprised at the number of clients who believe these connections do not require inspection because they are "trusted" connections.

Second, and just as important, the CSA states that strong IAM is also critical because the compromise of the IAM system can lead to compromise of both environments. There's a saying that identity is the new perimeter. Take this to heart when looking at cloud services. In a best-case scenario, federated identity management would be implemented so that there is only one source of identity that is tightly controlled and monitored. We will cover federated identity management (commonly referred to as simply *federation*) in Chapter 5.

Security services in a cloud environment are generally more automated than those found in traditional environments. Taking a "like for like" (also called *normalizing controls*) approach, in which you apply the same technologies and design patterns in the cloud as you would in traditional IT for security controls, is not the best approach to securing cloud environments. New approaches to security that use cloud native controls such as microsegmentation, event-driven security, attribute-based access controls, policy-based access controls, and other approaches can significantly improve security in cloud environments that have broad network access and limited perimeter capability due to their distributed nature. I will be covering all of these new approaches in upcoming chapters.

When considering having multiple datacenters connected to multiple cloud environments (some call this a *hybrid multicloud model*), network traffic can be routed through a *bastion network*. In cybersecurity, a *bastion* is a tightly controlled server that has all unnecessary services removed, and serves a single purpose. This server would be called a *bastion host*. For example, a DNS server would have all non-DNS services removed and network access to and from the server would be extremely limited. A bastion is also commonly used as a *jumpbox*. In this scenario, the strongly secured bastion host would be located in an accessible network (like a public subnet) and also have connectivity to a private subnet. As a use-case example, assume you needed to access a server in a private subnet inaccessible to the internet. To do this, you would securely connect to the jumpbox server using SSH (for example) and then "jump" to the private subnet by opening a secure connection to a server in the private subnet.

In relation to this subject, another concept you should know about is the *transit network*. Simply stated, a transit network is like the public transit system in a city. You would use the transit system to get to a destination. In networking, the network architecture has a transit network that all connections must go through on their way to a destination, like your cloud environment, for example.

So, taking this concept to the network, the bastion network is a secured transit network that all connections to cloud environments and the workloads within must go through. This approach of forcing all traffic through this tightly controlled network segment gives you the ability to centralize all network traffic and tightly control access to all cloud deployments.

If you haven't heard the term *bastion network*, that's OK. This seems to be a term that is fairly unique to the CSA CCSK documentation.

Setting up a bastion network is more a network architecture subject than a cloud security subject. However, I want to give you a high-level understanding of its implementation. Figure 4-4 depicts the implementation of a bastion network and a transit gateway.

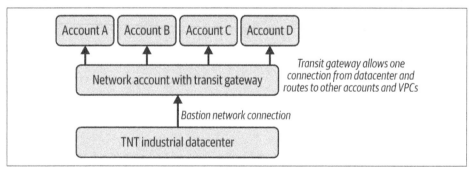

Figure 4-4. Bastion network and transit gateway architecture

In Figure 4-4, you can see that the TNT Industrial datacenter is connected to a single network account in AWS through a secure connection (this could be VPN or Direct Connect). From the network account, the transit gateway service supplied by the CSP (other CSPs have a similar offering) is configured with appropriate routes and other information to route traffic to different AWS accounts and VPCs within each account.

Exam Note

For the CCSK exam, you will need to know what a bastion network is and why it's used. You should also know what a transit network is, but you likely will not be tested on it directly.

Organizational Management for Multicloud Security

Although not a deployment model according to NIST, the term *multicloud* is used to describe the use of multiple IaaS/PaaS CSPs. Most of the time, this means multiple public cloud providers, but it could be used with a mix of multiple private and public clouds. The CSA mainly speaks to the use of multiple public clouds as being a multicloud model. The use of the multicloud model has grown substantially over the past few years. Now, most companies I speak with are using a multicloud model, such as AWS and Azure. From a functionality perspective, this can range from running one application in one CSP and other applications in another cloud, all the way to having cross-provider failover to support business continuity for critical workloads.

From a security perspective, the issue is that even though the providers have feature parity, the way the services work and are set up can be dramatically different. This requires an organization to have SMEs for each environment. To expect one person to be the SME for every CSP used is simply unrealistic. Sure, one person could know the generalities of multiple CSPs, but they can't be expected to have a deep understanding of all the unique characteristics of all CSPs that may result in security issues. Take virtual firewall services such as security groups, for example. Some providers have a default deny approach, so communication between systems in the same security group is denied unless a rule explicitly allows communication. Other CSPs may have a default allow approach, likely for simplicity. In other words, one CSP may restrict lateral movement by default, while the other doesn't.

The multicloud model can be very complex and will likely require different tools to be known and used in the different environments. Although some tools, such as Terraform for IAC and some CSPM tools, may be vendor agnostic, they are still platform specific. In other words, individuals still need to have deep knowledge of the CSP and will likely have to customize these tools based on the CSPs used. In most instances, CSP-supplied tools and services will need to be used to properly secure a cloud environment, and these tools will only work in the relevant CSP environment. The services and functionality delivered by these CSP services will then need to be understood and similarly implemented to the appropriate extent possible in the other CSP environments.

Due to these complexities, the CSA's perspective on the multicloud model is that it is better to stick with one CSP, become very good at securing it, and then move to a multicloud environment if required due to mergers, acquisitions, or business requirements. Even in the case of mergers or acquisitions forcing a multicloud model, the CSA recommends that users migrate the application to the single CSP used, where possible. In the event a second CSP must be used due to specific needs or because consolidation isn't realistic, the CSA recommends that all new deployments use the original primary CSP while the secondary is only used for limited or isolated deployments. Finally, only when an organization has an adequate level of cloud security expertise and effective management strategies should it support a full multicloud model with key security-shared services (e.g., SIEM, CSPM, IaC) designed for a multicloud environment.

One specific area of concern the CSA has regarding multicloud adoption is portability. Many organizations use portability (ease of moving workloads from one CSP to another) and avoidance of vendor lock-in (can't move without difficulty, technical or otherwise) as reasons to implement a multicloud model, but in reality they aren't very good at building truly vendor-agnostic implementations.

From a portability perspective, organizations will build cloud native applications that inherently lock themselves into a single vendor, as these services are unique to the single vendor. Take containers, for example. While a main goal of using containers is portability, the underlying supporting infrastructure, such as the management infrastructure for scheduling and orchestration, databases hosted on CSP-hosted PaaS platforms, CSP-supplied message queues, notification buses, and other services that underlie modern applications, is often not. These CSP services are commonly used because they typically offer economic, security, and operational benefits to the consumer. So, while the workloads in the containers themselves may be portable, the infrastructure used to support the containerized applications is not, unless CSP-specific services are avoided and third-party multicloud tools are used instead, potentially leading to a loss of the benefits realized when using CSP-specific tools. So much for multicloud being great for portability.

Tooling and Staffing for IaaS/PaaS Multicloud

As I mentioned earlier, it is not realistic for an organization to expect a single individual to be an expert on multiple CSPs. Having a deep understanding of one CSP is hard enough! An example of this I often use is the number of API actions in the AWS EC2 service. Can you believe there are over 600 different actions that can be granted or denied? Now imagine if an organization were using 10 services from a CSP. Sure,

EC2 may be an extreme case of granularity, and every action can be looked up in the CSP documentation, but still, that's a lot for a single person to handle.

The CSA states that you should have at least one SME per significant cloud service used. The fewer CSPs that are used, the fewer people that are needed to support an organization's cloud usage.

Finally, a smaller organization may engage a managed service provider (MSP) to implement and support the technical aspects of cloud services, but it is critical that the organization understand that, by law, it cannot outsource accountability in regard to security and governance. To paraphrase President Truman, the buck stops with the organization, and finger-pointing doesn't absolve it of being accountable for the actions of either the CSP or the MSP.

Organizational Management for SaaS Hybrid and Multicloud

SaaS presents possibly the hardest aspect of managing cloud services. This is because, for every IaaS used, there are potentially 20 SaaS solutions used. Who is reviewing and managing these contracts, identifying the shared security responsibilities, securing them, and managing identities and other critical items? In some organizations, leadership believes that "cloud" means all security responsibility is outsourced, and that's just not the case.

Beginning with the management of SaaS, there needs to be an authorization process in place that evaluates SaaS solutions for security and compliance. This includes reviewing available third-party reviews such as SOC 2 reports, ISO/IEC 27001 and 27017 certifications, and any other third-party (also called *pass-through*) assessments and certifications. In addition to these technical measures, the question of "Do we even need this?" should also be asked. After all, what is the sense of having five different CRM solutions when one can do everything the other four do? That just leads to 5× the effort and, more importantly, five areas where corporate data is being held.

The importance of assessing the security of a potential SaaS vendor cannot be overstated. There are so many SaaS vendors that really don't do a good job with security. I'm not saying this is inherent to the service model. It's just that some SaaS vendors don't prioritize security like major IaaS providers do.

SaaS solutions may interact with other SaaS solutions to deliver a complete business solution. In this case, you need to understand where your data is, how it moves between SaaS providers, and how it is secured.

The CSA lists the following types of security tools to help manage these SaaS solutions.

Federated identity brokers

Identity brokers will have prebuilt integrations for major CSPs, and a unified dashboard for user access to different services. These federated identity brokers ease the implementation of FIM and streamline the administration of user access and permissions for all cloud models, SaaS in particular. We will cover this in greater detail in Chapter 5.

Cloud access security brokers

Cloud access security brokers (CASBs) can be very useful for managing a SaaS portfolio by discovering the cloud services actually in use, not just the ones an organization thinks it is using. In other words, CASB can help identify Shadow IT. CASB also offers governance of SaaS, by helping with access control and monitoring capabilities that can enforce which SaaS solutions are utilized, who is using them, which devices (and device posture checks) they are using, and where they are located. It does this primarily by using access controls such as user roles and location. DLP (which may be internal to the CASB or may leverage an existing DLP system) and regular expressions (regex) that can look for specific text strings can also be integrated.

As an example of SaaS governance, say you are the CISO for a financial institution that has both stock brokerage and advisory services for publicly traded companies. In this scenario, you have a regulatory requirement that any recommendation comes with a disclosure that states whether there are any vested interests (e.g., recommending a stock to the public that you also have a corporate arrangement with). If a stockbroker posts on a website that they recommend people buy a stock without required disclosure, this must be blocked. However, if they post a marketing message saying that they are doing a free portfolio review, this will be allowed. By using both DLP and regex (on top of the access controls covered earlier), the CASB can understand which message must be blocked and which one is permitted. This allows your organization to meet both compliance and business needs well beyond what a simple allow or deny web filter can do.

On top of the monitoring and governance of connectivity to the SaaS, CASB can also work in API mode. This allows the CASB to see what users are doing within the SaaS application and perform policy enforcement, such as overseeing user actions, implementing configuration settings (such as sharing restrictions), and detecting anomalies within the SaaS application. Some vendors call this a *hybrid CASB*, as it performs both governance of user access and actions performed in a SaaS. To function, the CASB must be able to understand the APIs exposed by a SaaS vendor. This may lead to a lack of integration for less common SaaS solutions. It also requires the CASB vendor to be able to quickly address any changes made by SaaS vendors to its APIs.

API gateways

APIs are used to externalize an application's functionality. Consider an API gateway as a firewall for APIs. To be more specific, API gateways can bring visibility, control, and policy enforcement over API interactions by offering services such as authentication, authorization, encryption, rate throttling, logging, and more. Following is a list of the security controls an API gateway will typically deliver to protect API access and usage:

Authentication
: Validates the identity of the requester using tokens, API keys, OAuth, or JSON Web Token (JWT) before allowing access to the API

Authorization
: Determines what actions the authenticated user is allowed to perform, often based on roles, scopes, or policies

Encryption/SSL termination
: Secures data in transit using HTTPS, and may handle the SSL/TLS handshake to offload encryption overhead from backend services

Rate limiting/throttling
: Controls the number of API calls a client can make over a period to protect against abuse, DoS, or cost overrun

Request and response transformation
: Modifies API requests or responses (e.g., converting XML to JSON, adding/removing headers) to ensure compatibility between systems

Logging and monitoring
: Captures detailed logs and metrics on API usage for auditing, analytics, debugging, and compliance purposes

Threat protection
: Blocks malicious payloads or patterns (e.g., SQL injection, XSS) at the edge using predefined or custom rules

Caching
: Stores responses to reduce latency and load on backend services for repeat requests

Analytics and usage reporting
: Provides dashboards and reports on API consumption trends, user behaviors, error rates, and performance

Load balancing
   Distributes incoming API traffic across multiple backend instances to improve scalability and availability

IP filtering/geofencing
   Restricts or allows API access based on IP address ranges or geographic locations

Figure 4-5 shows how the API gateway is positioned and highlights its key functionality.

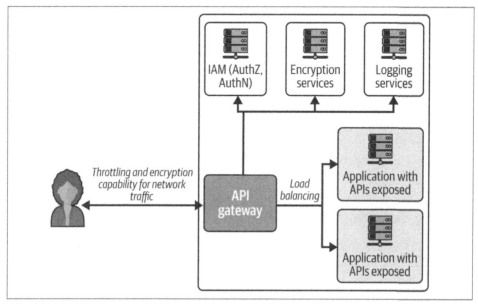

Figure 4-5. API gateway protecting application APIs

That's quite a large number of security controls available to protect your application APIs. But there's more! If you want to control or monitor the API interaction between SaaS solutions, you will need to implement your own API gateway solution and route traffic through it. This can be done via an API gateway vendor (e.g., Apigee, Kong) and major CSPs such as AWS API Gateway, Azure API Management, and Google Cloud endpoints. While this routing and inspection can introduce both complexity and latency, it may be justifiable if the data is deemed important enough to protect across different SaaS-to-SaaS or SaaS-to-enterprise solutions.

Summary

In this chapter, we covered organization management and how creating multiple isolated environments helps create strong isolation blast zones. We also covered organizational security controls and the use of multiple clouds.

For the CCSK exam, you should know the following:

- The importance of building organization hierarchy.
- The different hierarchy models (business and application based, environment and geography based).
- Hard security boundaries create limited blast zones in the case of an incident.
- Policies can be implemented in a top-down model that imposes organizational security on all accounts/subscriptions/projects and cannot be overridden at lower levels.
- Policies can be applied at different levels.
- Security services can be centralized to control all deployments.
- A multicloud model should not be pursued until an organization has mature cloud security capabilities in place.
- The concept of a bastion network for monitoring and controlling network traffic.
- What CASBs and API gateways offer for security.

That's it for the organization management domain. Let's move on to a critical subject in domain 5: identity and access management.

CHAPTER 5
Identity and Access Management

Identity is the new perimeter.
—Common Cloud Security Statement

Of all the security controls available, it's hard to say the most important one isn't identity and access management (IAM). IAM is the underpinning of successful security. Quite simply, this is the control that stops attackers from gaining access to your management console in the cloud and destroying everything in a matter of minutes. IAM is required for access controls to limit what entities can do in your cloud environment. It's also the control that stops corporate information from being exposed to everyone on the internet if held in object storage.

As I said in the last chapter, many say that identity is the new perimeter in the cloud, because if you don't have strong IAM in place, you can't have strong cloud security that applies the principle of least privilege. It's that simple.

This chapter covers IAM and cloud infrastructures such as users accessing IaaS, PaaS, and SaaS. It doesn't address configuring individual applications built in IaaS or PaaS with their own identities, because this isn't required for the exam. IAM on its own is a whole career path. That said, let's get into the IAM discussion, focusing on the knowledge you need for the CCSK exam (and then some).

How IAM Is Different in the Cloud

When it comes to IAM in the cloud, there are three major differences that must be appreciated.

First, IAM spans multiple locations. In fact, every cloud service will have its own identity repository that you can create accounts in. The problem is that these accounts need to be managed. Just picture a company with 1,000 employees using 100

97

different cloud services that everyone needs access to. Without FIM (which we'll soon cover in much more depth), that's 100,000 accounts and passwords to manage.

Second, not all IAM systems across these cloud providers will be the same. Some will have varying levels of access, while others won't. For example, some SaaS applications may have very fine-grained controls down to the database field level (e.g., only the HR manager can access payroll data), whereas for others, if the user has an account, they can access anything in the application that they wish.

 Always remember that there are no rules or regulations as to what a cloud provider must or must not do. Prior to authorizing any cloud provider, you must assess it to determine if its solution and security are appropriate for your organization.

Finally, the ability to perform any action, be it through the console or programmatically via APIs, is dictated by the IAM system in the cloud environment. If the CSP only allows or denies access to an application with no ability to restrict action within the application itself, you must accept the risk that the provider accepts. Again, going back to a previous discussion, this is something that you should discover as part of your provider assessment before signing any contract.

The CCSK exam will include questions about IAM, as IAM touches nearly every topic in the CCSK domains. Again, it's really important. In the next section, we'll review some IAM terminology, dive a little deeper into cloud identity, and then move on to access management.

Fundamental Terms for Understanding IAM

The following sections define terms you should be familiar with before diving any deeper into IAM. You aren't likely to be tested on the definitions themselves, but you'll probably get questions that use these terms.

Access Controls
> Access controls are the things that allow an entity access to a resource. You only want to allow access to what the entity should have access to, and nothing more; this is known as *least privilege*. Resources can be accessed in many ways, such as through the Create, Read, Update, and Delete (CRUD) operations, each of which can be a separately granted permission.

Entity
> An entity is anything or anyone in a computer system. For example, an entity can be a user, a device, an application, or a system that is identified and authenticated by an IAM system. Entities can have different roles and permissions via access control within the system. Any action or resource access should be monitored

and logged to ensure that it does not have excessive privileges to a resource. This is more than just a security issue. It is likely required for audit and compliance purposes as well.

Identity
This is a unique set of attributes that define a subject within a specific context. For example, your identity on a website like Facebook would be your email address, whereas your identity in an organization may be your username.

Identifier
An identifier is the artifact used to assert or represent an identity within a system. In digital systems, this could be a public key, a hashed biometric template (such as a fingerprint hash), or a subject claim (e.g., email address) embedded in a cryptographic token such as JWT. In the physical world, examples would be a driver's license or passport.

Authentication
Authentication is the process of verifying the identity of an entity. This is the first step in the entity gaining access to a system. This is also where MFA comes into play. We'll cover that shortly.

Authorization
Authorization refers to the decision to permit or deny an entity access to system resources after it is authenticated. Authorization enforces access controls.

Multifactor Authentication
MFA confirms that a user is who they say they are, by using two (or more) of "something you know, something you have, or something you are." Currently, MFA is usually implemented with passwords (something you know) and an authenticator app (something you have), text messages with random numbers, or even fingerprints (something you are). Given the broad network access essential characteristic of cloud offerings, MFA should be in place for all access to cloud management consoles, especially for privileged users.

Exam Note

Two-factor authentication (2FA) is a term commonly used to denote that two forms of factors are used in authentication. In MFA, two or three forms could be used. The bottom line is that both 2FA and MFA mean you need more than one factor for authentication. The exam writer may try to trick you by presenting two of the same factors in an MFA-related question. For example, you would need to know a password and the secret answer to a question (e.g., your mother's maiden name), both of which are "something you know."

Persona

A persona represents a type of user with specific responsibilities in a system. Grouping users by persona helps assign the right permissions based on what they need to do. For example, a developer might need access to coding tools, while a security analyst would need access to security logs. Each persona helps create roles that match the tasks users perform.

Attribute

Attributes can include a variety of information about the entity, the connection, or both. Examples of attributes include personal details, user roles, the time of an access request, the IP address of the entity requesting access, or the location from which the request is made.

Entitlement

An entitlement maps identities to authorizations and any required attributes. Basically, you can think of entitlements as permissions that also include attributes.

Entitlement Matrix

An entitlement matrix is where you would write down the different groups and their entitlements in a grid format (e.g., Excel spreadsheet). This is then used to implement technical policies.

Role

A role is something someone does in an organization, such as developer, administrator, or sales. Roles are used to define the access level (permissions) for users to perform specific tasks. Roles can be unique or shared. A single user might have multiple roles based on their responsibilities. For example, Larry the sales director could be assigned to multiple roles, such as corporate user, director, and sales. Roles are often closely associated with groups, but they are not the same thing. Multiple people who serve the same role in a company are often grouped together. Also, quite often it is the group that has the permissions assigned, but again, this is because the group members serve a certain role that requires access to appropriate organizational resources to do their job. This concept of giving permission to resources based on a user's role in the organization is referred to as *role-based access control* (RBAC).

> Remember this definition of the word *role*. AWS uses the term *role* differently. In the AWS world, a role is a pseudoidentity that can be used to grant permissions to entities. Just stick to a role being something someone does in an organization.

Attribute-Based Access Control

Attribute-based access control (ABAC) assigns access controls based on attributes of the user and/or the connection of the user attempting to access a resource. For example, beyond basic RBAC, ABAC could also allow or deny access to a resource based on the user having performed MFA as part of the authentication process or based on their IP address. In the cloud, access can also be granted based on resource tags. For example, users in the developer role may only be granted access to terminate a server instance that has the tag "environment" and the value "development."

Before we get into policy-based access control, I want to address the term *policy*. There are two types of policies that you need to know about. First, there are organizational policies. As you learned in Chapter 2, organizational policies state what is expected of people. This is good and all, but what about enforcing this written policy? This is where machine-enforceable policies such as access control policies come into play (and will be discussed next). The technical policy document will be evaluated, and a decision will be made if an action is allowed or not.

Policy-Based Access Control

Policy-based access control (PBAC) defines access requirements in a machine-readable policy document (e.g., JSON or XML), offering extensive flexibility and granularity with support for various conditions and variables such as attributes. For example, a policy could state that only developers can delete development VMs based on several conditions, such as that they are using a particular IP address and have used MFA during authentication (both examples of ABAC). This policy would be applied to the developer group (RBAC).

The key here is that PBAC uses both RBAC and ABAC to make authorization decisions. There aren't hardcoded permissions at the resource level. Rather, a centralized policy is created that is ultimately easier to administer due to version control repositories being available and can be used as part of IaC.

Figure 5-1 is an example AWS IAM policy in JSON format that would be used in this scenario. If all three conditions (attributes) are met, they can terminate an instance. If they do not meet all three conditions, the request will be denied.

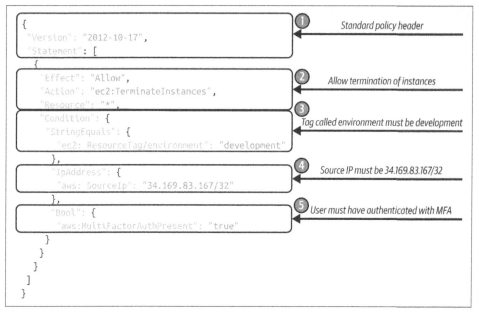

Figure 5-1. Sample IAM policy showing ABACs

Let's go over this policy statement to look at the attributes (conditions) of this policy:

- This is how all AWS IAM policies begin. You can ignore this.

- This is the statement of allowing or denying API action(s). In this case, this policy will allow whoever has the action of terminating (deleting) a VM applied to them. Note that this policy is assigned to a user or a group. That's where RBAC comes in.

- Systems can have resource tags assigned to them. This allows for identification of systems based on tags rather than IP addresses or server names. The CCSK material doesn't address resource tags, so I won't get into them in detail. Just know that they are a very powerful way to assign permissions based on server type. In this example policy, you see that a resource tag called environment is used to determine if a server has this resource tag with a value of development. If it does, the condition (attribute) is met.

- Here you see another condition (attribute) that must be met for the individual who has this policy applied to them. In this case, the person attempting to terminate the instance must have the IP address 34.169.83.167. The /32 means that only that single IP address is applicable. (Yes, this is an easter egg.)

- This condition states that the user must have been authenticated (logged on) with MFA.

Authoritative Source

The authoritative source is the source of truth for identity. Although an Active Directory system is often the authoritative source for identity, it could be the HR system that is the actual authoritative source. Identity is then propagated to Active Directory when changes to identities are made.

Federated Identity Management

Federated identity management (FIM) allows users to use one set of login credentials to access multiple systems or services across different organizations. This is critical, as FIM is strongly recommended for organizations that use multiple cloud providers. Federation allows your organization to own the identities for authentication and the CSP to enforce authorization. FIM also enables Single Sign-On (SSO). With SSO, users don't have credentials within the myriad CSPs. They log on locally using their corporate identity and then use a token (or assertion) to access the cloud systems they are granted access to. There are two systems you need to be aware of when it comes to FIM: the identity provider and the relying party.

Identity Provider

The identity provider (IdP) is the source of the identity in federation. The IdP holds the identities, performs authentication, and issues tokens to users accessing cloud services. These tokens can contain role mappings that map identities to roles at the CSP. These can be used to determine what users are allowed to do at the CSP. For example, the IdP administrator may configure a role mapping so that the internal Sales user group maps to the SFDC_Sales role in Salesforce. As a result, members of that internal group will be granted the permissions associated with the SFDC_Sales role when accessing Salesforce.

The system acting as the IdP could be installed locally, such as ADFS, or it could be a cloud-based identity broker solution, such as OKTA or Azure Entra ID. The IdP creates the tokens that users will ultimately use to access cloud services.

Relying Party

The relying party (RP) is the system that trusts the IdP to authenticate the user. When discussing FIM for cloud services, the RP, also sometimes known as the *service provider* (SP), is the CSP. The RP will enforce authorization based on the attributes or role mapping in the token generated by the IdP. In shorthand, this is often referred to as the *RP/SP* to denote that it is the relying party/service provider.

I'll be covering the IdP and RP in greater detail in on page 104. For now, the big takeaway is that the IdP does authentication and the RP does authorization based on instructions from the IdP.

Assertion

I've used this term a couple of times now, but assertions are statements from an IdP to an RP that allow users to access resources at the CSP. Assertions typically include a user's identity and may include attribute values or references to support authorization decisions. Assertions are generally related to the SAML federation standard, while OAuth paired with OpenID Connect generally uses JWT in place of assertions. In either case, it is these assertions that allow the CSP to make access decisions based on what is stated by the cloud consumer's IdP. We'll cover these standards later in this chapter.

Federated Identity Management

We've already addressed what FIM does and covered its main components (IdP, RP/SP, and assertions). FIM is incredibly important for cloud consumption, and many organizations using cloud services are very likely to use federation to manage user access to cloud services. You just can't allow employees to have usernames and passwords in potentially hundreds of different cloud environments. On top of that, you need to manage these accounts. Just imagine a scenario where a large organization that uses 100 cloud services lays off 1,000 employees. That means you need to deprovision 100,000 accounts. In fact, there are organizations that will not work with a CSP that doesn't offer federation services. It's that critical. Let's look at the standards that allow federation to work.

Common Federation Standards

The following standards are used for creating a federated link between customers and CSPs. There are other standards, but at this time, the following three standards are the most commonly available by CSPs and the only ones covered by the CSA CCSK material.

SAML
I like to refer to SAML as the king of federation standards for users accessing cloud services with a web browser. The SAML standard is currently at version 2.0 and is from the Organization for the Advancement of Structured Information Standards (OASIS). SAML uses XML for its assertions, which can contain authentication statements, attribute statements, and authorization decision statements. On a related side note, I've been hearing about the impending death of

SAML (mainly due to the complexity of its assertions written in XML format compared to the lightweight JSON that OpenID Connect uses) for over a decade. It still hasn't happened.

OAuth 2.0

OAuth is an authorization framework (memory tip: OAuth is for AuthOrization) used to delegate access between systems and applications developed by the Internet Engineering Task Force (IETF). It is solely used for authorization. OAuth is used in system-to-system communications that use API access and application access by third parties through the use of access tokens, such as an application accessing your Google Drive, for example.

OpenID Connect

OpenID Connect (OIDC) is an identity standard created by the OpenID Foundation. It is considered the identity layer on top of OAuth to build a standard for federated authentication widely supported for web services. You've likely seen many sites that allow you to log on with Google, Apple, and so on instead of creating an account on the website itself. This is the goal of the OpenID Foundation: to limit the number of identity stores on the internet.

How Federation Works

In this section, I discuss both OIDC and SAML federation in action. Both share similarities, but there are some details that you should be aware of. Also of note is that different standards use different naming conventions. We aren't covering specific naming conventions aside from IdP and RP/SP. We don't need to make this more confusing than necessary!

OIDC workflow

Federated identity allows an IdP to share identity information with an RP, based on a trust relationship established through cryptographic operations and credential exchanges. For example, when a user authenticates with the IdP (such as an internal directory service), the IdP and RP (such as a SaaS application) already have a trust agreement in place. Once the user is authenticated by the IdP, the IdP forwards necessary identity attributes to the RP. The RP trusts this information and grants access to the user without needing them to enter a username or password. From the user's perspective, it feels like an automatic login after authenticating with the IdP.

Figure 5-2 shows the workflow when a user wanting to access a website uses OIDC.

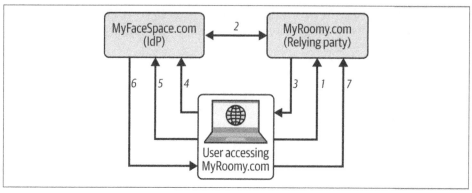

Figure 5-2. OIDC workflow

Let's look at an example of how FIM works. I'm using fake names to keep things light (and me out of a lawsuit). Using Figure 5-2 for the example, we have a website that a user wants to access, called MyRoomy, which is a service that connects potential roommates. For the OIDC IdP, we have a social network called MyFaceSpace. The user goes to the MyRoomy site, and they have the option to create an account using their email address and a password, or to log in using MyFaceSpace. The user decides to click the box that says "Log in using MyFaceSpace" instead of creating an account. The next screen they see is a MyFaceSpace page that says "MyRoomy wants to validate your identity." Then, underneath this, they will likely ignore the fine print that explains that, by continuing, MyRoomy will get access to their full name, email address, likes, friends list, and photos (these are called *claims* in OIDC). Once they click Agree, they are redirected and logged into MyRoomy (and MyRoomy collects all their data from MyFaceSpace). Please note that the user is being redirected from the RP to the IdP and back to the RP automatically.

Now let's take a slightly more technical look at what's happening here, by breaking down each step in a generic format:

1. The user visits the RP site and chooses to log on with a listed IdP.
2. The RP and IdP have a preestablished trust relationship, including a client ID and shared secret.
3. The user's browser is given an authorization request by the RP and is redirected to the IdP.
4. The user is prompted to log on to the IdP (if required).
5. After the user authenticates, the IdP redirects the browser back to the RP with an authorization code.
6. RP exchanges authorization code with IdP for an ID token.
7. RP verified ID token and grants the user access.

SAML workflow

I want to cover the SAML workflow as well, as there are some differences you should know about. It's not likely that you will see this information on the CCSK exam, as it's not in the CCSK material, but since we're already covering how federation works, why not see how the leading standard for users accessing SaaS applications works, right? Figure 5-3 shows the SAML workflow.

What I find interesting about SAML is that it supports both service provider–initiated (SP-initiated) and identity provider–initiated (IdP-initiated) workflows. This means a user could access a SaaS application like Salesforce directly, or they could access Salesforce by clicking on an internally hosted web page where they simply click the Salesforce icon and they're automatically logged in and have appropriate access to what they need to do their job.

You may have noticed that some websites you visit may just ask for an email address at the logon page, not an email address and password. This supports SP-initiated logons (there are other ways, but the goal is understanding SP-initiated logons). Once the user enters their organization email address (e.g., *IRoy@isaro.com*), the SP looks to see if there is a SAML configuration set up for that domain. This is called *home realm discovery*. If there is a SAML association established between the organization and the SP, the user is redirected to their IdP for logon. Once authenticated by the IdP, they get a SAML assertion (a.k.a. *token*) and are redirected back to the SP. The user's browser then presents the assertion and the user is logged in. If there is no SAML association, then the user is challenged for a password on the next screen.

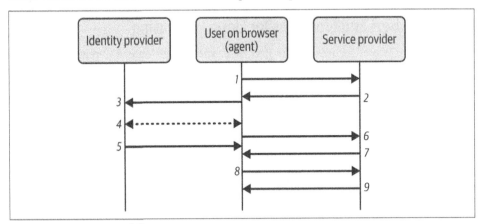

Figure 5-3. SAML workflow

Let's walk through the numbered elements of Figure 5-3. To begin with, you can see there is the identity provider on the left, the service provider on the right, and the browser in the middle. You may also notice there is no communication between the IdP and the SP. The browser in the middle is called the *agent* in SAML because it acts as the intermediary between the two. It relays requests and responses between the IdP and the SP.

The term *user agent* for a browser may seem familiar to you. In web standards, software (e.g., the web browser) acts as a user agent that acts on behalf of the user to interact with a service.

1. The end user accesses the CSP with their browser.
2. The SP redirects the SAML request to the browser.
3. The browser relays the SAML request to the IdP.
4. The user presents their credentials and is authenticated by the IdP.
5. The IdP generates a SAML assertion (an authentication and attribute statement, such as a role mapping) and sends it to the browser.
6. The browser relays the SAML assertion to the SP.
7. If the user is authenticated (passes validation), the SP creates a session for the user, sets a session token or cookie, and sends it to the user's browser. This token or cookie is used to prove the user has been validated, and tracks the session.
8. The user requests a resource from the SP.
9. The SP responds with the requested resource.

Managing Users and Identities for Cloud Computing

Identity management focuses on the processes and technologies for registering, provisioning, propagating, managing, and deprovisioning identities. Ideally, all identity management would be done centrally, but the reality is that you are likely to find multiple identity stores for individual applications. It should also be noted that identity management is not access management. Although they may appear to be the same thing, identity management deals with identities, and access management deals with the entitlements these identities are granted.

To begin with identity management, you have to first identify who the users are to be managed. This might include employees, contractors, service providers, customers, third-party providers (e.g., MSPs), and so on. There are different requirements for each, and one approach may not fit all. The approach used should be based on the risk associated with each type of access. For example, employees will usually be granted a long-term account with no predefined account for de-provisioning, whereas contractors will likely need to have an automated de-provisioning process when their contracts end.

When it comes to identity management in the cloud, several things must be considered. First, cloud providers will likely support internal identities, identifiers, and attributes for users who directly access the service. Many CSPs will also offer and support federation so that customers can centrally manage one identity store as the IdP and leverage the CSP to act as the RP/SP. In my experience, many organizations want to drastically limit the number of identities stored in different cloud environments and leverage federation whenever possible.

Cloud customers need to decide where they want to manage their identities and which architectural models and technologies they want to support to integrate with cloud providers. As a cloud customer, you can create all your identities in the various CSP IAM systems, but this is not scalable and leads to an incredible amount of complexity to manage for all but the smallest organizations, which is why I mentioned earlier that most organizations use federation.

There are two architectural patterns mentioned by the CSA that you should be aware of in preparation for the CCSK exam. These are the hub-and-spoke model and the freeform model.

With the hub-and-spoke model (see Figure 5-4), internal IdPs/sources communicate with a central broker or repository that then serves as the IdP for federation to cloud providers. An example of this would be a cloud service such as OKTA, Microsoft Entra ID, or Ping Identity. There are multiple reasons why an organization may choose to use an identity broker as part of a hub-and-spoke architecture. This includes reduced infrastructure cost, simplicity of management, and availability of a vendor-agnostic IAM solution that may offer more advanced solutions than a traditional on-premises freeform architecture. Additionally, as a cloud service, users can connect to the identity broker from anywhere to access any cloud service used by the organization.

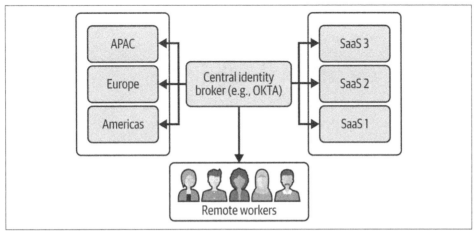

Figure 5-4. Hub-and-spoke FIM architectural model

With the freeform model, internal IdPs/sources (often directory servers) connect directly to cloud providers. An example in the Microsoft world would be ADFS. Implementing such a solution doesn't require a monthly charge, but it does require that local infrastructure such as SQL and IIS servers be installed and maintained. All federation connections will need to be manually created on a one-to-one basis with each CSP. Other issues are that the directory needs internet access, and users will need to connect to the organization via a VPN to access cloud services unless the ADFS server or ADFS proxies are made publicly available, which may be a security concern.

Figure 5-5 shows the freeform architecture. As you can see, when dealing with multiple domains, the amount of effort required to establish and maintain federation can become unmanageable very quickly. Additionally, remote users must connect via a VPN to their respective domain in order to access cloud services.

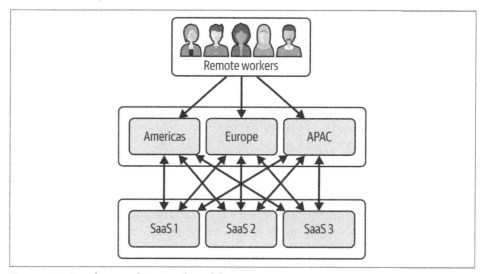

Figure 5-5. Freeform architectural model

Strong Authentication and Authorization

I defined authentication and authorization earlier in the chapter. Both items are critical to cloud security and need to be secured following industry best practices to minimize security exposure, especially considering that the cloud has broad network access as an essential characteristic.

Authorization

Authorization, or as the cool kids call it, AuthZ, essentially means allowing access to a resource. At a slightly more technical level, AuthZ determines user entitlements (permissions) to a resource. RBAC, ABAC, and PBAC are subjects we already covered. These are all forms of authorization. We'll cover entitlements shortly. For these entitlements, it is important to remember that the customer is responsible for defining and implementing desired access authorizations (and remains accountable for them!), and the CSP enforces these policies.

Authentication

In the realm of authentication (or AuthN), MFA is crucial. We already know the factors for MFA are something you know, something you have, or something you are. The "something you know" is a password, or even just a four-digit PIN that you set up for your bank card. The "something you are" is biometrics. There are multiple biometrics options, but the most common today are your fingerprint and your FaceID on your phone or laptop. Regarding the biometric data, it is held locally on the phone. It is not sent to the requesting website. As far as the "something you have," this could include hard tokens, soft tokens, and/or out-of-band tokens.

Hard tokens

These are physical devices that can be plugged into a computer via USB or wirelessly via Near Field Communication (NFC) or Bluetooth and that require the key to be close to the user workstation. A popular vendor that you may have heard of before is YubiKey. Fast Identity Online 2 (FIDO2) is the current standard that many vendors follow for their hard token authentication devices. FIDO2 credentials are now referred to as *passkeys*. Devices that use FIDO2 are generally considered to be phishing resistant.

This is not on the CCSK exam, but I should note that devices that support multiple authentication protocols (such as OTP, smart card, and FIDO2) may not offer phishing resistance unless FIDO2 is explicitly used. For example, OTP-based logins on the same device can still be phished. FIDO2 is *origin bound*, which ensures that authentication credentials are usable only with the intended domain, making FIDO2-based authentication phishing resistant by design.

Soft tokens

These are based on the Time-based One-Time Password (TOTP) standard. They are generally implemented as an application that is installed on your phone (e.g., Google Authenticator, Microsoft Authenticator).

Out-of-band tokens

Out-of-band tokens are one-time passwords that are sent via email or text. These are generally considered the weakest of all options due to account takeovers intercepting emails or SIM-swapping intercepting texts.

Just as a quick aside, passwordless authentication is gaining popularity these days. Passwordless authentication is often supported by FIDO2 passkeys and the WebAuthn protocol. Passwordless doesn't contradict MFA. Remember, you can have something you are as well as a second factor. A hard token combined with biometrics could be considered a stronger factor for authentication than the standard password and out-of-band approach. At this time, the CSA does not recommend passwordless methods for administrative-level cloud service accounts, as it considers this method a single factor for authentication (SFA, not MFA).

The current version of the CCSK study guide mistakenly refers to the WebAuthn protocol as the "webauthz" protocol. With the way exams are written and maintained in general, the CSA would remove any questions that refer to webauthz. The CSA won't change the question or answer to refer to WebAuthn instead, because that would contradict its material.

Privileged User Management

Privileged identity management (PIM) and privileged access management (PAM) are key components of IAM that focus on securing high-level accounts with elevated privileges. Let's dive into these two areas.

Privileged Identity Management

PIM is a security practice that is focused on managing and controlling access to high-level or sensitive accounts with elevated permissions within a system or organization. Imagine an administrator account as a simple example (more on this later). These privileged accounts can make critical changes such as system configuration changes, access sensitive data, or manage other user accounts. Misuse of these accounts, either accidentally (e.g., opening a malicious email as an administrator) or maliciously (e.g., account compromise), can lead to significant security risks. This is why your organization can't just trust users with this potential access level to do the right thing and only log on to their privileged account when absolutely needed. This is where PIM comes into play. PIM brings separation of duties into accessing privileged accounts. To obtain privileged access, a user must be granted such access by a manager or director. Access will be temporary in nature, not persistent.

Privileged Access Management

PAM focuses on controlling and managing what level of access privileged accounts have to critical resources, as well as the conditions that must be met for them to gain access. ABAC can be used within PAM to make dynamic authorization decisions based on attributes related to the user, the resource, and the context of the access request (e.g., time of day, location, device). In a cloud environment, ABAC allows for more granular control by evaluating multiple attributes before granting or denying privileged access.

Associated with PAM is another concept, called *just-in-time* (JIT) *access*, where an administrator gains administrative-level access as needed for a short time period as dictated by an automated or manual approval workflow. This allows the administrator to use a standard nonprivileged account and request elevation of permissions on an as-needed basis. The elevated permissions are automatically revoked after an established period of time. Actions performed during these sessions are also rigorously monitored. This reduces the risk associated with someone always being logged on with a privileged account.

Just remember that PIM is about who can become privileged and when. PAM is about what actions can be taken with privileged access. Since these are privileged accounts, you need to ensure that strong security measures such as automatic credential rotation, MFA, and detailed auditing and reporting are performed.

> I used an administrator account as a simple example of a privileged user. Privileged users are more than just administrators, though. For example, an HR manager who can see payroll data and government ID numbers (e.g., Social Security numbers) would be a privileged user. As such, their access to sensitive data should be tightly controlled, and all actions taken should be monitored and logged.

Summary

In this chapter, you learned about key concepts associated with IAM in cloud environments. Remember, identity is considered the new perimeter. Make sure you are comfortable with everything in this chapter. For the CCSK exam in particular, your primary focus should be:

- Knowing the benefits of FIM and why it is needed for user access to cloud systems.
- Knowing the fundamental terms associated with IAM.
- Understanding RBAC, ABAC, and PBAC.

- Knowing what the IdP and RP are. Remember, the IdP plays the key role of authentication, and the RP performs authorization based on attributes supplied by the IdP.
- Knowing the main FIM standards (SAML, OAuth, and OIDC) and what they offer.
- Remembering the hub-and-spoke and freeform federation architectures.
- Understanding the PIM and PAM concepts and the roles each serves.

Now that we have addressed everything regarding IAM to the depth required for the CCSK exam, let's move on to the next chapter, which covers another critical cloud security component in security monitoring.

CHAPTER 6
Detecting Threats in the Cloud

You can't defend what you can't see.
—Common Security Quote

It's critical to be able to detect a security threat so that you can adequately respond to it. Detecting potential issues requires the right monitoring for your environment. In a cloud environment, you not only have to monitor your servers and applications, like you do in traditional IT, but you also have to monitor what is happening in your cloud environment, such as who is logging in to the cloud management console, and log their actions. On top of this, you have to monitor cloud native applications such as serverless workloads, functions, containers, microservices, and other workload types that may not exist in traditional IT environments, which is a challenge on its own.

In this chapter, we will cover logging and events in single, hybrid, and multicloud environments. We will also address configuration drift detection in a holistic cloud security monitoring capability. Finally, we'll cover the role of AI in enhancing the security of cloud infrastructures.

Cloud Monitoring

Effective security monitoring in cloud environments requires an understanding of both the unique characteristics of the cloud and the specific responsibilities that come with using shared infrastructure. Unlike traditional IT environments, cloud platforms introduce new dynamics, such as global accessibility, rapid resource creation and destruction (a.k.a. velocity of change), and multiaccount architectures, which I addressed in Chapter 4. These are among the many items that significantly affect how monitoring must be approached.

The CSA identifies several key factors that must be considered when designing a monitoring strategy for cloud environments. Each of these areas brings distinct challenges for building a resilient, scalable, and automated security monitoring capability:

Management Plane

We know from Chapter 1 that the management plane is the place in the cloud environment where virtual resources are created, modified, and deleted. This is also where all security configurations are made. We also know this console is accessible from anywhere in the world, thanks to the broad network access characteristic of the cloud. Monitoring of the management plane is critical to maintain security in the cloud. I will discuss new tools that can be used to assist in monitoring this environment later in this chapter.

Velocity of Change

Cloud resources can be created and removed incredibly quickly. On top of this, many cloud resources are ephemeral (short lived). As such, responses to incidents must be automated. An example of this is event-driven security, an approach in which an action is detected and an automated response is performed. Take, for example, a scenario where a security group (virtual firewall) ruleset is changed. By monitoring the API calls used to modify the ruleset, you can automatically call on a function to revert the changes back to what the ruleset should be. In addition to this example of event-driven security, major IaaS CSPs offer many services you can leverage to build a strong automated response capability.

Distribution and Segregation

In Chapter 4, we covered the usage of hard security boundaries to limit the blast radius if an incident occurs. From a monitoring perspective, this requires the consolidation of logs and configuration items. Assuming your provider supports centralized monitoring (all large IaaS providers do, but ask your CSP to be sure), you can create a security monitoring account/subscription and monitor all the accounts/subscriptions from this centralized security monitoring environment.

Cloud Sprawl

Cloud sprawl is simply an extension of distribution and segregation across multiple CSPs. Cloud sprawl adds significant complexity, as each CSP environment would need to have a robust security monitoring system architected, implemented, and maintained. Although it is possible to centrally monitor all cloud environments through the forwarding of log data to a centralized SIEM and/or SOAR system, trade-offs of this approach, such as egress network charges and latency, should be carefully considered. Selectively forwarding high-priority events to a centralized SIEM/SOAR solution to have centralized visibility over high-priority metrics and security incidents may be a strong approach to balancing costs and latency. I will cover both SIEM and SOAR in greater detail later in this chapter.

Allocation of Responsibility
As mentioned in Chapter 1, understanding who is responsible for what as part of the SSRM must be known in advance of using a CSP.

Logs and Events

Logs and events are fundamental in monitoring, compliance, accountability, and risk management. Although these terms are often used interchangeably, there are substantial differences between the two.

Logs include detailed records of everything happening in an environment, from viewing a configuration to changing it. Essentially, they log CRUD operations. Logs are usually retained for a long duration (based on retention policies), and they are used for long-term analysis (e.g., forensics, troubleshooting). Log delivery can be delayed. For example, logs may only be written to storage in batches every 5 to 15 minutes.

Events offer immediate awareness of key changes in a cloud environment. In other words, events are Create, Update, and Delete (C-UD) operations (not Read operations) and are triggered by specific security alerts that have been set up in advance. This allows for rapid response (as well as automated response). Events are normally ephemeral (not typically written to long-term storage, unlike logs) and are high level, lacking the detail that log entries will have. You can create events based on log data. Some CSPs will enable real-time log streams being sent to an event management service that can generate events based on log data.

Essentially, logs capture all actions for historical purposes, and events deliver real-time monitoring for rapid response.

To drive this point home as far as the CCSK exam goes, logs and events are complementary to each other. Logs capture detailed records of all actions and are essential for a wide range of activities, such as investigating security incidents and providing auditors with evidence of compliance. Events deliver near–real time monitoring and alerting for rapid response. This is because an event can be used to kick off an automated response to an action. Let's take a look at a scenario that demonstrates the interconnected nature of logs and events. We'll use AWS as the example, but remember, there are no vendor questions in the CCSK exam, so don't get hung up on remembering the service names you're about to see. The goal is to understand logs and events, not a particular CSP's implementation. By the way, Azure and Google Cloud offer similar functionality.

For our example, we want to know if a security group ruleset for outbound (egress) traffic is changed to suddenly allow all outbound traffic out to the internet and possibly back to a command and control (C2) server. The API call that is invoked when this happens is `ec2:AuthorizeSecurityGroupEgress` and it is logged by the logging service called CloudTrail. CloudTrail is set up by default to work with another service, called EventBridge. In EventBridge, you can monitor for an API action from CloudTrail as an option. So you would add `AuthorizeSecurityGroupEgress` from the EC2 service as a pattern rule, and if this pattern matches, that is, if an outbound ruleset is changed, Simple Notification Service (SNS) will automatically send a notification to the administrator via email or text message that a security group's outbound rules have changed, and a Lambda function will be invoked that will automatically run a Python script that will set the security group back to what it should be. This is called *event-driven security*. Figure 6-1 shows this in action.

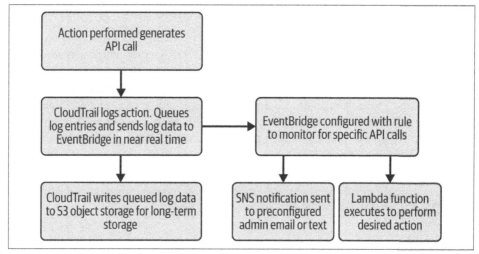

Figure 6-1. Logging and event workflow

This type of automated response is valuable today but will be critical in the near future due to the increasing threat AI poses to systems and infrastructures as a whole. The speed at which an automated attack operates can only be countered with automated defense.

Although the CSA doesn't talk about metrics, I think it's good to know these are also an important part of the overall telemetry of a cloud environment. Metrics are numerical measurements that can show the health, performance, and utilization of a system. Metrics can also support the initiation of incident response. Take, for example, a sudden spike in outbound network traffic at 2 a.m. Is this the result of data exfiltration? Metrics can also support trend analysis, which is important for capacity management and other areas for proper management of cloud environments.

Posture Management

In addition to the logs and events we just covered, another key component of monitoring in a cloud environment is posture management. Essentially, posture management is continuous monitoring of the configuration of your cloud environment. All major CSPs offer services that will monitor configurations for changes and can generate alerts of potential vulnerabilities and attack vectors, such as misconfigurations, which are a leading cause of cloud exploits. Some posture management tools can also measure compliance of the cloud infrastructure against major compliance standards such as PCI, HIPAA, NIST, and others.

In an upcoming section, we'll look at some cloud native security tools that include various posture management solutions.

Cloud Telemetry Sources

Cloud telemetry means the collection, monitoring, and analysis of data generated by cloud resources and applications. Telemetry sources include the logs, events, and posture management we just covered. Now we are going to investigate in greater detail the types of logs and tools that can be used to gain observability into cloud environments.

Management Plane Logs

As covered earlier, activities performed in the management plane need to be continuously monitored. Management plane logs capture the who, what, where, when, and how of actions in the cloud environment. They don't cover the services (e.g., network logs) or resources (e.g., workloads). Those activities are captured in service and resource logs, which I discuss in the next sections.

The CSA does reference the CIS benchmarks as a starting point for establishing management plane monitoring. CIS benchmarks are specific security best practices for many products, including those of the major CSPs. In general, the CIS benchmarks will address a wide range of CSP-specific security recommendations, including configuration of logging services.

Service Logs

Service logs are specific to a particular cloud service. Following is a partial list of common service logs:

API gateway logs
　　An API gateway is akin to an API firewall. These logs can be used to monitor access requests made to APIs and may detect malicious actions.

Storage logs
　　These logs capture access and actions performed in object storage. They are critical for proper data governance and are often a compliance requirement for an organization.

Network logs
　　These logs deliver a high-level view of network traffic (e.g., what are the source and destination IP addresses and ports as well as whether packets were accepted or rejected) in the cloud environment. Note that these are not used for packet analysis. They provide basic, high-level information about network packets.

DNS logs
　　DNS logs are just as important in the cloud as they are in traditional IT environments. DNS logs can be used to discover C2 servers that compromised resources will communicate with, as well as other indicators of compromise (IoCs) based on the domain names being accessed.

Function logs
　　Function logging is essential for monitoring and troubleshooting. These logs can assist with security by providing a record of executions, access patterns, and unauthorized attempts to execute functions, which may flag suspicious activity to be investigated. Due to their ephemeral nature and the fact that they run in systems maintained by the CSP (e.g., serverless environments), function logs are very important in detecting malicious behavior, as runtime monitoring may not be possible.

Cloud web application firewalls (WAFs)
　　The WAF is an application layer (layer 7) firewall that goes beyond the standard layer 4 firewall that grants or denies access based on a simple IP address and port. It understands the application code, such as HTTP and HTML, and can be used to prevent attacks against web servers, such as SQL injection, cross-site scripting (XSS), and other popular web server attacks.

Resource Logs

Resource logs are generated by systems and applications. Picture the system and security logs generated by Windows or Linux servers and workstations. Applications may likely generate their own logs as well. In a cloud environment, these logs should be written to some form of long-term storage, such as object storage. This is because servers in a cloud environment are often more ephemeral than servers in traditional environments. When you delete (terminate) an instance, you lose all the log data that is held on the server.

This is done through the installation of a CSP agent that will be configured to collect resource log data and send it to a centralized logging service such as AWS Cloud-Watch Logs, Azure Monitor/Log Analytics, or Google Cloud Logging. From there, the log data can be analyzed and used to generate alerts. Finally, the data is exported to long-term object storage for archival and compliance purposes. Figure 6-2 shows the resource log collection architecture.

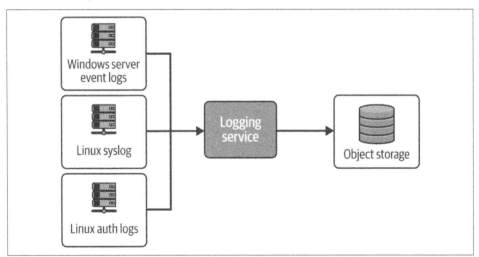

Figure 6-2. Resource log collection architecture

Auditors are likely to disapprove of log data that is missing because servers were deleted and the logs were never saved. Considering the requirement that many regulations and standards have for logfile retention, you will fail compliance checks if these logs are unavailable.

Cloud Native Security Tools

In the posture management discussion earlier, I referred to different posture management tools. The cloud offers a new generation of security tools that address the challenges the cloud introduces regarding the security of both the cloud platform and the new cloud native application architectures that take advantage of the new ways to run workloads, such as serverless functions. These tools are combined into a single platform known as the cloud native application protection platform (CNAPP). CNAPP is an emerging category of cloud security tools that provide protection across workloads, containers, applications, and cloud services.

Following is a short summary of some of the new cloud native security controls you should know about in preparation for the CCSK exam. I'm including some third-party products in this summary as well. As always, you don't need to memorize these vendors or products for the exam.

Cloud Security Posture Management

Cloud security posture management (CSPM) is a control that focuses on the protection of the cloud infrastructure (both IaaS and PaaS) itself. CSPM offers centralized implementation of continuous monitoring, compliance reporting, and automated remediation of the cloud infrastructure (although some third-party solutions may extend native CSPM solutions to address resources as well). This allows CSPM to identify misconfigurations, compliance violations, and security risks. All the major IaaS providers offer CSPM solutions, and there are third-party solutions that can manage multiple cloud providers from a single console.

Examples include Palo Alto Networks Prisma Cloud, Wiz, and Check Point CloudGuard.

SaaS Security Posture Management

SaaS security posture management (SSPM) is a security control that is used to manage and monitor (govern) the controls, configurations, and entitlements of SaaS applications. SSPM tools offer centralized visibility into security controls, configurations, and compliance status across supported SaaS applications. Think of SSPM as CSPM, but for SaaS apps instead of IaaS and PaaS.

I should point out that SSPM is different from CASB, which we touched on in Chapter 4. CASB effectively governs communication to a SaaS. The SSPM integrates with the SaaS's APIs to inspect the controls, configurations, and permissions inside the SaaS.

Examples include Adaptive Shield, DoControl, and Obsidian Security.

Cloud Workload Protection Platform

Cloud workload protection platform (CWPP) focuses on the security of resources in a cloud infrastructure. CWPP tools offer automated scanning for vulnerabilities and misconfigurations. They can also offer workload hardening recommendations, and runtime protection to detect and respond to threats in real time. These tools can be used as a control for both cloud native workloads such as containers, Kubernetes, and function as a service (FaaS), as well as traditional workloads running on VMs. CWPP tools can also integrate with SIEM/SOAR platforms for threat visibility and incident response.

Examples include Trend Micro Cloud One Workload Security, CrowdStrike Falcon Cloud Workload Protection, and Palo Alto Networks Prisma Cloud.

Data Security Posture Management

Data security posture management (DSPM) is a security control that offers continuous monitoring and real-time alerting of data security in a cloud environment to identify risks, user behavior analysis through anomaly detection of data access patterns, and compliance status with regulatory requirements. DSPM tools provide data discovery, classification, and encryption policy enforcement, and ensure that proper access controls are in place to safeguard data. They can be used to protect data in SaaS, PaaS, and IaaS systems. Unlike CSPM and CWPP, major CSPs do not generally offer DSPM services currently. Because you will likely require a third-party solution, you must ensure that your DSPM vendor supports the CSPs you use, as the tool used must understand the vendor APIs that are exposed to customers in order to work.

Examples include Varonis DSPM, Rubrik, and Sentra.

Application Security Posture Management

Application security posture management (ASPM) is a new security control that is focused on the application layer, from integration into the development process as part of DevSecOps through to real-time monitoring of application code, configuration, and behavior. It is complementary to CWPP in that ASPM tools are focused on the security of the application code, not the environment that hosts the applications, which is where CWPP tools are used.

Examples include Apiiro, ArmorCode, and Bionic.

Cloud Infrastructure Entitlement Management

Cloud infrastructure entitlement management (CIEM) is a control designed to manage and monitor entitlements within cloud environments. It is used to reduce excessive permissions and associated threats. In other words, it enforces least privilege. CIEM is often available as a third-party offering that can be used to govern access across multiple clouds through API integration.

Examples include Sonrai Security, Veza, and Ermetic.

Cloud Detection and Response

Cloud detection and response (CDR) is a security control that detects and responds to security threats and incidents within cloud environments. Think of CDR as endpoint detection and response (EDR), but for cloud infrastructures instead of endpoints. Like EDR, CDR uses advanced analytics, threat intelligence, and behavior anomaly detection to identify suspicious activities and IoCs. It is complementary to CSPM. CDR tools facilitate rapid incident detection, investigation, and response, helping to mitigate the impact of security breaches and unauthorized access attempts in the cloud. CDR tools can also integrate with other security controls, such as SIEM/SOAR platforms.

Examples include Lacework, Wiz (CDR module), and Gem Security.

SIEM and SOAR: The Detective and the Robot Guard

Having raw log data generated and centrally stored is great and all, but without tools to go through the logs and find the proverbial needle in the haystack, you may never discover the critical information these logs may contain. This is where SIEM and SOAR tools come into play.

This explainer of SIEM and SOAR is not exam specific. These technologies are being explained for those who may not be aware of them. The CSA study guide discusses their importance in cloud monitoring but doesn't cover what these technologies are or why they are critical for a strong security posture.

Security Information and Event Management

SIEM systems can aggregate, analyze, and correlate security logs and events across key components such as firewalls, operating systems, applications, and intrusion detection (and prevention) systems across an entire traditional or cloud environment. They detect anomalies, generate alerts, and have dashboards for incident detection. They can also produce reports for leadership and compliance purposes. Let's look at the key features of a SIEM system.

Log normalization

Log normalization converts different log formats to a single format. Take the following log formats for the same event, for example:

- Firewall log:

    ```
    ALLOW TCP 192.168.1.100 10.0.0.5 22 johndoe
    ```

- Windows log:

```
EventID: 4624 | User: johndoe | Logon Type: Interactive
| IP Address: 192.168.1.100
```

- Linux log:

```
sshd[12345]: Accepted password for johndoe from 192.168.1.100 port 52222 ssh2
```

These all essentially say John Doe accessed SSH (port 22) on server 10.0.0.5. Technology-specific parsers used by the SIEM system will understand the different log formats and extract relevant fields and normalize them into a common schema. These can then be displayed in a standard format (e.g., JSON). An example of the standardized SIEM entry would look like this:

```
{
  "event_type": "user_login",
  "username": "johndoe",
  "source_ip": "192.168.1.100",
  "destination_ip": "10.0.0.5",
  "protocol": "TCP",
  "logon_method": "password",
  "success": true
}
```

Now, if you were really paying attention, you noticed that not all the logs from different sources have the same information. By putting the pieces together, the standardized SIEM data can be used to correlate and detect actions performed across multiple systems.

Correlation and detection

Correlation and detection are core functions of a SIEM system, and they work together to raise alerts. Take, for example, someone who enters a building at 5 a.m., logs on to an engineering workstation, and copies data to a USB drive, then accesses a different workstation, plugs in the USB drive, and uploads 500 GB of data to an external IP address via encrypted SFTP. These actions on their own may not generate an alert (and let's be honest, no analyst will ever see these actions in raw logs).

But thanks to correlation of standardized logs across different systems, the SIEM system can see all the actions. If you had established a detection rule that triggers an alert if people are copying corporate data to the internet under unusual conditions, you would be alerted to this suspicious activity and start an investigation. (We'll continue this insider threat scenario in "Security Orchestration, Automation, and Response" on page 127.)

Integration with threat intelligence

By connecting a SIEM system with a threat intelligence service (there are numerous offerings, both free and paid), the SIEM system can receive threat feeds of IoCs, such as malicious IP addresses, domain names, URLs, and malicious files (via hashes, essentially a file's unique fingerprint) using open standards (e.g., STIX/TAXII). The SIEM system will then automatically scan your normalized log data for these IoCs and generate alerts if any are discovered. This can prove invaluable in a scenario such as an employee opening a malicious file that then connects to a known C2 server. By getting an immediate alert, the security team can remove the user workstation from the network before the attacker takes any further malicious actions. If the initial connection to the C2 server isn't detected, this will likely allow the attacker remote access to the machine, where they would then deploy additional malware to the system (e.g., ransomware, keylogger) and expand their attack by moving laterally to other systems the compromised workstation can access.

Incident response and forensics support

Quite often when a company realizes it has suffered a breach, the initial compromise likely happened weeks or even months before the discovery. The historical search feature of a SIEM system is invaluable in this scenario. The incident responders can query the SIEM system to reconstruct the timeline of events that led to the initial compromise, and take actions from that point on.

Going back to threat intelligence, we know file hashes are part of any threat intelligence capability. Let's assume the initial malicious file was only discovered by threat researchers and added to the intelligence service three months after your organization was initially compromised. You can use the historical information to determine exactly when and what systems were compromised to limit the effort of rebuilding systems.

This information can also be used by the forensics team to perform further collection activities for technical and legal actions. Additionally, this information can be used for compliance audits, in which an organization must have the capability to demonstrate that only authorized users have accessed a regulated system, for example.

User and entity behavior analytics

User and entity behavior analytics (UEBA) is a capability found in modern SIEM systems. By integrating with IAM systems, UEBA will be able to do heuristic and behavior-based detection of anomalies from both users and entities (everything on a network is considered an entity, including devices, applications, and systems). Heuristic and behavior-based detection uses algorithms and logic to infer potential malicious actions based on deviations from normal actions. This approach is complementary to traditional signature-based detection (e.g., file hashes). UEBA continuously observes what a user and/or device is doing and generates an alert if something unexpected occurs.

Let's say TNT Industrial has operations in both Ottawa and Miami. The company president, Tony Tuck, often travels between the two locations. It wouldn't be suspicious to see Tony logging in from both locations. But what if he logs in from Ottawa at 2 a.m. and then again from Miami 10 minutes later? That's called *impossible travel* and would generate an alert. For another example, what if a finance employee, Conrad Langhans, who typically accesses payroll data, is discovered accessing data that has nothing to do with his job, say, customer records, for example? Is Conrad's user account compromised, is his device compromised, or is he an insider threat? This would be a valid reason to raise an alarm and shut down access for his user account and his device until an investigation is performed.

The difficulty with UEBA is that it needs to understand what normal behavior is before it can determine abnormal behavior. This can lead to many false positives and "alert fatigue" for the security team. That said, despite these challenges, UEBA is a powerful tool that is a cornerstone of strong zero trust architectures to address insider threats and zero-day attacks that would evade traditional defenses.

Security Orchestration, Automation, and Response

Now that you know the importance of a SIEM system, you may have noticed something throughout the capabilities discussion. The SIEM system generates alerts for investigations, and humans perform the investigations. In today's threat landscape, manual activities need to be minimized as much as possible.

Make no mistake: this isn't about companies saving money by reducing security staff. This is about needing automated defense to protect from automated attacks, which are becoming more likely and more advanced by the day thanks to AI-driven threats.

Enter SOAR, a newer technology that, unlike SIEM, can be configured to automatically respond to security events. For the automated response, a SOAR system will require two things:

- The source(s) of event data that will be consumed by the SOAR system
- A playbook (instructions) on how to automatically respond to events

Event sources

For event data sources, the "best" implementation would leverage an existing, well-configured SIEM system. Although a SOAR system can integrate directly with event sources such as EDR, CSP event detection services (e.g., AWS GuardDuty, MS Defender), and others, the issue is the lack of broad event visibility, log aggregation, event correlation, and other benefits we covered in the section on SIEM.

As with other security tools, the quality of event data the SOAR system receives is of top concern. If a lot of bad alert data is sent to the SOAR system, you may have many false positives that will likely negatively impact operations. If this happens, companies may restrict automated responses, effectively disabling the ability for the SOAR system to do what it was procured for (much like an intrusion prevention system being downgraded to an intrusion detection system by stopping the automated response capability of the former when too many false positives occur, or a CEO missing an important email that was blocked).

Playbooks

Playbooks are a set of automated, step-by-step instructions on what to do when an event is identified. These instructions can include communicating with other security controls via API calls (such as instructing EDR on a workstation to quarantine a machine). Although SOAR tool vendors may supply preconfigured playbooks, an organization will also be required to generate custom playbooks and possibly customize supplied playbooks, which will be time-consuming. Alternatively, some playbooks may be configured to not automatically respond to an event, but rather, to pause the response until a human review is performed. This should be limited, as the goal of a SOAR implementation is to provide automated defense against automated attacks.

I should note that some vendors are beginning to leverage automated playbook creation via AI learning from previous event data, but this capability is generally in its infancy.

Collection Architectures

With so many logs and other telemetry being generated, many questions arise from both cost and management perspectives. The CSA does not promote any single architecture for the collection and retention of all this log data. It does, however, highlight some key areas that warrant consideration. Let's start with log storage and retention locations, and then move on to creating a logging architecture.

Log Storage and Retention

Although there may be no direct cost associated with the generation of log data, there are generally costs associated with the storage and copying of log data out of a CSP due to many providers charging for egress (outbound) network traffic. As a result, the CSA highlights the following considerations for architecting log storage that is both effective as a detection tool and keeps costs to a minimum:

- Availability, suitability, and cost of detection and analysis tools offered by the CSP
- Costs for storing the data in the cloud versus external storage (such as on-premises or third-party cloud storage)
- Costs of moving and exporting the logs from the cloud to external storage
- Requirements to integrate cloud logs with logs of other sources (i.e., an on-premises SIEM solution)

I'd like to add a few more considerations regarding log storage and retention in cloud environments. You can use the following considerations for log storage and retention requirements as part of assessing a cloud service:

- What is your SaaS log retention policy? Does it meet your requirements? What do you do if a financial SaaS provider only has a 30-day retention policy, but your policy requires five years to meet tax record retention requirements?
- Does the SaaS provider allow you to export your logs?
- What format are they in?

These questions need to be answered before procuring a CSP's services.

Above all of this, there is the question of working with multiple accounts and multiple CSPs. If your organization already has a SIEM or SOAR system installed on premises, you may want to integrate all logs back to one centralized location. This brings us to the next topic of our logging discussion: cascading log architecture.

Cascading Log Architecture

A cascading log architecture is a hierarchical approach to log management. Logs from multiple accounts are sent directly or replicated from one account to another centralized logging account. Figure 6-3 shows this architecture.

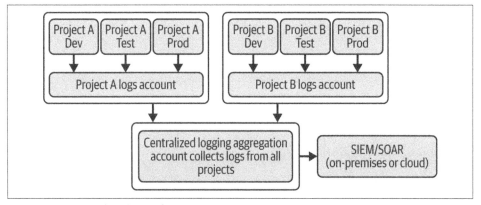

Figure 6-3. Cascading log architecture

In Figure 6-3, you can see two applications (projects) that have four accounts/subscriptions each (Dev, Test, Prod, Logs). Dev, Test, and Prod all forward or copy logs to a project-specific log account. These logs are then forwarded or copied to a centralized log aggregation account that holds all logs from all projects. At this aggregation account, you can install SIEM/SOAR provider tools to feed log data to the SIEM/SOAR product for alerting/response purposes.

How this is implemented will be highly vendor specific, both from a CSP and SIEM/SOAR perspective. The goal of this section is to understand the importance of centralizing logs and then integrating tools that can be used to analyze the log data to assist with incident response and other investigations.

AI for Security Monitoring

Security monitoring generates a huge amount of data. It is simply impossible for a human to sift through all the data manually. Both machine learning and AI have been used in security monitoring for quite some time now to assist with the following:

Anomaly detection
Using machine learning to identify unusual patterns in data traffic and user behavior, flagging potential security threats more quickly and more accurately than traditional methods.

Threat intelligence and threat hunting
Integrating AI to analyze vast amounts of data from various sources to identify emerging threats and provide real-time alerts.

Automated responses
Implementing AI-driven automation to respond to security incidents quickly, reducing the time between threat detection and mitigation. SOAR is an example of this capability.

Assisting analysts
Enriching logs, simulating attacks, patching vulnerabilities, and reducing the overall burden on security teams.

Summary

For the CCSK exam, it is important to have a solid understanding of key material in this chapter. Specifically, you should:

- Understand the complicating factors of cloud monitoring. These are the management plane, the velocity of change, distribution and segregation, and cloud sprawl.
- Understand that logs capture all actions (CRUD) and events capture changes (C-UD).
- Know that logs are for long-term storage and are useful in incident response, forensics, and evidence of compliance for audits.
- Know that events are for rapid response to actions performed.

- Know the telemetry sources (management, service, and resource logs) and which type of data each contains (e.g., DNS logs are service logs, O/S logs are resource logs).
- Understand the different cloud native security tools and the purpose for each.
- Know that many of these cloud native security tools fall under the category of CNAPP.
- Understand the basics of SIEM and SOAR systems.
- Know recommendations for a cascading log architecture for log management.
- Know that AI for security monitoring has been used for a long time, and understand the benefits of AI in SIEM and SOAR systems.

This concludes our coverage of the security monitoring domain. In the next chapter, you will learn about infrastructure and networking in the cloud, as well as CSA recommendations.

CHAPTER 7
Infrastructure and Networking

The network is the computer.
    —John Gage

This chapter covers infrastructure and networking in a cloud environment. Much of this chapter is focused on how an IaaS provider builds the infrastructure and network that customers access. It also covers security controls that are exposed to the customer, and how customers can use these controls to meet their own security policies.

I also address the concepts of cloud infrastructure secure architecture and infrastructure as code. The chapter concludes with related technologies in the areas of zero trust and SASE.

Cloud Infrastructure Security

As I've stated before, cloud security is a shared responsibility. It is up to the cloud customer to build and secure their usage of the cloud. In the IaaS service model, the provider simply wants to be the facilities provider. It offers advanced security controls; the customer must adopt and adapt the controls to meet their own security policies.

The CSA breaks down some key elements of security for both the consumer and the provider. We'll break them down in the following sections.

Cloud Customer Security Techniques

For the consumer, the official CSA materials list three foundational security techniques:

Secure architecture
    The architecture (the big picture of overall goals and high-level structure) and design (implementation details) of the cloud infrastructure is built with security as a key guiding principle. This includes segregation of resources and networks, enforcing least privilege access, and ensuring secure storage, communications, and service configurations.

Secure deployment and configuration
    By leveraging widely accepted security benchmarks such as the Center for Internet Security (CIS) benchmarks, the customer secures the deployments and configurations of all cloud infrastructure components. This includes VMs, containers, storage, and secure networking. There are multiple CIS benchmarks for a wide variety of technologies, including major CSPs. There are other frameworks that could be used, including the Well-Architected Frameworks published by major cloud vendors. Standards by leading industry groups (e.g., CIS benchmarks) and vendor-specific publications (e.g., Well-Architected publications) are what I refer to as "shoulders of a giant to stand on." Why go it alone when you can follow recommended approaches? Following these benchmarks and standards gives you (and your leadership) defensibility if and when something goes wrong.

Continuous monitoring and guardrails
    This involves the ongoing, real-time tracking and assessment of an organization's cloud infrastructure, including workloads, networks, and data to detect and respond to potential security issues as they arise. Major CSP vendors will offer a suite of tools to ease the implementation of continuous monitoring in the services they provide.

A *guardrail* is a set of automated, policy-based controls designed to enforce security best practices and prevent misconfigurations within the cloud environment. In Chapter 4, I covered organization management. In a scenario where you have multiple accounts/subscriptions, these policies can be established at a primary account and enforced at the lower-level accounts. For example, a *preventive guardrail* might prevent users from creating public-facing storage buckets, while a *detective guardrail* would alert security teams if an existing bucket is made public. A *reactive guardrail* would automatically revert the bucket permissions to block public access.

Controls have been used in security and risk management for decades. *Guardrail* is a fairly new term that really came about with cloud computing and DevOps. Guardrails are automated controls that are used to maintain boundaries, whereas controls are used to address specific risks and compliance requirements that could be manual or automatic. For example, in object storage, the control would be "no public buckets allowed." This could be done manually or established automatically using policies. A guardrail for preventing public buckets would proactively prevent anyone from being able to make an object storage bucket public in the first place.

CSP Infrastructure Security Responsibilities

The CSA points out some key responsibilities of the CSP when creating a secure infrastructure for customers to use. Security of the physical and logical infrastructure itself includes the following:

Facilities
This is the physical security of the datacenter. Physical controls would include restricting access of people to secure areas, CCTV cameras, and fire detection. As an interesting aside, even large CSPs may not own all the datacenters hosting customer workloads, and instead may use a colocation facility run by another company. They usually don't make this public. I wouldn't say it's a concern for customers—more of an interesting fact.

Employees
The CSP is responsible for performing background screening, training, and managing employees who have physical and logical access to the cloud infrastructure. This ensures that the personnel handling sensitive systems are both qualified and trustworthy (to the degree that background screening can assure). I think it is fair to say that major CSPs have the ability to hire top talent for positions such as architect, engineer, and security professional.

Physical compute components
The CSP secures and maintains the underlying pools of physical components of the cloud infrastructure, such as servers, storage devices, and networking equipment housed in datacenters.

Virtualization layers
CSPs are responsible for securing the virtualization technology that enables the creation and isolation of VMs and containers running on the physical infrastructure. Server virtualization is typically done through a hypervisor. The hypervisor used could be a commercial solution (e.g., VMware ESXi), be open source (KVM or Xen), or even be built by the CSPs themselves. The security of the hypervisor

is critical due to the hypervisor being responsible for isolation of workloads in a multitenant environment.

Management plane
The CSP secures and controls access to the web-based interfaces and API endpoints customers use to manage their cloud resources and services. This is a critical aspect of cloud security that will be covered on the CCSK exam.

PaaS and SaaS services
The CSP secures the platform and underlying servers used by customers in the PaaS model and the application itself in a SaaS model. Note that many PaaS and SaaS vendors use a CSP for the infrastructure. In this case, they are the cloud customer, just like everyone else using that IaaS to run workloads on, and they must understand the shared responsibility model of the cloud as a result. Be cautious if a SaaS provider claims security solely based on its use of a major IaaS or PaaS provider, as it is still responsible for securing its applications and customer data.

To wrap up this section, just remember that cloud security is a shared responsibility. The CSP secures the physical facilities, hardware, virtualization layer, and management interfaces that comprise the cloud infrastructure. The consumer must validate to the extent possible that the CSP does operate a secure cloud (due diligence of potential providers), and they are also responsible for securing their use of the cloud.

Infrastructure Resilience

Resiliency is simply the ability to continue operating in the event of some form of failure. In a traditional IT environment, this could be an active/passive server implementation in which a secondary server takes over in the event of a server failure. This is usually done in the same datacenter, but it could be done in two different datacenters in the same city if the organization has the resources and if the systems running on those servers are critical enough to warrant such a business continuity approach.

Things are different in the cloud. Major CSPs have a global presence these days, with multiple availability zones (datacenters, for our discussion purposes) across many regions around the world. This means that even though a CSP may not necessarily implement resiliency for your servers and applications, it is something that customers can leverage to ensure that their systems will remain available in the event of some form of outage at the CSP.

For cloud business continuity and disaster recovery, there are three (well, four, if you choose not to have resiliency) options at your disposal. We'll cover them in the following sections. But do know that CSP outages of any degree are fairly rare. That's not to say they don't happen, but when they do occur, outages are often expressed in minutes and hours, not days or weeks. There are, however, some examples of disasters that have severely impacted customers. I cover one such example in "Case Study: OVHcloud Datacenter Fire".

Before we move on to the different resiliency models, I want to share a Japanese proverb I once read in an airport: "When you are thirsty, it is too late to think of digging a well." This is appropriate when considering resiliency in a cloud environment. When the datacenter hosting your data goes up in flames or is underwater, it's too late to copy the data elsewhere. You must take a risk-based approach in advance. What is the impact of losing a key revenue-generating system versus losing the system that hosts the cafeteria menu? If the cafeteria menu is unavailable, does anyone really care? I'll bet leadership would take steps to make sure the revenue-generating system has resiliency. This is what is meant by a risk-based approach.

Single-Region Resiliency

Single-region resiliency is where multiple availability zones in a single region are used. Implementation is done by using CSP services such as auto-scaling and load balancing to handle sudden spikes in traffic and to be fault-tolerant against individual component failures. Many PaaS offerings managed by the CSP will also offer a simple means to implement cross-availability zone replication and redundancy. This form of resiliency is often the easiest and cheapest means for customers to address business continuity and disaster recovery planning, but it is subject to regional outages.

When the customer is responsible for implementing single-region resiliency, they must understand the physical distances between datacenters operated by the CSP. "Case Study: OVHcloud Datacenter Fire" explains why this is critical. Note that details of the case study will not be on the CCSK exam.

Case Study: OVHcloud Datacenter Fire

OVHcloud, a significant CSP based in Europe, suffered a catastrophic fire in a datacenter campus located in Strasbourg, France. The location housed four datacenters (labeled as SGB1, SGB2, SGB3, and SGB4 availability zones) in close physical proximity to one another.

The fire occurred in March 2021 and started in the SGB2 datacenter. Unfortunately, the SGB2 datacenter was destroyed as a result. The fire spread to an adjacent datacenter (SGB1), which was partially damaged (an approximately 30% loss). The other datacenters (SGB3 and SGB4) were shut down as a precaution. Hundreds of OVHcloud customers were impacted as a result, ranging from simple downtime if they were lucky enough to have resources in SGB3 and SGB4, to losing everything if they were unlucky enough to have all their resources in SGB2.

This resulted in a class action lawsuit and separate lawsuits launched by clients who lost all their data because of the fire. At this point, you may be asking yourself about backups and why the clients didn't back up their data to another location. Well, in two separate court cases that have been settled, it was determined that OVHcloud did offer customers an automated backup option as part of its virtual private server offering. However, contrary to the contract that stated OVHcloud would store backups in a separate, physically isolated location, these backups were stored in the same datacenter as the server the customers were using.

This case study demonstrates why you must assess the physical distances between a CSP's availability zones as part of single-region resiliency planning. The CSP likely won't give you physical access to the datacenters, but it should be able to demonstrate physical distancing between datacenters, which is a best practice that CSPs should follow.

Multiregion Resiliency

To address the unlikely event of a regional outage, customers may choose to implement multiregion resiliency. In this approach, you would replicate critical systems and data from one region to another. This requires more effort and money than the single-region approach, because some CSPs will require a customer to copy resources from one region to another since regions are fully self-contained from other regions as part of the CSP architecture. This requires customers to develop automation, and CSPs may charge for all data copied across regions as well as storage costs associated with having two copies of data stored in separate regions.

There are a couple of considerations regarding multiregion resiliency. First, are all the services and resources you use in one region available in the target region you plan to use as a business continuity/disaster recovery (BC/DR) point? Not all regions are guaranteed to offer the same services and have the same resources. Second, are there any jurisdictional issues with the target region used for resiliency? If you copy data from a region in the United States to Europe, are you in violation of any regulatory, legal, or contractual obligations?

Multiprovider Resiliency

Multiprovider resiliency consists of replicating critical systems and data from one CSP to another. An organization would use this model when it is attempting to reduce the impact of an entire CSP becoming unavailable. Using the risk-based approach we covered earlier, the multiprovider resiliency model should be reserved for only the most critical applications and data due to the effort and costs associated with it. This is the hardest resiliency model to achieve because every CSP is very different. It is also the costliest model due to the design, development, testing, and ongoing maintenance as well as the expertise required to manage multiple CSPs. In addition, there are likely to be charges incurred for copying data across provider networks.

From a workload perspective, containers (which we'll cover in the next chapter) may assist with portability between different CSPs, but there are issues that must be addressed in managing disparate networking, storage, and security models. Additionally, orchestrating deployments and operations across different providers may be challenging.

Implementing the multiprovider resiliency model proved invaluable for UniSuper, an Australian pension management firm with $135 billion in assets under management. UniSuper used Google for cloud services. Due to an extreme confluence of events, Google accidentally and irretrievably deleted all of UniSuper's data. Thankfully for UniSuper (and its clients), it had architected a multiprovider approach to resiliency and was able to retrieve its data from the other CSP to continue operations after a relatively short period of downtime (it took approximately two weeks for all the systems to be recovered). In this case, the importance of the data required UniSuper to plan for the most extreme scenario. In other words, UniSuper took a risk-based approach to its resiliency plans.

Cloud Network Fundamentals

Software-defined networking (SDN) is a network architecture approach used by CSPs to build and manage their cloud networks. SDN separates the network's control plane (which makes decisions about where traffic is sent) from the data/forwarding plane (which forwards the traffic). This separation allows network behavior to be programmatically controlled through software, enabling automation, centralized management, and rapid scalability. In essence, SDN allows CSPs to dynamically configure and optimize their network infrastructure using software rather than relying on manual hardware configurations. Figure 7-1 shows these architectural layers of SDP.

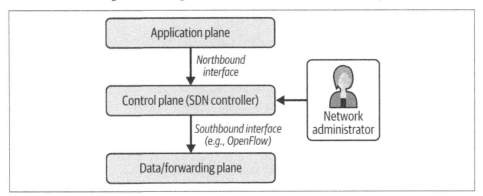

Figure 7-1. Software-defined network planes

At the top of Figure 7-1, you see the application plane. The application plane consists of network-aware applications that define desired network behavior or policies, such as load balancing or traffic shaping. These instructions are passed down to the control plane, which is managed by the SDN controller. There are open source (OpenDayLight, Floodlight) and commercial (Cisco ACI, VMware NSX) SDN controllers in the market. The controller acts as the central intelligence of the network, translating policies received from the application plane via the northbound interface into device-level instructions. The network administrator interacts directly with the control plane to centrally configure and manage network operations. Finally, the SDN controller communicates with the data/forwarding plane via the southbound interface using protocols, such as OpenFlow, that often consist of less costly commodity hardware than more expensive proprietary network devices that execute the actual data forwarding decisions. This separation allows for greater automation, programmability, and centralized management of the network.

In addition to enabling automation of network operations within a cloud environment, SDN also plays a critical role in enforcing network traffic separation and isolation. This is often achieved through packet encapsulation, a method that allows virtual network segments to remain logically isolated, even while sharing the same physical infrastructure.

For example, a packet generated by a VM may be encapsulated within a user datagram protocol (UDP) packet using a network overlay protocol such as Virtual Extensible LAN (VXLAN) or Generic Routing Encapsulation (GRE). While the encapsulation itself is performed by the overlay protocol, SDN is responsible for orchestrating the creation, configuration, and management of these virtual tunnels (e.g., VXLAN tunnels), ensuring that traffic is isolated and routed according to defined policies. Encapsulation is shown in Figure 7-2.

Figure 7-2. Ethernet frame encapsulation in a new VXLAN UDP packet

Network overlays are virtual networks built on top of a physical network (called the *underlay network*). Overlays enable features like traffic isolation, scalability, and dynamic provisioning. In the case of VXLAN, there is a VXLAN tunnel endpoint (VTEP) in the hypervisor that hosts the VMs. The VTEP is responsible for encapsulating Ethernet frames generated by the VM in a routable UDP packet that traverses a VXLAN tunnel built on top of the physical network on its way to the destination hypervisor hosting the destination VM. Once at the VTEP on the destination hypervisor, the UDP packet is decapsulated and the original Ethernet frame is delivered to the destination VM by the VTEP. It is this VXLAN tunnel that isolates network traffic in a multitenant network environment. VXLAN can also be used to present different physical datacenters as a single logical network.

Although you will not be tested on the details of VXLAN as part of the CCSK exam, you should know some important differences between a virtual local area network (VLAN) and network overlay protocols like VXLAN. The purpose of a VLAN is to create a single broadcast domain. It does not create an overlay network, like VXLAN does. Additionally, VLAN technology has a limit of 4,094 VLAN IDs (2^{12} bits). VXLAN has a limit of 16,777,216 VXLAN identifiers (called *VNIs*) because it uses 24 bits for its IDs. VLAN performs segmentation, not isolation. VXLAN and other overlay protocols such as GRE create isolated virtual network segments, which are critical in multitenant cloud environments.

The bottom line is that an organization does not need to implement VXLAN (or SDN) to use the cloud. Keep doing what you're doing. However, for CSPs, there's no question they will use VXLAN or some other form of network overlay technology instead of traditional VLANs.

Figure 7-3 shows this concept with the two hypervisors and the SDN network control logic that forms the overlay virtual network tunnels.

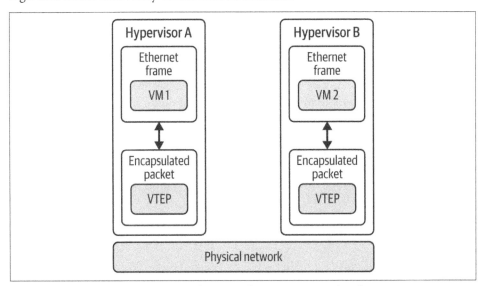

Figure 7-3. VXLAN packet encapsulation with VXLAN tunnel endpoints overview

From a cloud perspective, all CSPs will use SDN and overlay networks. As a customer, you always use this SDN network. CSPs are excellent at masking complexity from customers. Behind the scenes, the network established by a CSP is extremely complex, but it will present networking configuration options in a very similar way to traditional networking. This allows customers to benefit from the isolation of network traffic in a multitenant environment and avoid the burden of managing individual network components, such as routers, switches, and their access control lists (ACLs). Instead, they define logical groupings (VPCs, subnets, etc.) and network connectivity, and they let the provider, through its SDN technology, configure individual network components.

Now that we have a foundation of what SDN is, let's delve into some of the components that you are likely to work with on a regular basis.

Common SDN-Based Components

In the following sections, I'll discuss technologies that are commonly used in a cloud environment. Some are commonplace in traditional networking as well. You will need to know what these are to both pass the CCSK exam and work with any IaaS provider from a networking and security perspective.

> For the following networking discussion, remember that the CCSK exam is vendor agnostic. Focus on what capability each component delivers, and don't get hung up on the CSP-specific details.

Virtual networks/virtual private clouds

These are logically isolated network environments built through mechanisms like SDN and hypervisor-based segmentation. This ensures that traffic between your VPC and other customers' VPCs is isolated. They allow you to select IP addresses, create public and/or private subnets, manage routing, and determine traffic flows. I dislike the term *virtual private cloud* used by AWS. I much prefer Microsoft Azure's use of the term *virtual network*. There's nothing "private" about a VPC. You are still in a public cloud with workloads run on shared hardware, shared storage, and third-party administrators. These are not "hard security boundaries" in the same sense as what we covered in Chapter 4, which addresses the use of multiple accounts to segregate and isolate workloads to limit the blast radius of an incident.

Subnets (public and private)

Subnets are the same in the cloud as in traditional networking. Subnets allow for the grouping of systems within a VNet/VPC. IaaS providers will allow you to create public subnets where systems have a public IP address and are accessible from the internet, and private subnets that use internal IP addresses and typically use NAT to enable outbound internet access (though they can also be configured to entirely restrict internet connectivity for added security). Access control policies can be established to allow or restrict traffic between different subnets.

Route tables

Route tables direct traffic within a VNet/VPC. They are associated with a subnet and essentially act as a traffic cop for traffic leaving a subnet (systems within the same subnet are considered local traffic and are sent directly to the destination). Route tables are presented in a format that is very similar to traditional route tables. They can be configured to direct traffic to destinations such as internet gateways for public access, VPNs for secure connections back to an organization's datacenter, or peering connections for communication with other VNets/VPCs.

For instance, let's say you want to inspect all network traffic going from a subnet to the internet. Using route tables, you can direct all outbound traffic to an IP address that will inspect the traffic. From that point, the traffic would be sent to the internet via an internet gateway (we'll cover internet gateways shortly).

Security groups

Security groups are a cornerstone of network security in the cloud. They are like stateful firewalls (they remember outbound connections and allow returning inbound traffic) but are implemented as part of the SDN network fabric. Note that for our discussion, *network fabric* is a term for a virtual network infrastructure. Where things get tricky with security groups is where they are placed. Some providers, such as AWS, apply security groups at the virtual network card, while others, such as Microsoft Azure (which calls its implementation *network security groups* [NSGs]), allow customers to place them at the subnet level or the virtual network card. This is one of those examples of you needing to know the "how" of what CSPs do and how you secure your workloads. The goal is to have granular-level security for an individual resource or a group of resources.

By limiting inbound and outbound traffic based on IP address, ports, and protocols, security groups serve as the foundation for microsegmentation and microperimeters. Note that the microsegmentation is a small set of resources (e.g., servers), and the microperimeter is the security protecting the microsegment.

Network access control lists

Like security groups, network access control lists (NACLs) restrict traffic. However, they do it differently. NACLs are often applied at the subnet/network level and are *stateless*, meaning you have to establish rules to allow return traffic. Essentially,

NACLs are used to allow or deny traffic between networks. Security groups are used to allow or deny traffic to resources. Not all CSPs use the term *NACL*.

A strong defense-in-depth approach to network security would call for the use of both NACLs and security group layers. The NACL can be used as the initial broad-based filter, allowing or denying access to a subnet, and the security group can be used for fine-grained control of the resources within the network.

Load balancer service

Simply stated, load balancers are a service from the CSP that customers can use to distribute incoming requests to different web servers. They have auto-scaling capability and allow for redundancy by distributing traffic to web servers in different availability zones.

Load balancers may include basic DDoS protection to mitigate simple attacks. Load balancers will often be used with more advanced network controls to improve security, such as a WAF, which is a layer-7 firewall that can analyze and filter application-level HTTP/HTTPS traffic, block malicious requests, and offer enhanced DDoS protections to address more sophisticated attacks.

Internet gateways

As the name suggests, an internet gateway (IGW) is a service created and managed by the CSP that allows traffic into and out of a VPC/VNet and to/from the internet at large. This includes internet access to other CSP services, such as a server accessing object storage. As far as costs are concerned, some providers do not charge for network traffic coming in through the IGW, but they will charge for network traffic egressing the VPC/VNet. This is a factor that is considered part of Business Continuity Planning and Disaster Recovery (BCP/DR) cost planning.

Private endpoints

As mentioned, the IGW can be used to access the public internet–facing services such as object storage. CSPs will most likely also offer (and recommend as a best practice) a more secure connection to their services in their private endpoints. These private connections never leave the CSP internal network, and thus they avoid any exposure to the internet. They are service specific and are accessed via a unique DNS name or network address using internal routing.

Cloud Connectivity

Broad network access means CSPs make resources such as VMs, storage, and APIs accessible over the internet. While access can be restricted using security controls like security groups and ACLs, poor security configurations may expose resources to the public internet, increasing security risks.

CSPs also offer private networking options, such as VPNs and dedicated connections like ExpressRoute in Azure or Direct Connect in AWS, to securely connect on-premises datacenters to the cloud. These leased-line connections provide direct access to the CSP's network, avoiding the public internet.

However, private networking does not eliminate all risks. Configurations with overlapping IP ranges or inconsistent enforcement of security controls (e.g., security groups, ACLs) can leave gaps in protection. The key security control in these environments is effective traffic flow management, including inspecting and controlling traffic to ensure that malicious activity cannot propagate across networks. This reduces the potential blast radius of an attack, containing its impact to a limited scope.

Cloud Network Security and Secure Architectures

CSPs want customers to be as secure as possible when running workloads in their cloud environments. To support customers, all major IaaS providers offer best practices and reference architectures in the form of their Well-Architected Framework documentation. These Well-Architected documents are broken down into what the providers call *pillars*. The pillars include Security, Operational Effectiveness, Financial, Reliability, Performance, and Sustainability. You don't need to remember the individual pillars for the CCSK exam, as different CSPs may not have all six pillars. One thing they all do have, though, is the Security pillar. Let's address some of the preventive and detective controls that providers mention in the Security pillar.

Preventive Controls

In Chapter 3, we discussed the different control types and how preventive controls aim to reduce risk before it's realized. The following controls covered in the CCSK study guide are examples of controls that serve this purpose:

CSP firewalls
　　In addition to the security groups and NACLs we covered previously, major CSPs will offer network firewalls that can be used at the ingress/egress points of a VPC/VNet. The CSP offers these as a managed, scalable service. They can be configured by the customer to work at layer 4 and/or layer 7, so they can perform deep packet inspection (DPI) on all traffic entering or leaving the VPC/VNet if configured to operate at layer 7. These CSP firewalls can also be configured to inspect TLS-encrypted traffic and will often include IDS/IPS functionality, which is a gap in both security groups and NACL controls.

Virtual appliances
　　These are more advanced, next-generation firewall offerings by firewall vendors. They are available as *marketplace* service offerings, meaning you pay the vendor for the software and then run it on a server instance that you manage and keep

updated with the latest patches. As a best practice, these should be run in a load-balanced configuration for redundancy purposes. Vendors may offer different means for high availability, such as clustering and active/passive failover. You should understand these redundancy options before you make a purchase decision.

Web application firewall

WAFs are used to protect web-facing applications from common exploits such as SQL injection, XSS, and other Open Worldwide Application Security Project (OWASP) Top 10 vulnerabilities, as identified by the OWASP Foundation. All major CSPs offer WAF as a managed service, and some WAF vendors offer virtual appliances. As covered in "Virtual networks/virtual private clouds" on page 142, the managed service will offer scalability and is managed by the CSP; virtual appliances may offer enhanced capability compared to the CSP-managed service, but they will need to be managed by the customer.

I also want to note that beyond the two WAF deployment options just covered, there are also cloud-based WAF vendors that can be used. Two examples of this are Cloudflare and Akamai. This model may make more sense if you are operating multiple clouds or have a hybrid cloud environment, as these vendors provide globally accessible, centralized security and simplified management across diverse infrastructures. Additionally, cloud-based WAF vendors often include content delivery networks (CDNs) that can be used to stage web data across the globe, leading to enhanced performance for websites.

Detective Security Controls

In addition to the preventive controls just covered, there are multiple detective controls that CSPs also offer to customers. Detective controls are used for identifying and responding to security incidents by monitoring, detecting, and alerting on suspicious activities. Although the CCSK material just covers two of these, different providers will offer a variety of services, such as threat intelligence, SIEM, and EDR, among others. Following are some examples of detective security controls:

Flow logs

These logs capture high-level metadata information about network packets entering a VPC/VNet. They simply capture the source and destination IP address and port, protocol type, size of the packet, and accept or reject decision. For deeper packet inspection, you would need to install Wireshark, tcpdump, or some other network packet analysis tool.

DNS logs

These logs are very important for incident response. They will record domain name resolution requests and responses as well as client IP addresses. These can be used as part of incident response to determine things such as command and control (C2) servers, exfiltration of data via DNS tunneling (using DNS to send data as the payload), attempts to resolve domains associated with malware, and other security items. Correlating DNS logs with other sources of data can provide a comprehensive view of an incident.

Infrastructure as Code

One of the biggest differentiators of cloud versus traditional computing is automation capability. IaC is a core element of automation in the cloud. IaC allows for the programmatic building of complete architectures in a declarative form. *Declarative* means you define the desired end state rather than the steps to achieve it. This is a leading reason why IaC has become the dominant model for building cloud infrastructures and deploying cloud resources. If you plan to be a cloud engineer, this is an area that deserves your attention today and tomorrow. As I always say, it is better to be the person doing the automation than the person whose job is being automated.

Everything you can do graphically can be done programmatically using the APIs that vendors expose to customers. All major IaaS providers support IaC, and third-party IaC can be used to manage multiple cloud environments. Just note, though, that your organization still needs SMEs on the different CSPs when using a third-party IaC tool like Terraform by HashiCorp. Although Terraform will translate your scripts to the APIs of the target cloud environment, you still need someone who deeply understands the cloud environment to ensure that you are following best practices in that environment.

NIST defines IaC in its SP 800-172 document as "The process of managing and provisioning an organization's IT infrastructure using machine-readable configuration files, rather than employing physical hardware configuration or interactive configuration tools."

IaC takes advantage of the programmability of cloud environments by making it possible to create templates that will build an entire environment with a simple execution of the script. The build will be 100% accurate to the script. This is called *deterministic*. Because IaC is deterministic, it can also be used to eliminate configuration drift that occurs when manual actions are performed that deviate from an approved and established baseline.

Additionally, security teams can review the script and determine any vulnerabilities before it is executed. This allows an organization to *shift left* when securing a cloud architecture. Shifting left simply means that security is being introduced earlier in a process. Instead of security reviews taking place after the infrastructure is built, they take place prior to deployment. Reviews can either be performed manually or be automated compliance checks as part of a continuous integration/continuous delivery (CI/CD) pipeline within DevOps.

Another key benefit of IaC is automating rollback. As an engineer, I can tell you with 100% certainty that every change management request will (or at least should) always have the question "what's the rollback plan if things go wrong?" before approval. With IaC, a rollback can be executed incredibly quickly in case something doesn't go according to plan. With IaC, rollbacks are straightforward and efficient. If a deployment fails, the infrastructure can be reverted to a previous state by redeploying an earlier configuration from version control. This is key to addressing change management concerns and complexities.

The CCSK material states the following key concepts regarding IaC:

- Architectures can be described by code and defined in a machine-readable format, from low-level network design to high-level application components.
- Through the management plane, API infrastructure and services are deployed and configured.
- IaC is typically deployed using CI/CD automated pipelines.
- Security scanning for misconfigurations can occur in the pipeline.
- IaC enables full version control and change tracking.

Zero Trust for Cloud Infrastructure and Networks

We'll cover the nuts and bolts of zero trust in Chapter 12, but the CCSK material does have very important information regarding zero trust for cloud infrastructures and networks that we need to address here. As you go through this section, just know that zero trust is a strategy for improving security across a set of pillars (Identities, Devices, Network & Environment, Applications & Workloads, and Data). The following section is a discussion of two implementation models for network access in a software-defined perimeter (SDP) and Zero Trust Network Access (ZTNA) framework. These options are similar, but how they operate is quite different. In both cases, you have a policy decision point (PDP), various information sources called policy information points (PIPs), and a policy enforcement point (PEP). At a very high level (one that is appropriate for the CCSK exam), the PDP makes the access decision to a resource and the PEP enforces that decision.

Figure 7-4, from NIST SP 800-207, shows a high-level zero trust architecture and its various components.

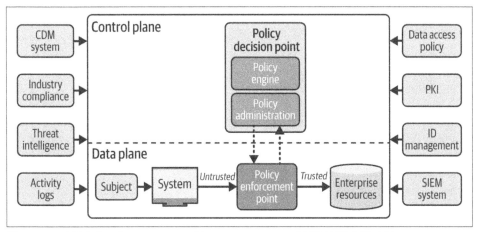

Figure 7-4. High-level zero trust architecture courtesy of NIST SP 800-207

It is important to note that SDP and ZTNA are not an either/or proposition. You could use SDP for high-value systems and ZTNA for lower-risk systems and access to cloud systems (SaaS, PaaS, and IaaS) to create a tailored zero trust security implementation.

Software-Defined Perimeter

SDP's claim to fame is its ability to create a *dark network*. This means resources protected by a gateway (the PEP) are not even visible to a requesting user until they are authenticated. After authentication (of both the user and the device), the SDP controller (the PDP) tells the gateway what resources the client is allowed to access. An overlay network (covered earlier) is used to expose the resources to the authorized user. This microsegmentation makes lateral movement by an attacker very difficult. After all, how can they attack what they can't see?

In fact, even the gateways are "hidden" until the user and device are authenticated. This occurs because an agent is installed on the device that will contact the SDP controller (the PDP). (Note that agents are normally used, but agentless may be an option using a browser plug-in, for example.) Once the authentication occurs, the controller sends the client a list of gateways they are authorized to access. It also sends the gateways a notification to acknowledge the client when they try to connect.

Next, the client sends a cryptographic message called a Single Packet Authorization (SPA) packet to open a connection to the gateway. Without an SPA packet, the gateway will drop any connection request. If the SPA packet is accepted, only then does the gateway respond with an mTLS request. This basically means both the client and the gateway validate each other and then a dedicated encrypted tunnel is created. Access to resources is time based and can be immediately revoked by the PDP if the client behavior changes (via UEBA), for example. SDP can also perform monitoring, logging, and reporting on authorized connections.

SDP can be used to secure local systems as well as hybrid cloud environments. It can also be used as a VPN replacement by exposing the controller to the internet. The key differentiator (and improvement) between traditional VPN and SDP as a VPN replacement is that with a traditional VPN, the remote worker (or attacker), once authenticated, has access to the entire network, as though they were physically located at a desk in the office. With SDP as the VPN replacement, remote users only have granular access to the resources they are permitted to access, as though they were in the office using SDP.

Zero Trust Network Access

ZTNA provides granular, application-specific access control, making it highly suitable for modern, cloud-based environments and local resources. Many of the vendors offering cloud-based zero trust solutions use ZTNA. Like SDP, ZTNA has controllers and gateways. ZTNA can also be used as a VPN replacement, just like SDP. ZTNA operates more on the identity and device layer than the network layer, like SDP does. ZNTA grants context-aware (user, device, geolocation, and other determining factors for authentication and authorization decisions) access only to specific applications or resources, but it does not create "dark networks," like SDP does.

For zero trust access to cloud systems (SaaS, PaaS, IaaS), it is common for an organization to use a cloud-based zero-trust-as-a-service (ZTaaS) offering. In this case, the vendor becomes the PDP and PEP, limiting access to cloud resources, just like internal access can be limited. User identities would be stored in an IdP that is accessible from the ZTaaS provider. This could be local, or more likely would be a cloud-based provider such as OKTA, Azure AD (now Entra ID), or another solution.

At the end of the day, many organizations use ZTNA because it offers "good enough" protection that follows zero trust principles and is easier to implement. This isn't a slight against ZTNA, nor am I saying there's no place for SDP. It's just that with a more complex implementation and rather limited vendor support compared to ZTNA, SDP is usually reserved for high-value systems and ZTNA is used for "general" systems. To remind you of a core security principle, everything is a risk-based decision, and the zero trust implementation models are no different. Organizations must assess their risk tolerance, system criticality, and operational requirements to determine the best fit.

Secure Access Service Edge

SASE is an emerging cybersecurity framework that integrates network security functions with wide area network (WAN) and proxy capabilities into a unified, cloud native service. It is designed to address the complexities of securing endpoint devices and access to applications and data in today's cloud-first, hybrid work environment, where users and resources are increasingly accessing systems from outside the traditional network perimeter.

Historically, traffic control mechanisms like firewalls were positioned at the perimeter of datacenters. These controls not only safeguarded the servers within the datacenter, but also protected users and their devices from malicious websites and data exfiltration. Common technologies in this category include:

- Firewalls and next-generation firewalls (NGFWs)
- Proxies
- Secure web gateways (SWGs)
- Data loss prevention (DLP) tools
- CASBs

These tools filter traffic based on factors such as IP addresses, ports, web URLs, content inspection, user attributes, behavior, and threat intelligence.

In a zero trust architecture, SASE plays a critical role by moving these filtering capabilities to the cloud. Instead of forcing users to use VPN to inspect their web traffic, or routing traffic back to a centralized datacenter for inspection using traditional security controls (a process known as *backhauling* or *hairpinning*), SASE leverages centrally managed endpoint agents and a global network of points of presence (PoPs) to enforce security policies near the user's location. Imagine the scenario where a US organization has remote workers in Singapore. Why route traffic from Singapore to the United States for inspection when a cloud-based solution can inspect it locally according to your policies, ensuring the same security with better performance and resulting in a better user experience?

I do want to add something that may not be on the CCSK exam but is worth knowing all the same. This industry is moving very quickly. From a security standpoint, the industry is increasingly focusing on the concept of Secure Service Edge (SSE), which represents the security-centric components of the broader SASE framework. SSE is composed of the security portion of SASE, such as CASB, firewall as a service (FWaaS), remote browser isolation (RBI), WAF, ZTNA, and SWG. To me, it makes sense to separate the network (SD-WAN, CDN, etc.) and security portions of SASE.

Even with just the security portions in SSE, make sure you are basing your vendor comparisons on your primary use cases. With so many different capabilities, not all vendors will have the best CASB option, for example, if that's your main reason for purchasing an SSE solution. You may also want to understand if there is one management plane for all functionality, or if each function has its own management interface and no communication between the different functions.

Summary

For the exam questions based on this chapter, you should ensure that you:

- Know the resiliency options for business continuity and disaster recovery.
- Understand what SDN is and why CSPs use it.
- Remember the SDN-based components.
- Know the difference between NACLs and security groups and where each should be used.
- Know the preventive controls listed and what they offer.
- Know the detective controls listed and what they offer.
- Understand what IaC is and that the automation it offers is a sought-after goal.
- Know the two zero trust architecture implementation options in SDP and ZTNA.
- Know that SASE is a suite of network and security tools.

This concludes our discussion of infrastructure and network security. In Chapter 8, you will learn about the different types of workloads in cloud environments and how to properly secure them.

CHAPTER 8
Cloud Workload Security

Security is not a product, but a process.
—Bruce Schneier

This chapter discusses securing workloads of all types. Workloads in the cloud have changed from solely running an application on a VM. New types of workloads include containers, serverless, FaaS, and now AI workloads. These different workload types have their own unique requirements, so security needs to be tailored for each. We'll cover the risks associated with these different workload types, as well as the platforms they run on. As with everything in cloud security, the SSRM must be understood by everyone engaged with cloud services within their organization.

Securing Virtual Machines

It's hard to believe that running workloads on VMs was the only means to run applications in the early days of the cloud. Although new options have been made available over the years, VMs are still widely used in IaaS. VMs offer robust isolation and compatibility for a wide range of applications. They are extensively used across various industries, especially for legacy applications and systems requiring dedicated resources. VMs in the cloud are commonly referred to as *running instances*.

Each VM has its own dedicated operating system stack. These are often available from the CSP itself and are referred to simply as an *image*. Although the CSP may patch these initial baseline OS images on a regular basis, they do need to be configured according to the customer's requirements. Examples of this could be removal of default running services, installation of endpoint protection or endpoint detection and response software, and meeting compliance. As the customer, you would then take this baseline image (different CSPs use different names, such as *AMI* or *VM image*) and make your own image that will be used to launch new instances. Once you do this, you are responsible for maintaining the security of your custom image and any instances built using it.

There are two key features you must be aware of regarding VMs in a cloud environment. These are auto-scaling and immutability.

Auto-scaling is a service that the major IaaS CSPs offer to customers. Essentially, you tell the auto-scaling service what image or operating system stack you want to use, the minimum and maximum number of servers you want, and when to launch a new server (e.g., CPU utilization for the servers in the auto-scaling group is 75%). The CSP can add and remove servers from the group based on actual demand.

Immutable means something is not subject to change. You don't update immutable servers; you replace them. This means you replace servers instead of patching them. The great security benefit behind this is that if a server is compromised by an attacker (after all, it is common that a server is unknowingly compromised and an attacker will install a backdoor to gain persistence), the immutable refresh process will replace the server that had a backdoor installed by an attacker with a fresh image that doesn't include the attacker's backdoor.

These two features can be combined. Using the auto-scaling service, you would follow the vendor process to use a new image for future servers. Let's imagine a scenario where you state a minimum of three servers are required for your auto-scaling group. If you delete one of the servers (some CSPs may automate the refresh cycle for you, so deleting may not be required; again, understand your CSP's functionality), the auto-scaling service will detect that you now only have two servers running. It will then take the new image to add a new server to the group of servers to bring the number of servers back up to three. You would then determine that the new server isn't generating any errors for users, and then repeat as needed to refresh the entire group of servers. This is also how a *blue-green deployment model* works. The original servers are the blue ones, and the servers using the new image are the green ones. If anything goes wrong, you have a fairly straightforward rollback by reverting to the previous image.

One important note about this process is that it is fairly simple to do for the servers themselves, but your application design needs to support it as well. If you keep data on the server, have a stateful architecture (a session stored on a particular server), keep logs on the server, or have any other data kept on the server, it will of course be deleted during this process.

Virtual Machine Challenges and Mitigations

Remember that VMs in the cloud need much of the same baseline security that VMs need in a traditional environment. In addition to the standard security requirements, you also need to manage the images and where they are stored.

The CCSK material states the following best practices for securing VMs:

- Enforce security using secure base images from a managed catalog, versioned and immutable.
- Regularly update images with security patches.
- Remove unnecessary OS components and harden configurations.
- Implement least privilege principles.
- Utilize automation for scanning, patching, and reporting.
- Use IaC for configuration management.
- Centralize and track monitoring and logging activities.
- Harden Secure Shell (SSH) networks and use host-based firewalls.
- Protect against pre-boot malware attacks.
- Monitor hypervisors continuously.

For most of these best practices, you're going to have to consult with the IaaS provider to understand what services it offers to implement them. For example, you can use secure base images in AWS with EC2 Image Builder and Service Catalog, whereas in Azure, you would use Azure Image Builder and Compute Gallery to build and store a managed catalog of baseline images. Don't worry about this for the exam, as vendor-specific tools are out of scope. For specialized security tools, this would of course be limited to private IaaS as the hypervisor is out of your control as a public cloud customer.

The main thing to remember regarding this list is that you need to manage these images and keep the instances created with them secure.

Creating Secure VM Images with Factories

One way to ensure that VM images are built with security settings established is to use an image factory. I just mentioned that the Image Builder service in AWS and Azure can be used to create images. That is a type of image factory service. What you need to know from a CCSK exam perspective is the concept of image factories, as shown in Figure 8-1.

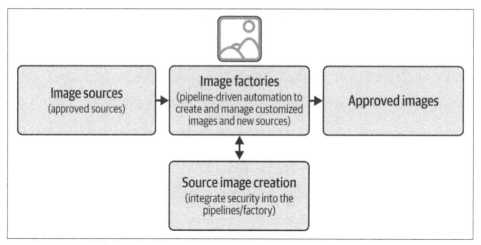

Figure 8-1. Image factory concept

Let's break the conceptual framework in Figure 8-1 into its parts. First, there's the image source. This could be a "quick start" image supplied by the CSP, or it could be an image that you import into the environment. Regardless of the image source, this is the barebones starting point. From that point, you have the security configurations and software automatically added to the baseline image. This ensures that consistent and repeatable secure images are being created as the output of the image factory process, and that they are the only images used in the cloud environment. Here's the formula to remember for the exam:

Approved Sources + Approved Process = Approved Images

There are multiple benefits to the image factory process:

- Building, testing, and fine-tuning VM images to ensure consistency across deployments
- Minimizing discrepancies that could lead to security vulnerabilities
- Streamlining the integration of security updates and configuration changes
- Preserving a library of source code and settings essential for creating VM images
- Incorporating security checks within the build process
- Keeping a comprehensive version history for easy rollback in case of issues

When it comes to image factories, the bottom line is that everything you normally do (secure configuration, patching, testing) is automated in a repetitive process.

Recommended Tools and Best Practices for VMs

The security tools that are used in cloud environments are quite different from those used in traditional IT environments. Not only that, but there are new tools coming to the market at a very quick pace. Following are some of the cloud-specific tools that are used to protect VM workloads in a cloud environment, as referenced by the CSA.

Cloud workload protection platforms

CWPPs came onto the scene in 2017 to address shortcomings of traditional vulnerability scanners in cloud environments. A main goal of a CWPP is performing vulnerability scans on VMs and other workloads such as containers and serverless. CWPPs can also offer features such as runtime protection, compliance monitoring, and integration with CI/CD pipelines for securing workloads during development and deployment. Findings can be prioritized based on exploitability and business impact. These can be used as a single console in a multiple-cloud implementation as well.

Configuration management tools

These tools, such as Ansible, Chef, Puppet, and SaltStack, can be used to keep VMs updated with the latest patches and configurations from a centralized console. Many of these are agent based. The agent will periodically check in with a centralized server and download (pull) the latest updates as instructed to by the central server. Alternatively, agentless systems such as Ansible will have the central server push changes to the managed servers.

Endpoint detection and response

EDR solutions use agents that perform runtime monitoring. You can think of EDR as a next-generation endpoint protection solution that goes beyond basic signature-based detection. In addition to traditional signature-based detection, it includes capabilities such as behavioral analysis, threat hunting, and incident response. Some EDR solutions may support vulnerability assessment as well.

SIEM and SOAR

Although SIEM and SOAR are two separate tools, they are often integrated to provide a more comprehensive approach to security operations. We already covered them in previous chapters. As a refresher, the SIEM platform can collect and process log data to uncover security issues. The SOAR platform can work with the SIEM data to automate responses (called the *workflow*) to security issues.

The Vulnerability Management Lifecycle

The goal of a vulnerability management program is to have a lifecycle that provides a systematic approach to handling vulnerabilities. The tools we just covered are part of a vulnerability management program from discovery to resolution. In the cloud, this cycle should expand to cover images and alternatives to patching, like immutable VMs (covered earlier in this chapter).

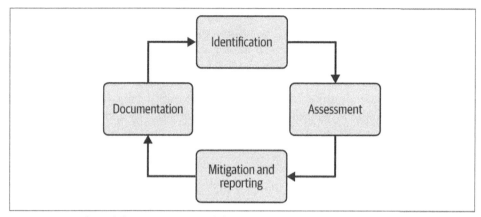

Figure 8-2. Vulnerability management lifecycle

The lifecycle, as shown in Figure 8-2, has the following phases:

Identification
　　This phase involves continuous monitoring for vulnerabilities using automated tools like the CWPP we covered earlier.

Assessment
　　Vulnerabilities are ranked for risk (impact + likelihood) once discovered. As this is a risk rating, you need to consider the system and data sensitivity themselves as well.

Mitigation and reporting
　　This phase involves applying patches in a timely manner, setting secure configurations, and employing workarounds to address vulnerabilities.

Documentation
　　This involves tracking vulnerabilities, assessments, and remediation actions for reporting and continuous improvement of vulnerability management capability and compliance. This phase also demonstrates vulnerability management practices and capabilities for auditing purposes.

Although the CCSK study guide states "mitigation and reporting," many other organizations reference "mitigation and remediation" as being part of a vulnerability management lifecycle. Mitigation addresses issues in the short term, like temporarily blocking network access to a vulnerable service, for example. Remediation is an actual fix, like applying a patch to remove a known vulnerability.

Snapshots, Public Exposures, and Exfiltration

In a cloud environment, snapshots are used to create nearly instant backups of storage volumes. These will be used instead of the traditional backups in a traditional IT environment. They are used for archival purposes and data recovery if needed.

Behind the scenes, the CSP will use a block-level differential or incremental approach to backing up data. So, even though snapshots look like full backups, the CSP is working magic to make it look like every snapshot is a full backup, and is only backing up the data that changed (deltas) since the last backup. This means the space consumed (and what you pay for) is nowhere near what it looks like. In other words, backing up data using snapshots is a lot cheaper than you may assume.

The security issue with snapshots is that users can easily copy them to other accounts and even make them public in many CSP environments. In fact, it is likely easier for an attacker to steal data stored in snapshots than live systems, as their security configuration is often overlooked. With this in mind, the CSA makes the following recommendations for snapshot security:

- Implement stringent access controls, limiting snapshot creation and retrieval to trusted personnel. In other words, the principle of least privilege should be used here as well.
- Encrypt snapshots to protect data, even if exposed. It is incredibly easy for a malicious insider to make a snapshot public if they have permission to do so. They can make the snapshot public and use their phone to take a picture of the snapshot ID. With that ID, they can download the snapshot at their convenience from their own CSP account.
- Regularly review and delete unnecessary snapshots to enhance security and optimize storage. This falls under the golden security rule that states "you don't need to protect what doesn't exist" (plus, you'll save money). Optimize storage by copying snapshots required for retention purposes to long-term archival storage, which is often much cheaper than online storage (assuming the CSP offers this).
- Use monitoring tools to detect unauthorized access and actions. For example, do you have the ability to be alerted to a snapshot permission being changed to public access?

Securing Containers

Now that we have addressed securing workloads that are on VMs, let's change our focus to another popular workload type: containers. In this section, you'll learn about two core technologies in container components and in scheduling and orchestration software.

The detail of coverage here will be limited to the depth of the CCSK material. If you are going to be the one to secure self-hosted containers on VMs such as Docker, there is extensive documentation, such as the 270+ page "CIS Benchmark for Docker" and the 270+ page "CIS Kubernetes Benchmark" that can be used for that purpose. Alternatively, you can use a container service from your CSP that will make securing the container platform the CSP's responsibility.

The goal is to understand the various high-level components in a container system and the security goals of each component, such as identity management, host OS security (e.g., nodes in Kubernetes), software version updates, container image security, network orchestration, network policies, firewalls, and load balancers.

Container Image Creation

The container image is the executable package that includes everything needed for the application to run in a segregated environment: the code, runtime, libraries, and settings.

The code could be a compiled executable or the source code, depending on the language used to create the application. There are several programming languages out there, but they will ultimately be either compiled or interpreted languages. With compiled languages, such as C, C++, C#, Go, and Rust, the source code is transformed into machine code (binary) by a compiler before execution. With interpreted languages, such as Python, JavaScript, Ruby, and PHP, the source code is executed line by line by an interpreter at runtime, without being precompiled into machine code.

The runtime within a container image is the layer that ensures that the application can execute as intended by providing the necessary environment, regardless of the underlying host system. This plays a key role in making containers portable, which is a major driver behind container adoption in the cloud. Without the proper runtime, the application code may not execute, or it could behave unpredictably. For example, a Python script requires the Python runtime (e.g., Python 3.9). A Java application depends on the Java Virtual Machine (JVM). By packaging this as part of the container image, you guarantee the proper runtime is available for the application. (Note that this relates to application runtime in the container image. There is also a runtime on the host, such as Docker and containerd, that supports the container system itself.)

Libraries refer to prewritten code modules that provide common functionality or services that the application can reuse. Instead of writing everything from scratch, developers leverage libraries to handle essential tasks such as connecting to databases, processing data, handling HTTP requests, or encrypting information. For example, if a Python application being built will interact with REST APIs, scrape web data, or integrate with external services, developers will likely need to include a library called *requests*. This library allows for the developer to simply call on the library instead of developing the functionality from scratch.

Although you don't need to know this for the exam, I want to address an issue with libraries and containers. You need to ensure that libraries are limited to what is needed to support the application. Including libraries that are not needed for an application to run is referred to as *container bloat*. This is a security, performance, and portability issue. It occurs for many reasons, including the thinking that "we may need it down the road" or "just in case." This thought process is a terrible thing for security across a wide range of functions, from IAM to containers. There's a saying in security: "You don't need to protect what doesn't exist." If you don't need it today, don't install it today.

Settings are the configuration parameters, environment variables, and application-specific options that dictate how the containerized application behaves during execution. These can be set in a configuration file that will be read when the application starts, and they are used for flexibility: you can customize an application by changing the settings, not the image itself. This is also where credentials may be hardcoded by developers, which is a security antipattern. The CSA recommends always using a secrets manager, including in containers.

All of these elements used to build the container image are defined in a *buildfile* (what is commonly referred to as a *dockerfile* in the Docker platform). The buildfile is like a blueprint or recipe that is followed to build the container image with the aforementioned components.

These container images should be based on a secure image and stored in a secure image repository, which is referred to as an *artifact repository*. When a container image is executed, it becomes a container. This is an isolated process that runs on the host system but uses the packaged components from the image. This isolation ensures that the application runs reliably regardless of the underlying infrastructure. This process is shown in Figure 8-3.

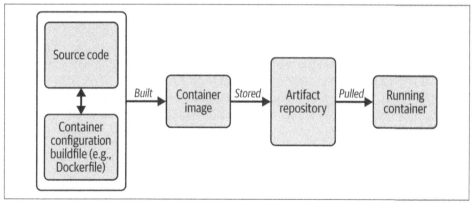

Figure 8-3. Container build phases

Containers are also immutable. Again, immutable means not subject to change. The container cannot be altered once created (aside from temporary data such as logfiles). When you need to make permanent updates to a container, update the images and launch new containers using the new container image to replace the original container.

Container Networking

Container networking extends the capabilities of the host operating system's networking stack. Containers run on a host using a container runtime (e.g., Docker). The container accesses network capabilities through virtual interfaces and network bridges created by the container runtime. This enables containers to communicate with each other, the host, and external networks while maintaining isolation and flexibility.

Each individual container typically operates in its own network namespace. This network namespace consists of separate IP addresses, unique routing tables, isolated firewall rules, and distinct virtual interfaces. The container runtime creates and assigns this namespace during container startup. The container's network namespace connects to the host system through a virtual Ethernet (veth) pair. One end of the veth pair resides in the container, while the other connects to a network bridge on the host. This setup allows the container to access the same networks the host is connected to, facilitating external communication.

Figure 8-4 is a simple diagram showing the container networking components together.

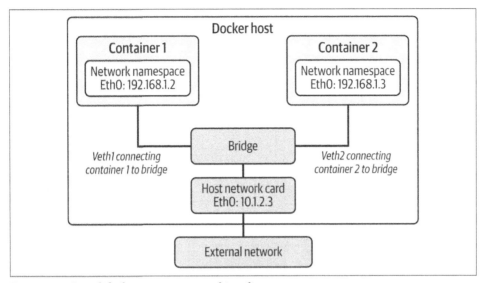

Figure 8-4. Simplified container networking diagram

The container networking concepts described here cover the fundamentals of standalone container networking. In the next section, we will explore networking in orchestrated environments using tools such as Kubernetes, where the networking model becomes more complex.

Container Orchestration and Management Systems

To use a large number of containerized applications in an environment, you'll likely need some form of orchestration and management to manage the containers. This is where systems such as Kubernetes (K8s) and Docker Swarm come into play (K8s is the most popular, especially for large-scale deployments). These systems are used to automate functionality such as application deployments, auto-scaling, and management across machine clusters. As is the case with the containers themselves, you have choices in a cloud environment. You can either build and manage these systems yourself, or you can leverage a CSP service that will handle much of the complexity of setup and management, and may include customizations for the particular environments with differing shared responsibilities.

Figure 8-5 depicts a simple Kubernetes architecture.

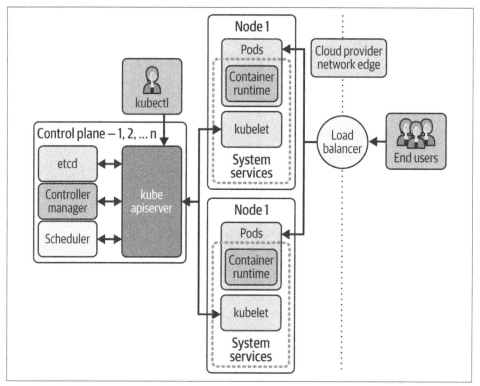

Figure 8-5. Kubernetes architecture with management and multiple pods

Let's define the components in Figure 8-5 that we haven't discussed yet: node, kubelet, pod, control plane, and cluster.

A node in Kubernetes is a computer, either a physical machine or a virtual one, that runs applications inside containers. Nodes are the machines that do the actual work in a Kubernetes cluster by hosting and running pods. Each node has the tools needed to manage these containers, including a container runtime (e.g., Docker) and a small program (agent) called the *kubelet*.

> In Figure 8-5, there are two nodes labeled node 1. This isn't a mistake. Although real-world nodes typically have unique identifiers, this diagram illustrates that pods can run on multiple nodes with the same configuration to balance the load and ensure high availability.

The kubelet agent monitors container pods and talks to the main Kubernetes system to make sure everything is running smoothly. Among its duties, the kubelet agent

164 | Chapter 8: Cloud Workload Security

performs health checks. If the health checks determine something is wrong with a container, the node helps restart it.

A pod in Kubernetes is the smallest deployable unit that encapsulates one or more containers and allows the containers to share the same network and storage resources. Kubernetes deploys containers by encapsulating them within pods. A pod can contain one or more containers that run together and share resources. A pod may contain multiple application containers if they are tightly coupled and require access to the same shared resources. An example of this tightly coupled scenario might be a web server and a log processing system. This is referred to as a *sidecar pattern*. In this scenario, functionality that could be run as a single service (web server and logging) is architected as separate containers for performance or other reasons. If multiple containers run in the same pod, they share an IP address. Pods are also ephemeral (short lived) and can be scaled as needed by the K8s system.

The control plane is the heart of the Kubernetes system. This is where all management is performed by the administrator via a command-line tool called *Kubectl*. The system that communicates between the control plane and the kubelets is called the *KubeAPI server*.

Although Figure 8-5 doesn't address clusters specifically, they are good to know about. A cluster is essentially all the nodes managed by the KubeAPI server as part of the control plane. You can have 100 separate applications with no dependencies or relationship between them in one cluster. There are also security controls (namespaces, network policies, RBAC, etc.) that can make this appropriate from a security viewpoint. However, there may be business reasons that restrict this, mainly based on risk (isolation) and compliance issues. For example, you may have to have all PCI-related applications in a dedicated cluster that is separate from the other application containers for true isolation. Alternatively, you may want to run all high-risk systems in one cluster, medium-risk systems in another cluster, and so on.

Container management and orchestration systems like Kubernetes can become much more complex than companies initially expect. Setting up and running a few containers is relatively straightforward, but as you scale to manage multiple applications across several servers, the complexity grows. To effectively monitor and manage the environment at scale, you'll need specialized tools and the right expertise.

This is where using a managed Kubernetes service from a cloud provider, such as AWS Elastic Kubernetes Service (EKS), Google Kubernetes Engine (GKE), or Azure Kubernetes Service (AKS), can be beneficial for most organizations. While you'll still need knowledge of Kubernetes and how to deploy workloads to meet your requirements, a managed service reduces much of the operational burden. The cloud provider handles tasks like cluster provisioning, scaling, patching, and upgrading, allowing your organization to focus more on application development and less on maintaining the underlying infrastructure.

Container Orchestration Security

We have covered most of the issues related to container orchestration security already, but I want to share here the CSA's list of what needs to be done to secure container orchestration:

- Leverage cloud provider tools for security.
- Disable unnecessary features, use secure base images, and enforce network policies.
- Regularly patch and update all components.
- Implement Kubernetes security and network policies.
- Follow CIS benchmarks and use standardization tools.
- Use private repositories with RBAC, image scanning, and signing.
- Start with robust, secure configurations.
- Harden host operating systems.
- Encrypt data, use access controls, and monitor access.
- Implement segmentation and firewall rules.
- Validate and sign images in the CI/CD pipeline.

Exam Note

For the CCSK exam, you need to know that securing the development environment is as important as securing the production environment. If an attacker can access the development environment, they can inject their own code into everything that is run in production.

Secure Artifact Repositories

The secure artifact repository is a secured area for storing all code, including container images. These repositories play a critical role in supply chain security, ensuring that only trusted, verified, and untampered artifacts are used throughout the software development lifecycle.

To properly secure the software supply chain and use these repositories in your organization, the CSA makes the following recommendations:

- Use trust mechanisms such as digital signatures to ensure the authenticity and integrity of container images. A digital signature verifies that the image originates from a trusted source and hasn't been altered. It does this by creating a checksum (a cryptographic hash usually generated by SHA-256 as a best practice) of the image and then signing this checksum with a private key. If the container image is modified in any way, the checksum will change and the signature verification will fail, indicating potential tampering or unauthorized changes.

- Implement access control to the repository. This limits access to only verified users who can push (upload) or pull (download) images from the artifact repository.
- Scan container images for vulnerabilities. New software vulnerabilities are discovered on a daily basis. By offline-scanning images regularly, you can address issues before they are introduced into a live environment.
- Container images should be immutable by default. When changes (e.g., updates) are required, a new version of the image should be made and deployed. This allows for rapid rollback if required and ensures consistency as well as reducing the risk of configuration drift.
- The origin and creation history of container images is well documented and secured, providing a transparent record of their sources and contributors. This is known as the *provenance* (the who, what, where) of the image software components. This is where a software bill of materials (SBOM) plays a key role. The SBOM lists all the software that is part of the container image, its dependencies, and the versions used. We'll cover SBOM in greater detail in Chapter 10.
- CI/CD pipelines are used to build, test, and validate container images before deployment. We'll cover CI/CD in greater detail in Chapter 10.
- Auditing (logging) of all access and actions must be performed. Remember, you can't respond to a security issue if there are no detective controls in place to alert on suspicious activity. Additionally, given the importance of software supply chains due to increased supply chain attacks, this log data will likely become more popular for auditors to assess.
- Keep repository software updated. Like all other software, new vulnerabilities in repository software can be leveraged by an attacker to compromise the security of your software supply chain. Regular updates and patching reduce the risk of such vulnerabilities being leveraged to inject malicious code or tamper with artifacts.

Now that we have covered container images and how to store them securely, we need to address securing these applications while in a live environment.

Runtime Protection for Containers

Runtime protection is exactly what it sounds like. The CSA makes the following recommendations for securing containerized applications while they are running. As you can see, these are the same recommendations for workloads of all types:

Real-time visibility
　Continuous monitoring for unusual behavior

Logging and auditing
　Detailed records for post-incident analysis

Microsegmentation
　Isolating containers to contain breaches

Container-specific firewalls
　Managing network traffic flow

Automated responses
　Immediate actions to isolate threats and maintain system integrity

Securing Serverless and Function as a Service

Serverless computing means the CSP is managing the servers that run a customer's applications. The CSP manages the provisioning, scaling, and maintenance of the servers. Customers can then focus on the security of their workloads and not on the commodity server hosting the application. There are many different serverless offerings from CSPs, ranging from applications to databases and even object storage. To determine what serverless means, just think of who manages the server. A typical example of serverless computing that we will focus on is function as a service (FaaS).

In FaaS, developers create code that performs a particular function. This is a different software architecture than most people are used to. You don't run a function 24/7. Rather, you execute a function through an event trigger, the function executes, and a result is delivered. You pay for processing time (which can be as granular as per millisecond) and the resources consumed during this time. When used appropriately, building a software architecture that includes FaaS for one-off operations can lead to a lower cost of operation.

Take a financial services company as an example. A customer accesses the company's website to see what a new-car loan would cost per month. The system may trigger a serverless function to perform the interest rate calculation. The system would pass over the principal amount, the interest rate, and the length of the loan. The function would then calculate that a $40,000 loan at an interest rate of 7% that lasts five years would equal a payment of $792 a month. This result would then be sent back to the website and presented to the user. Having done its job, the function shuts down and no longer generates charges.

Although FaaS may be cost advantageous in some scenarios, this does not mean it is a more cost-effective solution all the time. Software architects need to determine when using functions aligns with business and technical needs and when using a VM or containers to run workloads is more appropriate. This type of analysis is well beyond the scope of CCSK certification and cloud security in general.

From a security perspective, these ephemeral (short-lived) functions typically execute within a single-use container that resides on a single-use VM (as always, the behind-the-scenes architectural decisions made by a CSP must be understood by customers). This ensures that functions are isolated from each other. There is also no persistent, customer-managed server running for attackers to discover and exploit. That said, customers need to remember that they maintain responsibility for developing secure application code, managing access controls, and protecting data being transferred to and from the functions.

FaaS Security Issues

Remember that customers remain responsible for the application code. Using serverless FaaS doesn't change this. The CSA makes the following security recommendations for serverless computing, but these recommendations are applicable to all applications regardless of how they are executed:

- Do not overlook the security of APIs and other third-party services used in serverless computing. These are a large target for attackers. Although not required for the CCSK exam, I recommend that you look at the OWASP API Top 10 for examples of attacks against APIs, especially if you plan to work in application security.
- Dependencies are another area of concern for application security in general. A vulnerable dependency creates vulnerable applications.
- Misconfigurations are a leading cause of breaches. Take excessive privileges, for example. If an application runs with excessive privileges, negative outcomes can occur.
- Just like other types of workloads, serverless applications should have preventive controls to inspect and limit inbound/outbound internet traffic and detective controls established to protect them from attackers.

IAM for Serverless Computing

We already know the importance of strong IAM as part of strong security. IAM is important for serverless computing as well. Here are the CSA's recommendations for IAM for serverless, which of course are applicable for workloads of all types:

- Grant minimal necessary permissions and update regularly.
- Specify precise permissions for individual functions or resources. How this is done is highly CSP dependent.

- Use real-time attributes (e.g., user, device, time) to adapt access controls.
- Regularly audit and adjust permissions to align with evolving needs.
- Credentials should never be hardcoded in applications. In Chapter 10, we will cover secrets managers and their importance in application security.

Securing AI Workloads

The thing about IT in general is that it's always changing. The latest addition to workload types is AI workloads. This is, of course, an incredibly new (well, kind of) and exciting development in the world of IT. I say that it's kind of new because AI has been with us for quite some time now. Do you remember those CAPTCHAs that would ask you to click the boxes with traffic lights (or bicycles or whatever you were asked to select)? Those were being used to train AI systems years ago. Google Maps? AI. Self-driving cars? AI. Those social media algorithms that show you content? AI. General mass market acknowledgment really came about with the introduction of generative AI large language models (LLMs), starting with ChatGPT in late 2022. For the CSA documentation, much of the focus on AI is on the LLM aspect.

Why are we covering AI systems? AI workloads often use cloud computing. Of course, you can buy the GPUs and TPUs and build your own systems to handle AI workloads, but the reality is that many organizations will leverage the cloud for this.

For this section, we'll begin by looking at the assets involved in an LLM system, then move on to the risks, and finally look at some security recommendations.

Large Language Model Assets

Following is a list of the assets involved in an LLM system, according to the CSA. All of these assets need to have security properly addressed:

Data assets
　The datasets used to train, fine-tune, or infer with an LLM. This includes raw text, structured data, embeddings, and labeled datasets. Data quality and diversity directly impact the model's performance and accuracy.

LLMOps environment
　The infrastructure, tools, and processes that support the lifecycle of LLMs, including training, deployment, monitoring, and updating. It encompasses pipelines, version control, model registries, and security frameworks to manage AI operations at scale.

Model
> The actual LLM that has been trained on data to generate text, make predictions, or perform specific tasks. This includes foundational models, fine-tuned models, and distilled versions tailored for different applications.

Orchestrated service
> A managed service that integrates the LLM with other components, automating workflows, scaling deployments, and handling requests. This layer ensures efficient model invocation, load balancing, and integration with APIs and external services.

AI applications
> End-user products and services built on top of LLMs. These include chatbots, virtual assistants, content generators, code assistants, and other tools that leverage LLMs to deliver functionality to users.

Top Nine Large Language Model System Threats

Given the rapid changes in the AI field, it's important to note that the CCSK v5 material was created in 2024. It could very well be that those that are listed here as top threats to AI systems will change dramatically in the not-too-distant future.

The core of the material in the study guide is based on research by the CSA, called the "CSA Large Language Model (LLM) Threats Taxonomy," which lists the top nine risk categories to AI workloads. In a later section, we'll address the securing of these workloads. Here are the nine risk categories listed by the CSA:

1. Model manipulation
> This category involves attempts to evade detection or manipulate the LLM to produce inaccurate or misleading results. It encompasses techniques such as direct or indirect prompt injection (adversarial inputs), which aims to exploit vulnerabilities in the model's understanding and decision-making processes.

2. Data poisoning
> Data poisoning refers to manipulating training data used to train an LLM. This manipulation can be malicious, with attackers intentionally injecting false, misleading, or unintentional data points, where errors or biases in the original data set are included. In either case, data poisoning can lead to a tainted model that learns incorrect patterns, produces biased predictions, and becomes untrustworthy.

3. Sensitive data disclosure
> This category encompasses threats related to the unauthorized access, exposure, or leakage of sensitive information processed or stored by the LLM service. Sensitive data may include personal information, proprietary data, or confidential

documents, the exposure of which could lead to privacy violations or security breaches.

4. Model theft

Model theft (distillation) involves unauthorized access to or replication of the LLM by malicious actors. Attackers may attempt to reverse-engineer the model architecture or extract proprietary algorithms and parameters, leading to intellectual property theft or the creation of unauthorized replicas.

5. Model failure/malfunctioning

This category covers various types of failures or malfunctions within the LLM service, including software bugs, hardware failures, hallucinations, or operational errors. Such incidents can disrupt service availability, degrade performance, or compromise the accuracy and reliability of the LLM's outputs.

6. Insecure supply chain

An insecure supply chain refers to vulnerabilities introduced through third-party components, dependencies, or services integrated into the LLM ecosystem. Vulnerabilities in the supply chain, such as compromised software libraries or hardware components, can be exploited to compromise the overall security and trustworthiness of the LLM service.

7. Insecure apps/plug-ins

This category pertains to vulnerabilities introduced in plug-ins, functional calls, or extensions that interact with the LLM service. Insecure or maliciously designed applications/plug-ins may introduce security loopholes, elevate privilege levels, or facilitate unauthorized access to sensitive resources. Insecure plug-ins pose risks to both the input and output of integrated systems.

8. Denial-of-service attacks

DoS attacks aim to disrupt the availability or functionality of the LLM service by overwhelming it with a high volume of requests or malicious traffic and can render the service inaccessible to legitimate users, causing downtime, service degradation, or loss of trust.

9. Loss of governance/compliance

This category involves the risk of noncompliance with regulatory requirements, industry standards, or internal governance policies governing the operation and use of the LLM service. Failure to adhere to governance and compliance standards can result in legal liabilities, financial penalties, or reputational damage.

To address these risks, organizations developing LLMs need AI-specific security measures, ongoing risk assessments, threat intelligence, and proactive mitigation strategies. Let's look at those CSA recommendations in the next section.

AI Risk Mitigation and Shared Responsibilities

As mentioned earlier, this field is moving incredibly quickly. For the latest security recommendations by the CSA, consult CSA AI Safety Initiative resources on the CSA website. Let's review risk mitigation for AI systems and AI as a service.

AI systems

As AI systems handle vast amounts of sensitive data, ensuring robust data security is essential to protect privacy, integrity, and confidentiality. A layered security approach helps mitigate risks during data collection, storage, processing, and transmission. The following techniques are critical for safeguarding data throughout the AI lifecycle:

Encryption
   Protect data confidentiality during transmission and storage.

Differential privacy
   Introduce randomness into data or queries so that individual records can't be traced back to a person. It's like adding noise to a conversation to mask private details.

Secure multiparty computation
   Process data from multiple sources without exposing sensitive information, by anonymizing or tokenizing sensitive information as part of the flows.

Confidential computing
   Use Trusted Execution Environments (TEEs) to safeguard data during processing and protect AI model execution.

AI as a service

Many organizations are using AI-as-a-service (AIaaS) offerings such as OpenAI's ChatGPT, Anthropic's Claude, Google Gemini, and others. These are much like SaaS offerings in that they are turnkey solutions that are built for customers. Like other SaaS services, this removes the burden of securing the inner workings of the system from the customer, but there is still the requirement for customers to perform due care when selecting cloud services. AIaaS is no different. The CSA makes the following recommendations for data security in these AIaaS offerings:

- Clarify data deletion and retention policies.
- Understand data flow from company assets to services.
- Evaluate the provider's AI security measures against adversarial attacks.
- Understand SLAs, security practices, and regulatory compliance.

Data Security for AI

As AI technologies continue to play an increasingly vital role in critical business processes, safeguarding the security and integrity of AI systems has become essential. Ensuring data security for AI involves implementing robust measures to protect AI systems, algorithms, and data assets against a wide range of security threats and vulnerabilities.

Model Security

AI models are valuable assets, but they are susceptible to adversarial attacks, theft, and manipulation. Protecting models from these threats is critical to maintaining their integrity, accuracy, and value. The following strategies focus on strengthening model resilience, ensuring robustness, and safeguarding intellectual property throughout the AI lifecycle:

- Defend against adversarial attacks to enhance model resilience.
- Employ robust training techniques to improve generalizability (adapting to variations in data it hasn't encountered before) and reduce overfitting (memorizing training data).
- Strengthen AI models against attacks by incorporating manipulated examples into their training data.
- Embed unique identifiers (model watermarking) to assert ownership and deter theft.
- Protect intellectual property by altering the AI's responses to obscure its decision-making process.

Infrastructure Security

The infrastructure supporting AI workloads, including specialized hardware and cloud services, is critical to performance and scalability. However, this infrastructure can be targeted by various threats, such as DoS attacks or unauthorized access. Implementing robust security measures helps ensure the integrity, availability, and resilience of AI environments. The following practices are essential for safeguarding the infrastructure that powers AI systems:

- To maintain system integrity, utilize GPU and TPU hardware–based security features, regular firmware updates, and network security measures.
- Follow best practices in AI services for cloud services, including access controls and real-time monitoring.
- Apply quotas and rate limiting to identify and prevent DoS and DDoS attacks.

Supply Chain Security

AI systems often rely on complex supply chains, including third-party software, services, and dependencies. Securing the supply chain is essential to prevent vulnerabilities that could compromise AI models and infrastructure. By implementing rigorous policies, vetting third-party providers, and managing software dependencies, organizations can mitigate risks and ensure the integrity of their AI ecosystems. The following measures are key to enhancing supply chain security:

- Define and approve a cybersecurity policy for the supply chain.
- Practice software supply chain risk management by regularly auditing and updating third-party dependencies.
- Conduct security assessments by vetting third-party services before integration.
- Rely on and maintain an approved list of reputable sources for software dependencies.

By proactively addressing these threats with the outlined strategies, organizations can fortify their AI infrastructure against current and emerging dangers, ensuring the resilience of their AI systems. If you will be working on securing or assessing AI systems in the future, consult the latest best practices from organizations such as the CSA.

Summary

For the CCSK exam, be sure that you:

- Understand the definition and benefits of immutability.
- Remember the CSA best practices for VM security.
- Know what image factories are.
- Remember the security tools for VMs covered in this chapter.
- Know the vulnerability management lifecycle.
- Know that snapshots provide nearly instant backups.
- Know the components of a container system and container networking.
- Remember the elements of securing the container artifact repository.
- Know runtime protection for containers.
- Understand serverless and FaaS and how to secure them.
- Know the threats to LLMs.

In the next chapter, you will learn about the CSA's recommendations for data security.

CHAPTER 9
Keeping Data Safe in the Cloud

Data is a precious thing and will last longer than the systems themselves.
—Tim Berners-Lee

In this chapter, we will cover a primary goal of cybersecurity: protecting data. Attackers often target companies with the intent of accessing corporate data, which is frequently leveraged for blackmail or financial extortion.

To that end, we will address the different ways data can be stored and the best practices to secure it. We will cover the complexities of data security in the cloud, and investigate essential security strategies, tools, and encryption for protecting data both in transit and at rest. Additionally, we'll review technologies such as data security posture management (DSPM), data loss protection (DLP), digital rights management (DRM), and encryption that can be used for cloud data security to prevent breaches and uphold data privacy.

Data Structures

Before getting into the security aspects of data storage, I want to define the three different data structures that you will see in this chapter:

Structured data
    Data that is organized into a fixed schema, typically in tabular formats such as rows and columns (e.g., Microsoft SQL Server)

Unstructured data
    Data that does not follow a predefined data model or schema (e.g., social media posts)

Semistructured data
> Data that does not conform to a rigid schema but still contains tags or markers to separate data elements and enforce hierarchies (e.g., JSON, XML)

Storage Security Primer

Not all data is equally important to an organization. For example, does the cafeteria menu need the same security applied as the payroll system? Of course it doesn't. What's the best way to identify what type of data needs what level of security control? You can categorize data based on its type (whether it is financial data, personal information, etc.), sensitivity (how damaging exposure would be), and criticality (how vital the data is to the organization's operations or compliance). Once you categorize data, you can classify it into a small set of levels based on risk (e.g., Low, Moderate, High).

The terms *categorization* and *classification* are often used interchangeably, but there is a difference between them. Data is first categorized into broad categories and is then classified according to associated risk. Let's take an employee database with names, government ID numbers, and other sensitive information. This would be categorized as personally identifiable information (PII) and be assigned a classification level of High. This classification would be used to determine the appropriate security controls and access requirements.

Cloud Storage Types

There are two core forms of storage in cloud environments: object storage and volume storage. Many other types of storage, such as database storage, snapshots, log storage, and message queues, use these core storage services. For example, cloud databases typically use volume storage under the hood, while logs and backups use object storage for durability and scalability. We'll dive into these storage types in the following sections.

Object Storage

Object storage is accessible via the internet, meaning it can be accessed from anywhere and by anyone in the world if permissions are not properly applied. Because of this, object storage is often the source of information disclosure. Many organizations have had "misconfigurations" on object storage that led to embarrassing headlines because the permissions on object storage allowed anyone in the world to access the data held in object storage. Why would this happen? The answer is likely convenience, but also poor security practices.

Let's look at two common occurrences. First, there's the classical approach that someone like a developer or cloud administrator who quickly wants to do something, does it: "I'll just make the data public, copy the data, and then remove the public access." What usually happens in this case is the person then gets distracted and forgets to lock down the storage again.

Other times, it's security through obscurity (another approach that never ends well). In this case, they give the bucket name a long string of random characters, assuming nobody will ever discover the open bucket name. Well, that approach doesn't work when researchers and attackers fuzz bucket names. *Fuzzing* is simply testing random characters as a bucket name in a well-known URL format (like *https://my-bucket.S3.amazonaws.com*).

Here's the root of this problem: setting up permissions for object storage can be complicated depending on the scenario. You can set up public access, or you can create fine-tuned permissions that allow access to a specific account within your cloud environment. However, to implement access controls like this for individuals without accounts in your cloud environment, you need to build a frontend server that applies the access control and is then configured to securely access the object storage in the backend.

I have seen this with my own eyes, and I think it's a story worth sharing to drive home the importance of object storage security. I was on a project and brought up the subject of needing to review object storage permissions on a conference call with approximately 50 people in attendance. One of the people said, "Don't bore us with basics." Ouch. Long story short, about six months later, the company was in the news for a very public information disclosure involving over a million clients due to, you guessed it, public access to object storage. In this guy's defense, it was a third-party development company that left the storage publicly available. The thing about the basics is that they're basic because everyone needs to do them.

Technical aspects of object storage

Now that you have some context for the misconfigurations that can happen in the cloud, let's look at some of the technical aspects of object storage that you need to know for the CCSK v5 exam.

Object storage is a cloud native way to store data. In cloud storage, every file and associated metadata is an object that is assigned a unique identifier. These objects can be grouped together in buckets (for our purposes, they look just like directories). The key difference between object storage and volume storage (which will be covered next) is that object storage is accessible via APIs and URLs (as covered earlier).

Object storage is incredibly scalable and is primarily used to store large amounts of unstructured data (e.g., media files, backups, logs). Websites will often choose object storage as part of the architecture because many different web servers can access the backend storage at the same time (and because it is a scalable solution, as mentioned earlier).

From a shared responsibility model, the CSP is responsible for building and managing the object storage system itself, whereas the customer is responsible for securing data held within object storage. This includes governance, encryption, appropriate access controls, and backups.

One of these responsibilities may include implementing object storage versioning. When you enable versioning, whenever a file is modified, a new version of the file is created and changes are committed to this new version. In the case of a ransomware attack, where files are encrypted by an attacker, the customer can simply revert to the version of the file prior to the attack. This is not likely to be asked on the exam, but it sure is worth knowing about in real life.

Versioning is one of the most effective defenses against ransomware and accidental deletion (remember, not all security incidents are necessarily malicious). Additionally, when paired with immutable backups, even in a situation where access controls allow deletion of data, backup data cannot be altered. This serves as additional defense-in-depth security for data held in object storage.

Object storage security

Even though we addressed what object storage is and some of the issues associated with it, there are a few additional items that we need to cover regarding object storage security.

We already know that object storage is internet accessible and the source of many misconfiguration risks due to a myriad of reasons; mainly, buckets being open to the public. To address this common misconfiguration, many CSPs offer a public block feature now by default. This guardrail ensures that objects cannot be accidentally or purposefully made public without taking steps to remove the public block feature.

CDNs can also be an option to enable safe public access to private storage by caching copies of the objects held in object storage. In this scenario, the CDN implements access control to the cached data by creating a unique access token (a signed URL or signed cookie) that is given to the authorized end user who is then allowed time-limited access to the data.

Encrypting data with the CSP's key management service offering adds additional security by separating encryption keys and permission settings to limit access to data. These keys are securely stored and rotated and can be used to meet security and regulatory requirements.

Continuous monitoring with tools, such as CSPM to monitor and maintain object storage security configurations such as public buckets, IAM policies, and other risks, and DSPM (DSPM is covered later in this chapter), can be used to protect data through controls such as classification, access monitoring, and compliance enforcement.

Volume Storage

To the customer, volume storage, also known as *block storage*, is much like taking a hard drive out of an antistatic bag, opening a server, and attaching a cable. From there, you format the drive and voila! In a Windows world, you would now have a D: drive available.

Of course, this doesn't physically happen in a cloud environment, because everything you do as a customer is virtual. What really happens when you create a new volume is that the storage controller allocates storage from the storage pool, such as a storage area network (SAN), to create the new volume. From there, you attach it to your VM. Volume storage is known for its low latency, flexibility, and legacy support. These characteristics make it ideal for structured data such as SQL databases and legacy enterprise applications.

In addition to traditionally working with VMs, volumes can also work with containers. As we know from Chapter 8, containers are ephemeral. Volumes can be attached to a single or even multiple containers to store persistent data. This would be set up in the container runtime itself (e.g., Docker) or in management and orchestration software (e.g., Kubernetes).

Database Storage

Database storage can use either object storage or volume storage. Which scenario uses which type of storage is pretty inconsequential for the CCSK exam. The important things to know are the different types of databases that exist. There are reasons behind using one or both as part of an application architecture that we will touch on briefly, but remember, this is a cloud security certification, not a database certification. That said, let's look at the different types of databases that are referred to by the CSA.

Relational databases

Relational databases are the original SQL database format that stores data as rows and columns in structured tables in a logical structure called a *schema*. Generally, this type of database uses block (volume) storage. Examples of this would be traditional SQL servers such as Oracle, Microsoft SQL Server, and MySQL. In the cloud, you can run these on your own VM in an IaaS service model. CSPs will also offer PaaS relational databases such as Amazon RDS, Azure SQL, and Google Cloud SQL, among others.

Nonrelational databases

A nonrelational database (commonly referred to as *NoSQL*) can store large amounts of different data types (video, audio, documents, key-value pairs, etc.) using a mix of volume storage and object storage (depending on the data type) and is highly scalable. Like relational databases, you can choose to run these in an IaaS service model by installing the database software on a server you manage, or you can leverage a CSP PaaS offering such as Amazon DynamoDB, Azure Cosmos DB, or Google Cloud Datastore, among others.

It is highly likely that a complex system may very well use both types of databases (i.e., a hybrid model) in its architecture. Let's take a very simple look at a social media website as an example. The site would keep user information and connections with other users in a relational database because this is fairly static information. The posts that people make would be held in a nonrelational database because the posts could be hundreds of characters, they could be pictures, or they could be videos.

Other Types of Storage

There are a myriad of different storage types that again will use either volume (block) storage or object storage. Examples are log data, message queues that store messages for reliable communication between distributed applications, streaming services, caching, and in-memory databases.

The biggest "other type" of storage that you may be very familiar with are SaaS cloud storage offerings such as Box, Dropbox, Google Drive, and OneDrive. When using these services, it is paramount that you understand where your data is actually being stored. For example, Microsoft OneDrive and Google Drive are likely to use their own storage services, but there are still questions that remain. For example, do these offerings store all user data in one datacenter in the United States, or do they leverage a datacenter near the user (e.g., India)? This may have significant implications from a jurisdictional perspective. Alternatively, with other storage vendors, such as Box and Dropbox, is your data stored within the storage provider's datacenter, or does the provider use another CSP to store your data? Does this change based on the service you're using (e.g., free versus business)? After all, if you work for a US company with a requirement that all data be stored in the United States, it would become an issue if your CSP decided it would be a good idea to save money by using a discounted subservice as your storage vendor, and you don't know that it stores your data in a different country. Remember, you need to do your due diligence, and understanding that CSPs can and do outsource to other CSPs is part of that.

Data Security Tools and Techniques

In the following sections, we will address the tools and techniques for data security in the cloud, starting with data classification.

Data Classification

We touched on data categorization and classification at the beginning of this chapter, but let's get deeper into it.

Data classification is essential for safeguarding data throughout its lifecycle. It is the classification level of data that dictates what level of security needs to be applied to the data itself. This is the definition of a *risk-based approach*. A risk-based approach is always recommended by the CSA (and others) because not everything carries the same amount of risk. By taking a risk-based approach, you are applying appropriate controls to data and avoiding applying overly restrictive measures (as well as the cost and effort of doing so) to low-risk data.

You want to keep classification levels to a minimum; think three, maybe four at most. For example, the US government keeps it to Low, Moderate, and High. Too many classification levels can lead to confusion, and misclassified data as a result.

Another thing to keep in mind is that data classifications can (and do) change. For example, consider a financial report for a publicly traded company. Prior to release to the public, this data would be labeled as highly sensitive or confidential depending on the classification scheme used by the company. Once released to the public, the data classification becomes public.

Data classification can also assist with incident response. This is because it can help prioritize the focus of the incident response team. When data is classified according to its sensitivity and criticality, security teams can respond more efficiently and effectively by prioritizing high-risk assets and applying appropriate measures based on the impact of potential breaches.

From a regulatory perspective, data classification is also critical. Many data protection laws and frameworks require organizations to identify, manage, and protect sensitive data according to its risk and impact. Proper classification and clear ownership assignments ensure that data handling aligns with legal mandates, reduces liability, and prevents costly fines for noncompliance.

The best example of regulations and data security that I can think of is the one in which a ransomware group (AlphV/BlackCat) advised the Securities and Exchange Commission (SEC) that a company they compromised (MeridianLink) didn't pay their blackmail demand. They told the SEC that it should launch an investigation based on new SEC cybersecurity disclosure rules mandating breach disclosure within four days. Talk about bringing "lawfare" to a whole new level! As a funny side note to this story, the rule was not yet in force when the attackers turned into whistleblowers. MeridianLink stated that the attack did not disrupt operations or access sensitive production environments, and it did not face any SEC penalties.

Now that you understand the importance of data classification, let's look at the different ways data can be classified. This isn't covered as part of the CCSK exam, but I think it's worth considering nonetheless.

Classification techniques

First off, you need to understand how data is classified technically and how classifications can be applied. Let's review some important classification techniques and how they work:

Marking
When a document is marked, it is human readable. For example, there could be a header or footer on a document that states "Confidential – Internal Use Only."

Tagging
Tagging adds metadata (data about the data) to a cloud resource such as a file or database. This makes it machine readable. These tags are embedded in the file, so the metadata remains if the file is moved from one location to another.

Labeling
The label can be a catchall phrase that is visible to the user and/or it can be machine readable through the implementation of metadata.

Watermarking
Watermarking is another human-readable format that makes a permanent, semi-transparent marking across a page of a document (and remains when printed). For example, if you've ever seen a document that says "DRAFT" in a diagonal direction on every page, that's an example of a watermark. Watermarking can also be hidden in AI-generated content (which is a completely different subject that we won't get into here).

Naturally, it makes sense that tools such as DLP (covered later in this chapter) will require machine-readable classification to function.

Here's a mnemonic to remember the difference between marking and tagging: M is for Me to read; T is for Technology.

Classification approaches

Now that you know there are both human-readable and machine-readable ways to classify data, let's look at the three different ways data can be classified:

User-based classification
   Users could classify data themselves when they create it. This could be done by marking the document with a watermark. It could also leverage a technology that would allow for a tag to be applied by stating the classification level. The main issue here is that users may make mistakes when applying a label.

Content-based classification
   Data is classified automatically by analyzing the content. The technology scans for keywords, phrases, data patterns (e.g., credit card numbers, PII), or file types to determine the appropriate classification level.

Context-based classification
   Data is automatically classified based on external factors (metadata) rather than the actual content. This could include who created the document, where it was created, or the application used.

Those are the main ways data can be classified when it is created. Also, some DLP systems (covered shortly) can scan storage and classify data that hasn't been classified in the past.

Identity and Access Management

Identity and access management (IAM) obviously plays a critical role in data security. This is true for both users interacting with data and systems accessing data via APIs. In a cloud world, IAM determines the level of permissions that internal users and service accounts get when accessing resources. In short, IAM plays a critical role in enforcing who has access to which resources (i.e., who has access control).

For unknown external users, this is where different access controls come into play. Access controls may be applied directly on a resource using a resource policy or ACL. Taking Amazon's S3 object storage service, for example, access controls in the form of S3 bucket policies for external users to specific data resources can be applied by an administrator using the S3 Bucket Policy editor.

In both scenarios, access controls limit the access an entity has to a resource.

Access Policies

Access policies are directive, stating who and what can access a resource, whereas access controls are the mechanisms that enforce the policy. You can apply access policies to both individual resources and the network the resources are on. Both resource and network policies help build a defense-in-depth security boundary to protect data from unauthorized access and limit the potential attack surface.

In short, access policies state who is allowed access to which resources, and access controls enforce this policy. If you recall the coverage of zero trust in Chapter 7, I discussed the concepts of both PDPs and PEPs. You can think of access policies as the PDP and access control as the PEP.

Data Loss Prevention

I'm going to start this section by clearing up a common misconception about DLP. DLP can stand for either data loss prevention or data leak prevention. What's the difference? Data loss prevention means protecting data from being stolen (lost), whereas data leak prevention means protecting against accidental exposure. At the end of the day as far as the technology involved, there is no difference. Whether protecting against malicious exfiltration or accidental data exposure, DLP solutions operate by monitoring, detecting, and blocking sensitive data transfers across endpoints, networks, cloud environments, and email systems.

Cloud DLP can be challenging due to the amount of data stored and its distributed nature in IaaS and PaaS. Although some IaaS/PaaS CSP DLP tools do exist (albeit limited in scope), and data security tools are being developed to address these challenges, DLP is more often seen as a built-in tool offered by SaaS providers at this time.

For an effective cloud DLP strategy, the CSA recommends prioritizing high-risk areas and using cloud native and third-party DLP tools. Using a risk-based approach, implementing appropriate access controls, and deleting data that is no longer required (data minimization) help address cloud DLP challenges. For the last part, you don't need to protect (or spend money on storing) data that doesn't exist.

Cloud Data Encryption at Rest

Encryption of data at rest is a key security control to protect the confidentiality of data stored in a cloud environment. In the upcoming sections, we will look at encryption key management options and the different options for key generation and storage that are common in cloud environments. I promise, there's no math in these sections or on the CCSK exam. You don't need to know how cryptography works; you just need to understand the encryption options available in cloud environments.

Encryption and Key Management

The most critical aspect of encryption is the key management system that stores encryption keys. Without the keys, you lose all access to your data. There are different ways that encryption and key management can be done in a cloud environment. We will start by discussing the options in the cloud for key storage services, and then look at some of the implementation models.

Key Management Service

Cloud providers will often offer a key management service (KMS) to customers. A KMS built and managed by the CSP is typically a software-based service that may leverage hardware appliances such as hardware security modules (HSMs) for enhanced security. Leveraging a CSP-supplied KMS allows customers to easily manage the entire key lifecycle, including generation, rotation, expiration, and deletion, ensuring that encryption practices align with security policies and regulatory requirements.

Hardware Security Module

The HSM is a physical device designed to securely generate, store, and manage cryptographic keys (among other things) used for encrypting and decrypting data, ensuring that sensitive keys are protected from unauthorized access and tampering.

HSMs provide a high level of security by operating in a tamper-resistant Federal Information Processing Standards (FIPS) 140-2/3 environment. The level of tamper resistance is defined by the FIPS 140-2/3 certification level. There are four certification levels, ranging from level 1 to level 4. Generally, tamper resistance is a feature of levels 3 and 4. Most CSPs will use a FIPS 140-3 level 3 HSM to protect keys created and stored in the KMS they offer. At this level, the HSM will have tamper protection and detection capability that will erase (zeroize) the key store if physical or logical tampering is detected. This is why a backup HSM system is critical.

Some CSPs also offer HSM services in addition to their standard KMS offerings. Such a service can be used to not only store encryption keys, but also safeguard digital certificates, encrypt sensitive data, and facilitate secure transactions in industries that require strict regulatory compliance, such as finance, healthcare, and government sectors. Of note, HSM offerings are often dramatically more expensive and have less integration with other services than standard KMS offerings.

Encryption Key Options

There are different options for key generation and management in cloud environments. In this section, we will cover the different options you have to both generate and securely store encryption keys using a KMS offered by the CSP.

Client-side encryption

Client-side encryption is when a customer encrypts data locally and uploads it to the CSP in an encrypted format. Generally, this is used for *dumb storage*, in which the CSP does not need to access or work with the data. An example of this would be a client using a CSP to store information in object storage. Primary data stored like this would be backup and archive data as well as rarely used data.

If you are using a service that requires access to do its job, such as a SaaS that processes data to deliver a service such as a CRM or data analytics, this model cannot be used, as the CSP would need the encryption keys to do its job.

Server-side encryption

In the server-side encryption model, the CSP creates and manages the encryption key used by customers. This model is the easiest for customers to implement and could be as simple as checking a box in some instances. The security relies on the provider's encryption protocols and key management.

Customer-managed encryption keys

In this model, the customer leverages the KMS built and managed by the CSP. The customer creates a key and this key is held within the KMS. Customers do have the ability to assign permissions to administer and use the key, and the ability to manage the key lifecycle by managing CRUD operations. This implements a separation of responsibilities in which the customer maintains the keys and the provider maintains the encryption engine.

Customer-provided encryption keys

When the customer provides the encryption key, this is often referred to as a *bring your own key* approach. While this model does allow customers to have a trusted key generation process, I do wonder about the security benefits of doing so. You are copying this key to the provider, so there is still the risk of the CSP accessing the key to view your encrypted data, or being compelled by a court of law to give the key to law enforcement, which can use a Stored Communications Act warrant to view the data.

Hold your own key

Hold your own key (HYOK) will not be on the exam, but it's good to know about. In this scenario, the customer generates and maintains the encryption keys used in a cloud environment. The primary keys are never shared with the CSP. Rather, when cryptographic operations are required, a derivative data encryption key (covered later) is used in a cloud environment and wiped after use. HYOK is particularly valuable for organizations that must meet stringent compliance requirements, maintain privacy for sensitive data, or mitigate risks associated with CSP access to their data.

Encryption Implementation Options

Encryption of data stored on a disk (known as *data at rest*) can be implemented at different layers, from volume storage or object storage all the way up to within the application itself. In the next sections, we will discuss these implementation options, which are shown in Figure 9-1.

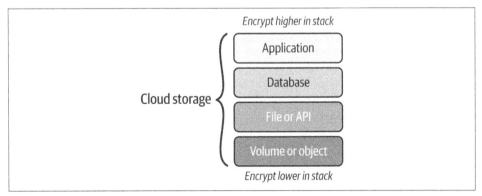

Figure 9-1. Encryption implementation layer options (from the CSA study guide)

Volume storage or object storage encryption

Object storage encryption and volume storage encryption are the lowest levels of encryption and the easiest way for a customer to implement encryption to protect data at rest. We'll cover object storage first, then address volume storage.

Object storage encryption is often automatically implemented by the CSP and is transparent to the customer without impacting performance. If not done automatically, customers can implement encryption on individual objects or across entire buckets and folders, protecting both data and metadata. Object storage encryption can be used to meet regulatory and security standards like GDPR, HIPAA, and PCI DSS. Common use cases for object storage encryption include securing backup and archival data, media storage, and big data analytics. By encrypting object storage, organizations can safeguard compliance-sensitive data, enhancing confidentiality while protecting against unauthorized access.

Volume storage encryption secures data on virtual disks in cloud environments. This encryption protects data at rest, including stored data on the volume as well as backups and snapshots. Volume encryption is implemented either by OS agents or by dedicated storage encryption services (e.g., KMS), providing encryption and decryption without requiring user intervention, thereby ensuring a minimal impact on performance. You can often enable encryption by default or through simple configurations to automate data protection. Volume storage encryption plays a critical role in securing data in multitenant environments, isolating sensitive data to meet compliance standards like GDPR, HIPAA, and PCI DSS.

By implementing both object storage and volume storage encryption, organizations can enhance their cloud security posture, ensuring comprehensive protection across various data types and storage architectures. This dual approach mitigates risks to confidentiality and supports regulatory compliance.

File/API encryption

File/API encryption refers to encrypting data at a more granular level than volume storage or object storage does, targeting specific files or data accessed through APIs. This approach provides a focused method of securing sensitive information, offering distinct advantages over broader encryption methods like volume storage or object storage encryption. This approach would be used when only a subset of data is sensitive or is in scope for compliance standards such as PCI, HIPAA, and others. By limiting the amount of data encrypted, you reduce the overhead and resources associated with encrypting all data and limiting the performance impact and complexity of key management for nonsensitive data.

For API encryption specifically, APIs can encrypt and decrypt data on the fly. Although encryption in transit using TLS is often performed, API encryption can be performed using message-level encryption on the content of API messages such as request and response data. This additional level of encryption ensures that data is protected if intercepted and/or processed by intermediaries. API encryption can be performed via an API gateway. These gateways often include TLS enforcement, encryption, and integration with KMSs. API encryption can be used in multiple scenarios such as users accessing data via mobile devices through system-to-system transactions like microservices in distributed application architectures.

Database encryption

You can perform database encryption in two ways. The first (and more popular) approach is transparent database encryption (TDE), which encrypts the database files themselves as well as logfiles and database backups. The other approach is field-level encryption, in which specific tables or columns containing sensitive information are encrypted. In either approach, compliance for encrypting regulated data is achieved. When TDE is used, the database system encrypts data that is written to disk and decrypts data as it is read, and thus it has a minimal performance impact. When field-level encryption is used, the application accessing the database encrypts and decrypts certain fields when committing and reading data from the database. This approach is computationally more expensive and more complex to implement.

Both database and volume encryption can be used together to provide increased defense-in-depth protection of data at rest. Database encryption works at a more granular level than volume storage. Database encryption will protect data at the database level (as well as backup data), whereas volume encryption is broader and protects against theft of the physical drive hosting the database.

A key advantage of both database encryption approaches is that they secure database backups or copies, even when they are written to a different, unencrypted volume. This ensures that sensitive data remains encrypted and inaccessible without proper decryption keys, offering additional protection against unauthorized access or theft.

Application encryption

As mentioned in the previous section, application layer encryption supports encryption of certain types of sensitive data, such as the field-level database encryption I mentioned earlier. In an HR system, for example, application encryption could be used selectively to only encrypt an employee's government ID and no other information, to minimize performance overhead. That said, application encryption can be used in a variety of scenarios to protect data at rest and in transit. Examples of such are API payloads, message queuing services between systems, email, encrypting backup data, protecting IoT communications, and end-to-end data exchanges between clients and servers. As you can see, the list of use cases is quite diverse and essential for data security.

For an example of end-to-end data exchanges, take a scenario of a client at the office using a custom-built application in the cloud. Assuming a symmetric key is used, the client uses the shared key to encrypt data locally, which is then sent to the application for processing. This encrypted application data is sent to the cloud-based application that then uses the same key to decrypt and process the data. When sending the response, the application uses the shared key to encrypt the response, and this is then decrypted by the client. If you own the application, you can use whatever encryption keys you want. In this scenario, portability may also be increased when you use and manage your own custom keys instead of relying on the CSP to generate and manage the encryption keys.

Symmetric Versus Asymmetric Encryption

The CCSK study guide doesn't discuss the difference between symmetric and asymmetric encryption, but I think it's important for any security professional to understand the difference between these two types of encryption key models, even if it won't be on the CCSK exam. If you're already familiar with this topic, feel free to move to the next section.

Symmetric encryption

Symmetric encryption is where both parties (e.g., Nathan and Ryan) need to share information confidentially. In the symmetric encryption model, both Nathan and Ryan need to have a copy of the same key. At the time of writing, Advanced Encryption Standard (AES)-256 is the de facto standard for symmetric encryption and is the default in many cloud environments. The 256 stands for the key length in bits. In general, the longer the key length is, the harder it is to guess the encryption key. Guessing the key is often referred to as a *brute-force attack*. Different values are tried in order to determine the encryption key. The longer the key length is, the more guesses are required. This is referred to as the *work factor*. The work factor to successfully guess the AES-256 key is many trillions of times longer than the age of the universe. In other words, a brute-force attack being successful is highly unlikely, to say the least.

Here is an example of an AES-256 encryption key:

60f94c7f7440e7804abec9873db90d0098aef10a6f39baf42fbf69e3e1f32d22

You may be thinking, *That's 64 characters, not 256 characters!* And you would be correct. Every one of those characters you see is 4 bits each (e.g., the character "f" is "1111" in binary format). So, take the number of characters (64) and multiply it by 4 to get 256 bits.

On top of this, there is the concept of an initialization vector (IV). An IV is a fixed-size, random, or pseudorandom number that is used alongside the key in an encryption operation. It is used to introduce randomness into the ciphertext output to further abstract the output, making inferring the key value even more difficult.

Let's say a user sends a plaintext "hello world" message. The encryption system uses the AES-256 key shown previously to convert it to the ciphertext of 8bce4b17cc54558bee843c89738bad18. This is sent to the destination. At the destination, the system uses the same key to convert the ciphertext back to plaintext. Figure 9-2 shows a symmetric key scenario of this.

Figure 9-2. Symmetric key known by both parties

All this sounds fairly simple on a 1:1 basis, where both parties are in the same room. There are more considerations in a larger context, though. What about a scenario where you want individuals to have their own keys for nonrepudiation purposes (answering the question of who really sent this) or to allow different individuals access to different data; this can spiral out of control rather quickly. Take, for example, a scenario in which security is paramount and 100 people need their own individual keys for 10 different systems. That equals 1,000 keys that need to be managed. This "key explosion" scenario greatly complicates management of symmetric keys.

Then there is the question of how the parties get a copy of the symmetric key. You can't just email the key, because it may be intercepted. There are different ways to do this, including using preshared keys, where the key is transferred via a USB key or face-to-face meetings; Diffie-Hellman key exchange, which allows for the creation of symmetric keys; or out-of-band distribution, where you could use a secure messaging app to send the key to a recipient.

I'm sure at this point you can appreciate how a seemingly simple symmetric key system can become very complex very quickly. Because of this, larger encryption implementations (especially public-facing web servers) would likely call for an asymmetric key model. We'll cover that topic shortly.

For cloud systems, this is where a KMS comes into play. The KMS is used by systems to generate a data encryption key (DEK) to encrypt/decrypt information and is short-lived. It does its job and is then wiped. To protect the DEK, it is encrypted by a key encryption key (KEK) generated by the primary key held within the KMS. This primary key is held in the KMS and never leaves it. This is referred to as *envelope encryption*. Figure 9-3 shows the relationship between these different keys that form this key encryption hierarchy.

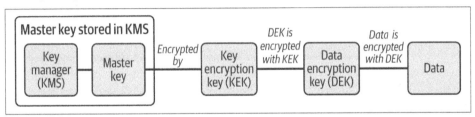

Figure 9-3. Key encryption hierarchy for envelope encryption

Asymmetric encryption

Unlike symmetric encryption, which uses the same key for both encryption and decryption, asymmetric encryption relies on a pair of keys: one public key and one private key. This model solves many of the challenges associated with symmetric encryption, especially in scenarios where scalability, individual accountability, or secure multiuser access is critical. This model is commonly used to securely access web servers (e.g., *https://www.intrinsecsecurity.com*). The *https* is indicative of a website that uses TLS, which relies on asymmetric encryption when a client connects to a web server. We will cover this in more detail shortly. First, let's understand what these keys are and how they are used before getting into specifics about securely accessing websites:

Public key
  Used to encrypt data that can only be unencrypted by the holder of the private key, or to decrypt data encrypted with the private key. This key can be freely shared with others, allowing them to securely send encrypted data to the key pair owner.

Private key
> Used to encrypt data that can only be unencrypted by holders of the public key, or to decrypt data encrypted with the corresponding public key. The private key is kept secret and is unique to the individual.

I know that sounds pretty confusing. Just think that whatever is done with the public key can be undone with the private key, and vice versa.

To address the scalability issue with symmetric keys, imagine the same scenario as before, where 100 individuals need secure access to 10 different systems. Instead of centrally managing 1,000 symmetric keys (100 individuals × 10 systems), each individual would have their own public/private key pair. The public key of each individual can be shared with the systems they need to access, and those systems would use the public key to encrypt any sensitive data sent to that individual. Only the individual with the corresponding private key can decrypt this data.

Public-facing web servers, like those hosting websites with HTTPS, use asymmetric encryption to securely initiate a session with users. This process involves two keys: a public key and a private key. The public key is shared openly with anyone visiting the website as part of its TLS certificate, while the private key is kept secret and stays securely on the server.

When you visit a secure website, your browser retrieves the server's public key and uses it to encrypt a small piece of data called a *session key* (a symmetric key used for the session). Only the server, with its private key, can decrypt this session key. Once the session key is securely exchanged, both your browser and the server use it to encrypt all further communication using symmetric encryption, which is faster for ongoing data exchange.

This method ensures that sensitive information, such as passwords or credit card details, is encrypted and protected from interception during transmission. The entire process, known as a *TLS handshake*, happens automatically every time you connect to a secure website, ensuring that your connection is private and trustworthy.

Additionally, asymmetric encryption supports nonrepudiation, which means actions like digital signatures can be tied directly to a specific private key owner. For instance, when a user signs a document or a transaction, their private key is used to create the signature, and anyone can verify it using the corresponding public key. This ensures accountability and makes it impossible for the user to deny their involvement.

Asymmetric encryption addresses scalability challenges, simplifies key management, and provides additional security benefits like nonrepudiation, making it the preferred model for many applications, such as securing email communications (e.g., PGP), establishing secure web connections (e.g., HTTPS), and protecting sensitive messages in distributed systems.

At the time of writing, there is concern that when quantum computing is readily available in real life (often referred to as *post quantum*), it will be able to break encryption as we know it today. Here are a few of my thoughts on this. For symmetric encryption, it is expected that the "gold standard" AES-256 will be half as effective in a postquantum world. Asymmetric encryption is another matter. Due to the way that asymmetric encryption works (prime factoring), it is expected that quantum will be able to break the RSA standard that is widely used today. Efforts are underway to create and standardize on a "quantum-resistant" asymmetric encryption. This isn't an issue for today, nor for the exam, but it is something to keep an eye on in the future.

Data Encryption Recommendations

The CSA makes the following recommendations for data encryption for improved security, compliance, and data protection in different environments.

Use a CSP-supplied KMS

Unless the data being encrypted is extremely sensitive and an HYOK approach is required, using a KMS that the CSP supplies will greatly help you manage cryptographic keys.

Encrypt SaaS applications

As mentioned earlier, SaaS applications that need access to data to perform their job will likely require access to the encryption key used to encrypt data that is processed by the SaaS application. As such, a CSP-managed KMS may be your only option in this scenario. There may be a possibility of using the same keys as used in IaaS/PaaS if both the customer and the SaaS provider use the same underlying CSP.

Use the default encryption with care

This encryption option may be "good enough" to meet compliance, as it is convenient and often a free option for customers. However, customers need to address their own threat models regarding this option to determine appropriateness. Scenarios where using default encryption may not be appropriate can include insider threats in which the CSP gains access to encryption keys, delegation of key management being prohibited by regulations, and vendor lock-in.

Use different keys for different services

Using different encryption keys for different services and deployments is a good practice. Taking this approach limits a compromised key potential impact.

Apply IAM policies on keys

Only appropriate entities (users, systems, etc.) should have access to encryption keys. This least-privilege approach to who or what can use keys and what actions they can perform can be implemented by applying IAM policies on keys.

Align with threat models

Threat models are about understanding your assets and the potential threats and vulnerabilities to implement appropriate security controls. Remember that encryption is just one part of the security puzzle. For example, how effective is database encryption if the DBA account is compromised? For sensitive data, always take a defense-in-depth approach. For this example of a compromised account, field-level encryption would protect data in the event of a DBA account being compromised. Are database backups protected at rest when located on a different system? These are examples of questions that need to be addressed when designing a system, not after the system is in production. We'll cover threat modeling in Chapter 10.

Data Security Posture Management

DSPM is a newer security tool that is focused on data-centered security. DSPM includes the data discovery and classification capability that we covered earlier in this chapter, and much more, such as data flow analysis, anomaly detection, and continuous compliance monitoring. DSPM can also address access controls on data, IAM policies, resources, and network policies to assess what entities have access to data and how they access it. They can make recommendations and/or manage remediation by integrating with tools such as those that generate IaC templates or policies. DSPM is a powerful tool that can assist organizations in meeting compliance requirements from regulations such as GDPR, HIPAA, and more.

Summary

For the CCSK exam, you should be comfortable with the following data security topics:

- Know the different cloud storage types (e.g., volume, object, database).
- Know that many PaaS offerings (logging, etc.) will leverage volume or object storage.
- Understand that cloud storage vendors may use other CSPs to store data, and know the potential jurisdictional issues.
- Understand the importance of data classification.
- Know what DLP is, its core features, and its benefits.

- Know the data encryption layers (from volume/object storage through to application layer encryption).
- Remember the encryption key management options.
- Know what DSPM is and what it is used for.

This concludes our coverage of data security. In the next chapter, you will learn about application security in cloud environments.

CHAPTER 10
Building Secure Applications

It's cheaper to build security in than to bolt it on.
—Gary McGraw

Application security is a wide-ranging area that is very complex for security professionals. It begins with security architecture and design and continues through development, testing, deployment, and ongoing management. To make matters worse, this is an area that, quite frankly, a lot of security professionals who are not developers struggle with.

This chapter won't turn you into a software developer or engineer, and we won't be diving into the specifics of any single programming language. Instead, my goal is to give you a big-picture view of application security, with a special focus on the unique challenges and opportunities in the cloud. We'll explore the basic components of modern application design and the tools used to build and secure cloud native architectures.

Let's start by looking at the complexities associated with securing today's cloud native applications:

- Applications are often built as a constellation of microservices and external services, which necessitates a more detailed analysis of attack surfaces and control boundaries.
- The attack surface often includes significant exposure through API interfaces.
- In a cloud context, applications are often developed using development and operations (DevOps) approaches with rapid feature development, which can be a risk as well as an opportunity.

- Applications can be built on libraries that are under the control of the provider (e.g., PaaS provider or serverless), which requires attention to the shared responsibility model.
- Applications frequently leverage third-party libraries, including open source components, introducing supply chain risks and additional attack vectors.
- Security features, such as identity management, logging, and monitoring, are often sourced from a cloud provider, which may or may not match the application requirements.
- Applications are often deployed on programmable infrastructure (IaC, orchestrators such as Kubernetes, etc.).
- Applications operating at scale within cloud environments necessitate a keen awareness of the underlying infrastructure's vulnerabilities. Stateless architectures, which prioritize scalability and resilience, are commonly employed to mitigate the impact of infrastructure failures. However, while these architectures offer flexibility and agility, they also introduce complexities that can undermine the overall security posture.

Secure Development Lifecycle

Secure software development starts with a plan. The CSA calls any structured plan that secures software development a secure development lifecycle (SDLC). An SDLC (also called *SSDLC*, which stands for secure software development lifecycle) breaks software development into a staged approach that consists of a series of process gates and related activities. Figure 10-1 shows the Microsoft Security Development Lifecycle as an example.

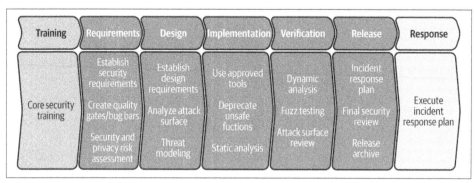

Figure 10-1. Microsoft Security Development Lifecycle

Another SDLC you can use is the CSA's Development, Security, Operations (DevSecOps) staged approach to secure software development, which identifies key processes, tools, and design patterns to be implemented in successful DevSecOps programs (see Figure 10-2).

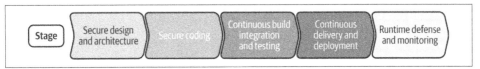

Figure 10-2. The CSA's DevSecOps SDLC (courtesy of the CCSK study guide)

I present these two options because, although the stages are different, the common thread between them is that software development is well managed through the implementation of SDLC stages. It should be noted that, although the focus of the stages is on software development, this approach is also valid for IaC, building secure server instances, container scanning, and other deployments.

Stages of the CSA DevSecOps SDLC

Let's go through the CSA DevSecOps SDLC stages and the related activities, technologies, key processes, tools, and design patterns implemented in successful DevSecOps programs.

Secure Design and Architecture stage

The first stage is Secure Design and Architecture. Security gets introduced at this stage. When you look at Figure 10-2, you can see why this is called a *shift-left* security approach. You are shifting left when you introduce security earlier in the application creation process.

It may seem counterproductive to spend time ensuring that architecture and design security is performed before any code is written, but it is generally recognized that shifting left is a good practice that reduces the time to deliver secure software. Applying security only at the end of the build stage often results in unforeseen issues, increased troubleshooting time, and, in many cases, insecure software being shipped. By shifting security to the left, organizations can address vulnerabilities proactively and reduce both development time and security risks.

> ### From the Trenches: A Lost Opportunity
>
> Here's a real-life example of the consequences of trying to apply security at the end of development. A SaaS provider wanted to sell its product to the Canadian government. There was also a need within the government for the provider's product. Perfect, right? Well, the members of the government's Cloud Center of Excellence (CCoE) team reviewed the product and discovered security issues they were concerned about. They told the SaaS provider they wouldn't approve the application for use, but would be open to reviewing it again once the security issues were fixed. About three months

later, the SaaS provider told the CCoE team it was unable to implement the security fixes because doing so broke the application, and the provider couldn't find a way to fix it. Opportunity lost.

Secure Coding stage

Coding security controls that leverage automation and AI provide a more efficient, scalable, and consistent method for identifying weaknesses and vulnerabilities in code compared to traditional manual reviews. Begin with tools such as GitHub Copilot. This real-time, AI-based vulnerability filtering system will detect and prevent bad practices such as usage of hardcoded credentials, SQL injection, and other vulnerabilities as the developer creates the code.

Continuous Build, Integration, and Testing stage

This is the heart of the CI/CD pipeline that forms DevSecOps. In this stage, integration and testing includes the tools and processes to security-test the functionality of an application/product when there is a code commit (meaning the code is checked into a repository). Tools used in this stage include static application security testing (SAST), dynamic application security testing (DAST), software composition analysis (SCA), and other security controls. We will cover these tools and the CI/CD pipeline in greater depth later in this chapter.

Automated testing should not be the only security review performed. I recall a conversation that took place many years ago with a security manager who fought for (and lost) the idea to remove all manual checks in favor of automated checks. His argument was, "If the exploit code is well written, an automated system won't catch it, whereas a trained human will." He has a point. Depending on an organization's risk appetite, it will likely need to strike a balance between automated and manual security testing.

Continuous Delivery and Deployment stage

This stage includes final predeployment checks, and it is the last stage before software is introduced into a production environment. Think of it as the final checks a pilot makes before takeoff. In this stage, the following types of final validation testing are performed:

Functional testing
    Ensures that the software meets intended business and technical requirements

Regression testing
    Confirms that new changes do not break existing functionality by rerunning previous test cases

Integration testing
> Verifies that the application correctly interacts with other software, databases, APIs, and infrastructure components

Final security testing
> Ensures that the system is hardened against vulnerabilities before deployment

Performance testing
> Validates that the application can handle expected workloads without performance degradation

User acceptance testing
> Validates that the application meets business and end-user use cases

Disaster recovery and failover testing
> Validates that the application backup and recovery functionality works as expected

I would also like to add here that staged deployments need to be used whenever it makes sense. Say, for example, you are deploying software to 1,000 workstations. Please, for the love of all that is good, do not just deploy to all 1,000 machines at once. Deploy to a handful of machines for a period of time and see if there are any unforeseen issues. CrowdStrike learned its lesson on this. CrowdStrike had always done "big bang" deployments for its signature updates to every customer workstation around the world. Its testing didn't catch a critical error in the code, and thousands of workstations and servers around the world went offline as a result. At the time of writing, CrowdStrike is in the process of defending itself from multimillion-dollar lawsuits as a result.

Runtime Defense and Monitoring stage

At this stage, the software is in production. This is where runtime defense and continuous monitoring and continuous improvement of security posture come into play. Although we covered some of these tactics earlier, a refresher is not a bad thing. Security tools such as the following are involved with runtime defense and monitoring:

Runtime application self-protection (RASP)
> Enhances application security by embedding runtime protection mechanisms directly into the application runtime environment. It actively detects and blocks threats such as SQL injection, XSS, and remote code execution.

Endpoint detection and response (EDR)
> Implemented at the endpoints (workstations, servers, mobile devices) and provides real-time threat detection through behavioral analytics. It also offers both automated and manual remediation to contain security incidents.

Extended detection and response (XDR)
> An evolution of EDR that integrates and analyzes threat signals across endpoints, networks, cloud environments, and user behaviors. XDR provides a unified view of security incidents, enabling faster detection, investigation, and automated responses to sophisticated cyberattacks.

Cloud workload platform protection (CWPP)
> Can secure VMs, containers, and serverless environments by providing real-time visibility, vulnerability management, and runtime protection. CWPP platforms help prevent misconfigurations, detect cloud native threats, and enforce security policies across multicloud and hybrid environments.

Security information and event management (SIEM)
> Provides centralized log management, threat detection, and incident analysis by collecting and correlating security data from across an organization's infrastructure. SIEM can help security teams identify anomalies, investigate incidents, and generate compliance reports in real time.

Security orchestration, automation, and response (SOAR)
> Can enhance incident response efficiency by automating repetitive security tasks, orchestrating workflows across multiple security tools, and streamlining investigations via integration with a SIEM platform. SOAR platforms reduce response time, improve coordination, and ensure standardized security operations through automated playbooks and threat intelligence integration.

All these tools can help a company detect and respond to incidents that happen in production. Without the ability to detect incidents, there is no ability to respond. The better an organization's telemetry is, the faster its detection is and the faster its response can be.

Threat Modeling

Threat modeling is used in risk management to identify, assess, and address potential threats to an organization's assets. It is normally performed during the application design phase.

Given the importance of threat modeling, there is surprisingly little coverage of it in the CCSK material. Although there are multiple approaches to threat modeling (PASTA, DREAD, ATASM, etc.), the CSA focuses on the STRIDE threat model (STRIDE can be combined with other approaches for a more complete threat model). STRIDE is an acronym for the following (listed along with a very high-level description of each term):

Spoofing
> Pretending to be someone else to gain access to a system

Tampering
    Changing or altering data without permission

Repudiation
    Denying that an action took place to avoid accountability

Information disclosure
    Exposing sensitive data to unauthorized people

Denial of service
    Overloading a system so that it cannot function properly

Elevation of privilege
    Gaining higher system access than allowed

To perform software threat modeling, you need to understand the system architecture and security objectives, and analyze the potential threats that could affect those objectives. Working through this process and addressing areas that are more vulnerable to attack will result in a more secure system design. Let's go through a scenario in which STRIDE threat modeling is used for a new payment gateway API.

The first step in the threat modeling process is defining the system's scope. Key components of the payment gateway include authentication and authorization mechanisms (such as OAuth 2 for API security), transaction processing workflows, secure data storage, and encrypted communication channels. The primary actors in this system are customers initiating transactions, merchants receiving funds, and payment processors or banks that complete the transactions. The assets at risk include user credentials, credit card details, transaction logs, and API keys.

Applying STRIDE to this system, the security team works to identify several potential threats. After some discussion, the team comes up with the following threats for each part of the STRIDE model.

Spoofing

Spoofing is a major threat because attackers could impersonate legitimate merchants or customers to conduct fraudulent transactions. To mitigate the risk, the team decides that OAuth 2 with short-lived access tokens, enforcing multifactor authentication (MFA) for merchants, and using mutual TLS (mTLS) for verifying merchant connections will be implemented as part of the system.

Tampering

An example of tampering could be attackers performing unauthorized modifications to API requests or stored data. By changing or altering the data, attackers could manipulate payment amounts, execute injection attacks, or alter transaction logs. To mitigate this risk, the system is designed to use hash-based message authentication

(HMAC) signatures to ensure API request integrity by verifying that the request has not been altered and that it originated from an authorized sender, the system enforces parameterized queries to prevent SQL injection, and the system maintains immutable logs with cryptographic hashing so that any tampering of log data is evident.

Repudiation

I defined nonrepudiation previously as proving that someone did something. Repudiation is where users deny executing transactions, potentially leading to disputes and fraud. This issue is addressed through comprehensive audit logging, requiring digital signatures on payment requests, and using tokenized transaction identifiers to ensure unique traceability to serve as sources for nonrepudiation.

Information disclosure

This is when information is obtained without authorization. Disclosure of sensitive payment details could lead to severe regulatory fines and reputational damage, resulting in loss of revenue. Mitigation measures include enforcing end-to-end encryption of data in transit using TLS 1.3, tokenizing credit card numbers, and implementing field-level encryption for sensitive customer data stored in databases.

Denial of service

DoS (and DDoS) attacks can disrupt payment processing by overloading the API with excessive requests, resulting in upset legitimate users who cannot access the system. To prevent such incidents, the system incorporates rate limiting and API throttling through the inclusion of an API gateway, deploys DDoS protection through cloud-based services like AWS Shield or Cloudflare, and continuously monitors traffic for anomalies using SIEM tools.

Elevation of privilege

This is a threat in which an attacker increases its level of privilege in a system. An example of this could be an attacker exploiting a misconfigured role to execute administrative functions or gain unauthorized access to encryption keys. To mitigate this, privileged access management (PAM) with just-in-time authorization is implemented, role-based access control (RBAC) and attribute-based access control (ABAC) are enforced, encryption keys are securely stored in an HSM, and WAFs are used to prevent server-side request forgery (SSRF) attacks.

Risk Assessment Matrix

To prioritize threats to the system, we use a risk assessment matrix that considers both impact and likelihood in order to assign a risk score, as shown in Table 10-1.

This helps the team categorize threats as high, moderate, or low risk, allowing it to prioritize security efforts accordingly.

Different organizations use different formulas to assign risk scores. The main idea is that you are coming up with a risk score based on the likelihood (probability) and impact of a threat being realized.

Table 10-1. Sample risk assessment matrix

STRIDE category	Threat example	Impact (1–5)	Likelihood (1–5)	Risk score (impact × likelihood)
Spoofing	Token hijacking via phishing	5	4	20
Tampering	API request manipulation	5	3	15
Repudiation	Customers denying transactions	3	4	12
Information disclosure	Leaked payment details	5	5	25
Denial of service	API rate-limiting bypass	4	4	16
Elevation of privilege	Admin privilege escalation	5	3	15

Now, you might be thinking, what's the sense in prioritizing risks when everything needs to be addressed before the application goes into production? Well, in a perfect world, that makes complete sense, but few things in life are perfect. There may be legitimate reasons why some lower risks need to be addressed in a later release. This could be due to lack of people, knowledge, money, and so on. By prioritizing risk, you ensure that the highest risks are addressed as part of the initial system design and not postponed until later. You can also consider what lower-risk controls and countermeasures must be applied immediately based on the probability of the system breaking if not incorporated as part of the initial design.

Finally, there are a multitude of tools that can be used to assist with the threat modeling process. Tools include (but are not limited to) Threat Dragon by OWASP, threat model design tools by Microsoft, and even the Elevation of Privilege (EoP) card game (yes, card game) by Microsoft that can help teams brainstorm ideas during a threat modeling session. None of these tools will be part of the exam, but they're good to know about all the same.

Testing: Predeployment

Now that the design has been reviewed from a security perspective through the use of threat modeling, you'll move to the security testing that is performed while the system is being developed. I'll discuss testing tools for this phase in the following sections.

Static application security testing

SAST, also known as *automated security code review*, is a structural testing approach that is conducted offline, prior to execution. It has complete access to the source code to identify security flaws or vulnerabilities in the application code itself. For example, it can read the code and alert to the use of hardcoded credentials (API keys, passwords), potential SQL injection flaws when user input is not sanitized, weak encryption (e.g., use of MD5 or SHA-1), buffer overflows, and other vulnerabilities.

SAST can be a powerful security tool when used as a plug-in to a CI/CD pipeline (covered later in this chapter), or when used as an extension to the developer's IDE during application code development. SAST extensions and CI/CD plug-ins such as Semgrep, SonarLint, and Snyk are commonly used to implement SAST functionality in both IDEs for early-stage security scanning and CI/CD environments to catch code vulnerabilities before entering the repository and deploying to production.

SAST tools can generate false positives by incorrectly flagging safe code as a security vulnerability (the opposite is a false negative, which occurs when a vulnerability is not discovered). These false positives can increase development time (and developer frustration) by necessitating manual reviews and suppression of false positives. To improve accuracy and efficiency, SAST tools require tuning, such as configuring rulesets, suppressing irrelevant findings, and refining detection thresholds based on the application's context.

Software composition analysis

SCA looks for open source components that are part of the software being built. SCA detects outdated dependencies or known vulnerabilities. It also can track what type of license model open source components are using to identify potential licensing issues.

SCA can also create an SBOM. The SBOM documents what third-party software is in use in various software products in an organization for rapid response to a newly discovered vulnerability, for example. Additionally, an SBOM may be required or recommended by a variety of standards and regulations, such as ISO/IEC 27001 and PCI.

For the CCSK exam, you need to know these tools and understand that they are used while the application is being developed. Once the application is built, it is ready for a different set of tools that can be used to perform security tests on an application that is running in a test (also known as *staging*) environment.

Secrets, images, and IaC template scanning

Finally, from a CCSK exam perspective, the environment that software runs in also needs to be secure. This includes the server and/or container images that host the application and the infrastructure it runs in. In IaC, the scanning templates (scripts) used to build the infrastructure can be assessed for security issues as part of a manual process, or this can be done using automated tools within the CI/CD pipeline.

Testing: Post Deployment

The term *post deployment* might imply that the application is now in production, but this is incorrect. Generally, once developed, an application is deployed from the development environment to a test (staging) environment, where final tests are conducted prior to deployment to production. In the previous section, we focused on code analysis as the application was offline. Now we are using dynamic testing tools to test the application as it is running (or online). Let's dive into the tools referenced by the CSA.

Dynamic application security testing

DAST is a functional testing model in which you do not have access to the code or knowledge of how the application runs ("online"). A security tester would use DAST to simulate attacks against a running application to uncover runtime vulnerabilities. As the DAST system does send malicious inputs and payloads to discover vulnerabilities (e.g., SQL injection, XSS, API security issues), there is a chance of these tests crashing an application (unlike SAST).

Interactive application security testing

Simply stated, interactive application security testing (IAST) is a hybrid of both SAST and DAST. It uses an agent (known as a *sensor*) that is embedded in the application runtime. It will then monitor the application from inside while it executes. Monitoring examples include HTTP requests, database queries, authentication mechanisms, and API calls. It acts like SAST by analyzing code as it executes, looking for insecure coding patterns. It acts like DAST by monitoring runtime behavior for runtime vulnerabilities that only appear during execution.

Penetration testing

A penetration test is a simulated cyberattack on a computer system, network, or application conducted by security professionals to identify and exploit vulnerabilities before malicious actors can do so. It is often said that a penetration test (pentest) is part art and part science. The goal of a pentest is to have the penetration tester successfully exploit a target (application or infrastructure) vulnerability by either structural testing, functional testing, or both. This can be done either manually or with automated attacks.

Pentesting has significant legal risks associated with it. The difference between pentesting and hacking has to do with permission. A pentest will have rules of engagement (RoEs) associated with it that limit the scope of the pentest. If the pentester goes beyond the RoEs, they no longer have permission and can wind up in jail. Key takeaway: always get permission in writing before starting any pentest, and stick to the RoEs. I'm serious. People have literally been jailed for breaking the project RoEs.

Bug bounty program

Companies run bug bounty programs to identify vulnerabilities in their systems. Bug bounty programs reward ethical hackers, security professionals, and security researchers for discovering vulnerabilities and advising the company under responsible disclosure terms. These programs have created their own industry sector, with companies offering platforms for managing submissions, validating reports, and paying rewards.

Once a vulnerability is discovered, the individual claiming a program reward submits the discovery, steps to reproduce the issue, the potential impact, and remediation steps to remove the vulnerability. Once the sponsoring company accepts and fixes the vulnerability, it pays the reward and allows the individual to disclose the vulnerability publicly (responsible disclosure).

I want to reiterate the importance of compliance in case you missed it earlier. This is a program run by a company, and it includes a defined scope, rules, and RoEs, just like pentests. You cannot simply attack a company and expect a reward for doing so. That makes you both a "bad actor" and an extortionist. And no, saying "I'm a bug bounty hunter" is not a viable defense in court, meaning you will likely spend time in jail.

Architecture's Role in Secure Cloud Applications

I think it is important to take a moment to address the difference between architecture and design, as the terms are often used interchangeably but have different outcomes. Architecture comes before design. It is a high-level, strategic framework that defines how security principles and controls are structured. It establishes a high-level view of security policies, standards, and guidelines while ensuring alignment with business objectives, regulatory requirements, and risk management strategies.

Design serves as more of a detailed blueprint that specifies how security controls will be implemented in a system or solution. In other words, architecture defines the big-picture strategy, while design translates that strategy into specific configurations, technologies, and implementations.

As an example, architecture would identify the need for a cloud-based identity provider that supports MFA. Design would then select a specific product (e.g., Okta) and define the configuration settings required to implement the architecture's security objectives.

The Impact of the Cloud on Architecture-Level Security

A traditional IT infrastructure consists of a mix of hardware appliances and software applications. In cloud computing, everything is software defined and highly automated. Although this allows for benefits such as increased agility and streamlined operations, it also requires a modern security strategy.

To build effective cloud security strategies, it's essential to understand how architectural options have changed. The following sections highlight key differences that demand a modern, cloud native approach to securing systems and data.

Infrastructure and application integration

Cloud architecture must consider the distributed and scalable nature of cloud computing. Cloud usage will often include federated identity management (FIM), distributed databases, and ephemeral workloads (e.g., FaaS).

Application component credentials

In a default deny environment such as the cloud, different services must be accessed with some form of credential. These credentials must be assigned least privileges to only the services required, as exposure or mismanagement may lead to security incidents.

Infrastructure as code and pipelines

IaC and the use of pipelines are commonly defined in IaaS and PaaS cloud environments. As discussed, these offer the ability to have security shift to the left by assessing IaC for security issues prior to usage and integrating security tests into the continuous integration pipeline.

Immutable infrastructure

As mentioned previously, immutable infrastructure is defined as something not subject to change. The use of immutable infrastructure replaces workloads rather than updating them, and can provide additional resiliency over traditional approaches.

Architectural Resilience

Resiliency in the cloud can be achieved by using redundancy by duplicating critical components across different availability zones or regions, load balancing to distribute incoming requests across different resources, and auto-scaling to increase (or decrease) available instances to meet demand.

The discipline of site reliability engineering (SRE) plays a crucial role in ensuring the reliability, scalability, and efficiency of large-scale cloud systems by applying software engineering principles to IT operations, infrastructure, and applications. Reliability of systems is the primary goal of SRE, and it uses automation in support of this goal. Applications should be designed and maintained to be resilient.

IAM and Application Security

Proper IAM is critical for application security. IAM includes the technologies and policies that are designed to manage identities and the access levels granted within an organization. It is critical to safeguard the credentials used by both humans and systems. One leading way to protect these credentials is by using a secrets manager.

Secrets Management

Secrets are more than just passwords; they are digital authentication credentials that include certificates (used for TLS encryption, authentication, and code signing), API keys (unique identifiers used to authenticate API requests), access tokens (temporary credentials for programmatic access), encryption keys, and database connection strings (which may contain embedded credentials), along with other sensitive data that must remain protected. Exposed secrets are a major cause of cloud security breaches. A secure way to store, manage, and control access to these secrets is through a secrets management system or secrets manager service supplied by a CSP or a third-party solution.

Effective secrets management ensures that sensitive credentials are securely stored, accessed, and managed, preventing unauthorized access and reducing the risk of data breaches. A secrets management system enforces tools and policies to systematically create, distribute, rotate, and revoke credentials. Some systems also include secret leak detection through logging and behavior analytics, such as identifying an IP address accessing a secret at an abnormal time. These measures safeguard the integrity and confidentiality of data across the infrastructure.

Hardcoded credentials should be avoided whenever possible. Modern cloud providers offer alternatives to the use of static secrets by enabling identity-based access control. Depending on the deployment scenario, applications and services can use IAM roles or service identities that reduce the need for hardcoded credentials. When secrets are necessary, all major IaaS and PaaS CSPs offer secure secrets manager solutions that integrate with IAM, preventing secrets from being hardcoded in application code, configuration files, or other insecure locations. Additionally, third-party secrets management solutions are available for multicloud and on-premises environments.

Secrets Management Workflow

Figure 10-3 shows the use of the AWS Secrets Manager solution and the process flow.

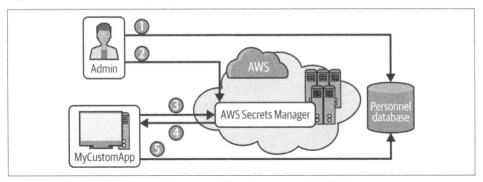

Figure 10-3. AWS Secrets Manager workflow (courtesy of AWS)

Let's go through each step:

1. The database administrator creates a set of credentials for MyCustomApp in the Personnel database, granting it the necessary permissions.
2. The administrator stores the credentials as a secret in AWS Secrets Manager, naming it MyCustomAppCreds. AWS Secrets Manager encrypts and securely stores the credentials as protected secret text.
3. When MyCustomApp needs access to the Personnel database, it sends a request to AWS Secrets Manager for the stored secret (MyCustomAppCreds). AWS Secrets Manager verifies MyCustomApp's IAM permissions to ensure that it is authorized to access the secret.
4. AWS Secrets Manager retrieves, decrypts, and securely transmits the secret to MyCustomApp over an encrypted (e.g., TLS) connection.
5. MyCustomApp extracts the credentials and uses them to authenticate and connect to the Personnel database.

DevOps and DevSecOps

Many people describe DevOps as a culture because it represents a shift in how software is developed, tested, deployed, and maintained. It is a software development and IT operations methodology that emphasizes collaboration, automation, and continuous delivery to accelerate the SDLC. DevOps is a natural fit for cloud computing, where it enables dynamic infrastructure, rapid deployments, and operational agility, making it a critical practice for modern software engineering.

By integrating development (Dev) and operations (Ops) teams, DevOps enables organizations to build, test, deploy, and maintain software more efficiently. It incorporates key principles such as continuous integration (CI) and continuous delivery (CD), which automate code deployment to testing or even production environments, ensuring rapid and stable releases. Because DevOps fundamentally changes how software is built and managed through automation, it requires a cultural shift within an organization to fully embrace its benefits.

Simply stated, DevSecOps extends DevOps by embedding security throughout the DevOps lifecycle. This includes automating security tests within the CI pipeline, ensuring that security is an integral part of software development rather than a separate step. Since CI is at the heart of DevOps, integrating security into this workflow is essential for securing modern applications.

The DevOps/DevSecOps Lifecycle

Figure 10-4 illustrates the various processes in a DevOps (and DevSecOps) lifecycle, which help organizations understand how continuous automation and collaboration improve software delivery.

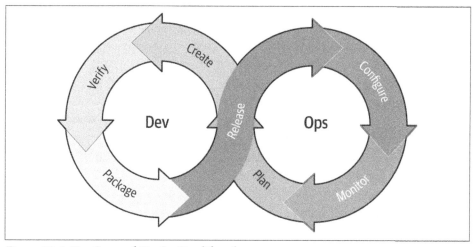

Figure 10-4. DevOps and DevSecOps lifecycle

The lifecycle consists of the following phases:

Plan
    In this phase, requirements are defined, goals are established, and security considerations are made from the outset. Teams collaborate to outline features and potential threats.

Create
: In this phase, code is developed with secure coding practices. Automated tools are used to detect vulnerabilities early in the development process.

Verify
: This phase tests the code for functionality and security using static analysis, unit tests, and vulnerability scans before moving forward.

Package
: This phase consists of bundling the code and dependencies into deployable artifacts (e.g., containers). Ensuring supply chain security and integrity is a key security element of this phase.

Release
: In this phase, code is deployed to production or staging environments through automated pipelines with built-in security and compliance checks.

Configure
: In this phase, teams create the infrastructure and environment with secure configuration settings. This often involves using IaC with policy enforcement.

Monitor
: Finally, in this phase, application behavior and infrastructure are continuously observed to detect threats, anomalies, and compliance issues in real time while in production.

As you can see, just like the SDLC we covered earlier in this chapter, DevOps and DevSecOps have a series of stages that application development goes through, from initial planning through to continuous monitoring while the application is in production. That's the main takeaway for the CCSK exam.

CI/CD Pipelines

A CI/CD pipeline is an automated series of steps that software development teams use to deliver new versions of software quickly, reliably, and with high quality. It's a core practice within DevOps, aiming to bridge the gap between development and operations teams. Figure 10-5 shows a conceptual CI/CD pipeline.

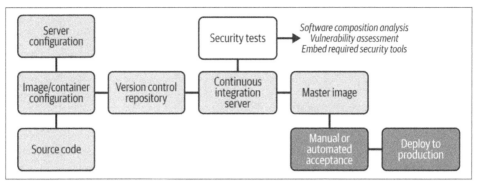

Figure 10-5. CI/CD pipeline (diagram courtesy of the CSA CCSK v5 study guide)

As you can see from Figure 10-5, server and container configurations, images, and source code can be uploaded into the version control repository. From there, a CI server will perform additional security activities. Once this is completed successfully, a primary image will be created that can then undergo additional acceptance checks and finally be deployed to the production environment. The key to DevSecOps is the automation the CI/CD pipeline delivers. Let's cover the main pipeline components in the version control repository and CI server.

Version control repository

A software version control repository is a system that stores, manages, and tracks changes to software code, configuration files, and related assets over time. It enables teams to maintain a history of code changes, collaborate efficiently, and ensure version control in software development. Examples of a version control repository include GitHub, GitLab, and Atlassian Bitbucket.

The version control repository is where artifacts, such as application code, configuration files for server or container images, and IaC templates, are stored and versioned.

Continuous integration server

At the heart of the CI pipeline is the CI server. It automates the building, testing, and integration of code changes in the software development process. It can also be used to create server and container images and inspect IaC templates. From a security perspective, the CI server can be used to enforce security and compliance checks in an automated fashion as well. It plays a crucial role in DevOps by enabling faster feedback loops, automated testing, and smoother deployments. Some examples of popular CI servers are Jenkins, GitHub Actions, GitLab CI, and Travis CI. CSPs also offer their own CI servers; examples include AWS CodeBuild, Azure Pipelines, and Google Cloud Build.

Although I mentioned various vendors, the CCSK exam won't ask any questions on the different CI server offerings in the marketplace. You must know what they do, though.

When a change is committed to the version control repository, a notification is sent to the CI server. The CI server then "pulls" the updated artifact and executes predefined tasks, such as performing security tests like SAST and DAST, conducting vulnerability assessments, or embedding security tools into images. If the artifact fails customer-configured security thresholds, the primary image is not created, and the CI server tells the submitter why the build failed and what needs to be addressed.

How does the CI server do all this? It uses plug-ins to perform whatever you request as part of a defined workflow. In the case of Jenkins, there are more than 1,800 plug-ins available to support DevOps activities, including integrations with products from major security vendors.

Post build

Once all tests pass and the artifact is successfully built, it moves to the deployment stage. This is where the CD part of CI/CD comes into play. The artifact can be deployed either to a different environment such as a test environment, or directly to the production environment. In many cases, the artifact would be deployed to a test environment for additional security and functionality testing that will be performed by humans.

> ### From the Trenches: Trimming, Not Tossing, Manual Reviews
>
> In one financial services environment that I worked in, the organization implemented a CI/CD pipeline to support its DevSecOps initiative. It didn't do this to automate all security testing or to deliver directly to production. Rather, its goal was to reduce the number of business days allocated to manual security reviews from 15 to 5. Again, adoption of DevSecOps and the level of automation comes down to the organization's culture.

Web Application Firewalls and API Gateways

WAFs and API gateways serve as critical security layers for protecting HTTP/S traffic directed toward cloud workloads. A WAF primarily secures web applications by filtering and blocking malicious HTTP traffic, defending against common attacks like SQL injection, XSS, and other OWASP Top 10 threats. WAFs can also help block unknown zero-day attacks. In contrast, an API gateway focuses on API-specific security concerns, such as authentication, authorization, rate limiting, and request/response transformations.

Additionally, WAF solutions often integrate with other security features, such as DDoS protection, SSL/TLS termination, and traffic inspection, further strengthening cloud security.

The following sections discuss the common deployment models for WAF and API gateway protection in cloud environments.

Agent-Based Deployment

When deploying web applications on IaaS instances, a WAF agent can be installed directly on the operating system to provide application-layer protection. While this approach helps defend against web-based threats, it typically lacks built-in DDoS mitigation, because the WAF operates at the host level rather than at the network edge. As a result, attack traffic still reaches the VM, potentially overwhelming its resources before the WAF can filter it. Additionally, this model may require extra configurations for scalability and high availability.

Cloud Native Provider Services

Major cloud providers offer load balancing services with built-in WAF and DDoS protection, often integrating with CDNs. These managed security services provide scalability, automatic updates, and reduced operational overhead.

By leveraging a CDN, organizations can distribute web content across multiple global edge locations, improving performance, reducing latency, and enhancing availability for end users.

Third-Party Marketplace Solutions

CSPs typically offer cloud marketplaces that feature a range of commercial WAF solutions. These solutions are deployed on dedicated VMs or cloud appliances, and their pricing includes both the WAF software license and the underlying compute resources required for deployment.

When considering this solution, ensure that you understand the product offering as opposed to just purchasing based on the vendor you use in your traditional environment. You may find that the cloud marketplace offering doesn't do everything the traditional offering does.

Unlike managed WAF services, these third-party solutions require customer oversight for deployment, configuration, and ongoing maintenance. This includes managing routing, redundancy, load balancing, and instance upkeep to ensure high availability and performance.

WAF and DDoS Protection as a Service

This model provides offloading of security processing while benefiting from advanced threat intelligence and managed security services, usually delivered as a cloud service (e.g., Cloudflare, Akamai). Traffic is routed through the third-party WAF provider using DNS redirection, where it undergoes inspection and filtering before being forwarded to the web servers running in a cloud provider's environment.

Summary

Here are the key exam takeaways from this chapter:

- Know the changes the cloud introduces to application development and the need for automation.
- Know that the purpose of any SDLC is to establish process gates and that security can be implemented in each phase.
- Understand that the term *shift left* means incorporating security earlier in the SDLC.
- Remember the tools used for runtime defense and monitoring.
- Know that threat modeling is used to identify threats to software during the design phase.
- Know the different types of security testing (SAST, DAST, etc.).
- Remember that SRE focuses on reliability, scalability and efficiency in operations.
- Understand when secrets management systems are important and that credentials should never be hardcoded.
- Remember that DevSecOps allows for rapid deployments with automated security checks.
- Know what WAFs and API gateways are.

This concludes the application security chapter. In the next chapter, you will learn about incident response and resilience in cloud environments.

CHAPTER 11
Incident Response: From Detection to Recovery

> *In preparing for battle I have always found that plans are useless, but planning is indispensable.*
> —Dwight D. Eisenhower

Incident response is the structured approach an organization takes to prepare for, detect, contain, and recover from cybersecurity incidents such as data breaches, malware infections, insider threats, or DoS attacks. Incident response must be planned before an incident occurs. Unfortunately, it is a matter of when, not if, an organization will experience a security incident and possibly a breach. These incidents and breaches can occur for numerous reasons, including accidental reasons.

While organizations likely have incident response plans for internal IT systems, the cloud introduces a new virtual environment that requires expert knowledge of incident response processes, tools and technologies, governance, and new complexity for every cloud platform used.

The CSA references several key tools for its incident response recommendations, including NIST SP 800-61 Rev. 2, the CSA Cloud Incident Response (CIR) framework, ISO/IEC 27035, and ENISA's "Strategies for Incident Response and Cyber Crisis Cooperation" document. The CSA adapts these recommendations to reflect cloud-specific incident response challenges and processes.

This chapter identifies and explains best practices for incident response in the cloud. These can be used as a reference to develop an organization's incident response architecture, plans, and processes that must be established in advance of an incident.

Incident Response

Every incident is an event, but not every event is an incident is a common saying in incident response. The distinction between the two is their impact. Figure 11-1 shows the different levels of damage an organization can face.

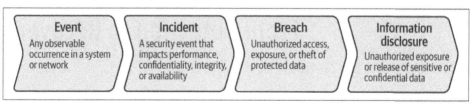

Figure 11-1. Security event escalation model

As Figure 11-1 shows, an event is any observable occurrence in a system or a network. Events can be routine system operations or anomalies. If an event negatively impacts performance, security, or availability, it is classified as an incident. If an incident results in unauthorized access to protected data, it may be classified as a breach. This is where notification to regulators or law enforcement may be involved and an organization may face fines. Finally, if sensitive or confidential data is exposed, whether through theft, accidental disclosure, or misconfiguration, it is classified as information disclosure. At this stage, the organization may face additional legal and financial consequences, such as providing credit monitoring for affected individuals or potential class action lawsuits if negligence in data protection is established.

Incidents require immediate attention to contain and mitigate their impact and prevent further escalation. The response must be performed as soon as possible and in a structured way to minimize damage, protect sensitive assets, and ensure business continuity. The structure and required actions of a proper incident response lifecycle are covered in the next several sections.

Incident Response Lifecycle

Figure 11-2 is the NIST incident response lifecycle that is used by the CSA.

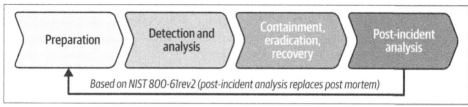

Figure 11-2. NIST incident response lifecycle

As you can see, there are four phases in the lifecycle, and the final phase informs the first phase to create a continuous improvement loop. Following is a generic list of considerations for each phase. In later sections, we'll look at the considerations that the cloud introduces to incident response.

Phase 1: Preparation

In this phase, an organization establishes an incident response capability to respond to incidents. This entails the following:

- Establish an incident response process.
- Build a team and assign roles and responsibilities.
- Train the team and run exercises.
- Establish a communication plan and facilities.
- Provide responder access to environments.
- Provide responder access to tools, such as incident analysis services, hardware, and software.
- Create internal documentation such as port lists, asset lists, and a network traffic baseline.
- Evaluate the infrastructure through proactive scanning and monitoring, as well as vulnerability and risk assessments.
- Subscribe to third-party threat intelligence services.
- Evaluate CSPs and their capabilities to aid in incident response regarding the services/resources consumed.
- Implement audit logs, snapshots, forensics capabilities, and e-discovery features.
- Conduct backup restoration testing regularly and disaster recovery tests at least once per year to ensure that incident response plans are up-to-date and effective.

Phase 2: Detection and Analysis

In this phase, the organization builds the ability to identify security incidents and analyze their impact. This entails the following:

- Establish detection engineering.
- Establish alerts. This includes cloud security posture management (CSPM), SIEM, workload protection, and network security monitoring.
- Validate alerts (reduce false positives) with escalation.
- Estimate the scope of the incident.
- Assign an incident manager to coordinate actions.

- Build a timeline of the attack.
- Determine the extent of the potential data loss or impact.
- Notify and coordinate activities.
- Communicate the incident containment and recovery status to senior management.

Phase 3: Containment, Eradication, and Recovery

In this phase, the organization builds on its capability to isolate the incident to prevent further damage and remove the root cause. This entails the following:

- Contain the incident by isolating identities and workloads, taking systems or services offline, and considering the trade-offs between data loss and service availability.
- Eradicate and recover by cleaning up compromised assets, restoring systems and services to normal operation, and deploying controls to prevent similar incidents.
- Document the incident and gather forensic evidence (e.g., chain of custody).

Phase 4: Post-Incident Analysis

Finally, in this phase, the organization benefits by improving its ability to learn from the incident, document, and improve future responses. This comes from a lessons-learned exercise that attempts to address the following:

- Which detections worked?
- Which alerts fired properly?
- What detections and protections need to be created based on the event?
- What improvements does the incident response process need to make?
- Did the incident responders have the necessary tools?
- Do the incident responders need additional training?
- What indicators of compromise (IoCs) were discovered, and were they shared with the community?

Many security incidents are not necessarily confined to a single environment. Attackers may be able to move laterally across cloud platforms, on-premises infrastructure, and various endpoints such as mobile devices, workstations, and IoT systems. This complexity requires incident responders to maintain a full view of the entire attack surface and avoid tunnel vision, which could lead to incomplete investigations and missed threats.

Now that we have covered the highlights of the various phases of incident response in general, we will dive into the cloud-specific recommendations the CSA provides for cloud computing.

How the Preparation Phase Changes in Cloud Environments

The changes that the cloud introduces to the incident response preparation phase include the following:

- Changes due to the relationship with the cloud provider
- Changes in responder training
- Changes needed to support the cloud incident response (CIR) process
- Changes required to support CIR technologies

Cloud incidents are inherently shared incidents, even when a customer owns and manages all the affected resources. This is because cloud environments operate under a shared responsibility model, where security and operational duties are divided between the CSP and the customer. However, the boundaries of responsibility vary based on the cloud service model (SaaS, PaaS, IaaS) used.

For effective incident response, organizations must have a clear understanding of their contractual agreements with CSPs, including the following:

Service level agreements (SLAs)
    Define guaranteed service uptime, availability, and support response times

Incident management responsibilities
    Clarify which incidents require CSP intervention versus those the customer must handle independently

Log and data access
    Identify what security logs and forensic data the CSP provides, as some logs (e.g., hypervisor logs) might not be accessible

Notification obligations
    Understand when and how the CSP will notify customers about security incidents affecting their cloud services

Organizations must review their incident response capabilities in the cloud and determine how to coordinate effectively with CSPs when incidents occur. Unlike traditional IT environments, where internal teams control all infrastructure and security tooling, cloud incident response often involves interacting with the CSP through predefined support channels. Depending on the relationship with the provider, the customer may experience limitations such as the following:

- Lack of direct security contacts if they don't have premium support
- Delayed response times if relying solely on standard support tiers
- Restricted access to system-level logs or forensic data due to multitenancy constraints

It is critical that customers have a premium support contract that will enable them to get in contact with the CSP in the quickest way possible. A CSP support package for IaaS primarily offers services that enhance incident detection, investigation, containment, escalation, recovery, and forensics. However, these support contracts can cost thousands of dollars per month, making them cost prohibitive for small organizations.

Beyond general support contracts, some providers may offer additional incident response support packages. It is the customer's responsibility to investigate and select the appropriate support given the criticality of the cloud-based workloads.

Additionally, customers should consider incidents that affect the CSP. History has shown that CSPs can be affected by public vulnerabilities, large-scale DoS attacks, and other security events that may disrupt cloud services. While customers may not have control over the CSP's infrastructure, they are not entirely powerless. They do have to plan for these, however. Although the vast majority of CSP outages are short in duration, there are a handful of examples of prolonged outages caused by both physical and logical incidents.

Training for Cloud Incident Responders

Although cloud incident response shares many characteristics and processes with traditional incident response, it is important for responders to understand the process and technology differences. This applies to every CSP an organization uses, as the "how" to respond to an incident will be different.

The CSA makes the following recommendations regarding training for cloud incident response staff:

- Generalized cloud incident response training helps build the foundational skills that work across cloud providers. This is also a good choice to improve cloud awareness, even with responders who won't be dedicated to cloud incidents.
- Provider-specific technical training is essential for any responder working on a major platform, particularly IaaS. This training should not be limited to just using the incident response tools offered by the provider, but should get into the

deep details, such as how to quarantine an exposed service credential, how to analyze logs, and so on.
- Scenario-based exercises in simulated environments help responders gain practice at core skills such as log analysis, threat hunting, and resource quarantining.
- Full exercises and red-teaming are designed to test the entire incident response process.
- Tabletop exercises (walking through a hypothetical scenario) with distributed cloud teams and leadership help ensure that different teams can work together and coordinate efforts. Tabletop exercises may also include simulations of large-scale incidents, such as a provider breach.

Individuals tasked with responding to cloud incidents require persistent read access to all deployments (AWS accounts, Azure subscriptions, etc.). As with other accounts, all activities should be logged and reviewed.

As for what these accounts should be able to read, there are two levels of access that need to be understood. The first is *metadata read access*. This is information about the resource (e.g., instance), but not access to the resource itself. Think of what is visible when looking at a resource in the CSP management console. The second level is referred to as *full-read access*, which does allow the incident response team member to access and read the contents of the workload itself (files stored on a server, snapshot data, etc.).

Generally, you should grant incident response team members full-read access under just-in-time principles. Access to the resources themselves should only be granted after approvals by management, and they should be time-bound by having these enhanced privileges automatically revoked after a period of time.

An additional requirement is access to the cloud deployment registry. We covered the cloud registry previously, but given its importance, it's worth repeating. The cloud registry needs to be continuously updated with the latest information on what cloud products are in use in the organization as well as all the services consumed. Most importantly, this registry must have entries for the business owner and technical leads for the deployment so that they can be quickly determined. This will assist the incident response function by knowing where to inspect for evidence collection and who to contact in the event of an incident. After all, the incident response team, business owner, and technical leads will need to work with one another to effectively respond to incidents.

Other elements the team will require access to are the CI/CD pipelines, code repositories, and other locations that may be compromised during an event. They will also require access to all logs generated by these items. After all, if an attacker can access the deployment pipeline, they would be able to push their own code to a production environment, install backdoors in software, or perform other malicious activities.

How Detection and Analysis Change in Cloud Environments

The principles of incident detection and response in traditional IT extend to the cloud, but the details of how detection and analysis are performed change significantly in a cloud environment, and they will also differ on a per-platform basis. Key differences that must be understood for cloud detection and response include the following:

- The new telemetry for detection and analysis that the cloud introduces
- The additional attack surface of the management plane, which must be the primary focus during any response
- The higher rate of activities in the cloud, which include the speed of attackers (who are highly automated) and the speed of change of the cloud environments themselves
- The lack of a traditional network perimeter and the addition of an IAM blast radius
- The API-driven nature of the cloud and the ephemeral nature of resources
- The decentralized management of infrastructure by cloud and development teams
- The impact of automation, IaC, serverless, and other cloud native technologies

The next few sections will address these differences and how to adjust detection and response activities for cloud services versus traditional IT.

Impact of the Cloud on Incident Analysis

In cloud environments, incident analysis will primarily be focused on the management plane, which provides a centralized view of cloud activities through its logs. These logs are essential for detecting unauthorized access, misconfigurations, and other anomalies that may indicate a security incident. Given the dynamic nature of the cloud, where resources are rapidly provisioned and decommissioned, incident response teams must include leveraging automation and machine learning (e.g., AI-enhanced SIEM and SOAR platforms) to efficiently monitor changes and detect threats in real time.

When a CI/CD pipeline is used in an organization, incident analysis must include pipeline security and its supply chain. As mentioned earlier, this software supply chain is a high-value target for attackers, as compromising the deployment process can enable malicious code injection, backdoor deployments, and unauthorized infrastructure modifications.

The shared nature of cloud services makes it critical to incorporate external threat intelligence into detection and response workflows. These threat intelligence systems collect and analyze data from global attack trends, security vendors, government sources, and dark web monitoring. This information allows organizations to proactively detect zero-day vulnerabilities, malware campaigns, and advanced persistent threats (APTs) before they impact cloud workloads.

Threat intelligence is not just knowledge; it can be automated to dynamically detect and mitigate security risks in real time. Modern threat intelligence platforms (TIPs) and SIEM systems integrate with firewalls, XDR platforms, SOAR tools, and CWPP to automate threat detection and response. For example, security tools can automatically block malicious IPs, quarantine compromised workloads, or revoke compromised credentials based on real-time intelligence feeds. CSP security services can leverage threat intelligence to detect suspicious activity, while firewalls and WAFs can dynamically update rules to block known attack sources.

By leveraging both knowledge-based and automated threat intelligence, organizations can build adaptive security defenses that continuously evolve to counter emerging threats. In modern cloud environments, integrating automated threat intelligence into security workflows, firewalls, and incident response processes is essential for maintaining proactive and resilient cloud security operations.

Cloud System Forensics

Digital forensics is the process of identifying, preserving, analyzing, and presenting digital evidence in a legally admissible manner. Forensics is a highly specialized discipline that requires deep expertise and should never be performed by individuals who lack formal training and experience in digital forensics. While forensics is often seen as a component of incident response, it is also a critical legal process, with significant implications for compliance, litigation, and criminal investigations. Errors in the forensics process can lead to evidence being inadmissible in court, potentially resulting in cases being dismissed. Even the credibility (experience, credentials, etc.) of the individual performing the forensics activities will be scrutinized by opposing lawyers. Both the forensics expert and the data they present in court must be beyond refute.

Figure 11-3 shows the workflow involved in forensics activities.

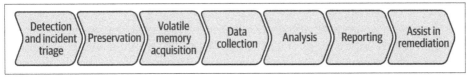

Figure 11-3. Forensics workflow

For a general overview of the digital forensics workflow, I will first provide a high-level view of the seven steps shown in Figure 11-3 and then cover specifics on certain items as addressed by the CSA. Following are the seven steps, in brief:

Detection and incident triage
Suspicious activity is identified using alerts, monitoring, or user reports.

Preservation
Activities here include taking snapshots of VMs, containers, and storage volumes. Logs are exported and preserved; systems are isolated from the network and volatile memory is acquired.

Volatile memory acquisition
Running memory is captured. Tools that were used are documented, along with any impact they may have had during the collection process.

Data collection
Data such as disk images, memory dumps, logs, and metadata is collected. Cryptographic hashes are used to verify integrity to ensure that no data collected was altered prior to being presented in court.

Analysis
Snapshots and memory are scanned for file changes and any malware or injected code.

Reporting
Findings, timelines, and evidence-handling procedures are documented.

Assistance in remediation
Findings supporting remediation and lessons learned are shared to improve incident response processes.

In a cloud environment, forensics has two areas of focus: the management plane and the workloads themselves. Because everything is virtual, forensics teams will be reliant on snapshots, specialized forensics software, and CSP support. Let's cover the recommendations by the CSA for these items. You will see how the CSA recommendations cover much of the general forensics workflow we just covered.

Snapshots and storage volume forensics

Snapshots will capture everything on a disk when the snapshot operation is performed, which is critical for forensic analysis. Most CSPs and container management systems support snapshots. Customers need to understand how to take storage volume snapshots immediately upon detecting an incident to preserve the state of a VM or container for later analysis. These snapshots help forensics teams recover files, analyze malware, or reconstruct system states. Forensic snapshots should be protected to ensure that they are not overwritten or deleted due to retention limits.

Volatile memory acquisition and live response challenges

Volatile memory refers to computer memory that requires power to maintain the stored data. Once the system is powered off or rebooted, all data in volatile memory is lost. Collecting this volatile memory during a forensic exercise is critical, as it holds active processes and network connections, user credentials, and malware operating in memory. Capturing this volatile memory in cloud environments presents significant challenges because customers don't have direct access to the hardware that is abstracted by the CSP. Unlike traditional on-premises forensic investigations, cloud forensic responders must install software-based memory acquisition tools within the compromised VM or container, which can potentially alter system state and impact forensic integrity. Some cloud native forensic tools may provide partial solutions, but memory forensics remains a challenge in cloud environments. Courts will accept what is technically possible in place of perfect in scenarios such as this. They care more about the integrity of the process following forensic best practices than demanding things be done the way they have been done in the past with traditional IT.

Log analysis and correlation with management plane activities

Forensic analysis in the cloud relies heavily on log analysis, as logs provide insight into system, application, and user activity even when direct VM/container forensics are limited. Management plane logs give visibility into API calls, privilege escalations, IAM changes, and administrative actions. These logs are crucial for tracking attacker movements, detecting lateral movement, and identifying unauthorized API calls.

Forensics chain of custody in cloud environments

The chain of custody is a critical process that must be adhered to throughout the identification, collection, documentation, transfer, and preservation of evidence. Maintaining the chain of custody in cloud environments requires a thorough understanding of the following:

- Cloud provider backup and retention policies (e.g., snapshot expiration, log retention)
- Legal and compliance considerations (e.g., GDPR, ISO 27037 digital evidence handling)
- Chain of custody protocols to maintain forensic integrity
- Tamper-proof storage options such as Write Once Read Many (WORM) offerings available from the CSP

Forensic evidence must be collected, stored, and transferred securely while adhering to jurisdictional requirements and cloud provider data retention constraints. Without proper evidence preservation strategies, key forensic data may be deleted by the CSP, rendering an investigation incomplete.

Forensics Blast Zones

When conducting cloud forensic investigations on VMs, it is critical to perform these activities in a segregated forensic environment that is completely isolated from any development, test, or production environments. These isolated areas are known as *blast zones*. This isolation is essential to prevent accidental activation of malicious payloads that could spread within the cloud infrastructure or disrupt business operations. If an infected VM is analyzed in a live production environment, there is a significant risk that malware could propagate, C2 connections could be reestablished, or the attacker could detect forensic activities and attempt to erase evidence.

We covered the key aspects of forensics in a cloud environment in a previous section. Now let's put all this together. To safely analyze a compromised VM, the forensics process typically involves creating snapshots to quickly copy and preserve the data on a drive and an image of the system without rebooting the instance to capture everything about the compromised instance, including memory contents. This approach ensures the quick preservation of data through the snapshot and memory (RAM) contents, active network connections, and other volatile forensic artifacts. Rebooting a compromised server will clear memory, reset system states, or trigger self-destruct mechanisms by malware, making forensic reconstruction more difficult.

Once the team creates a forensic snapshot or image, it must transfer the snapshot or image to a dedicated, isolated environment. This environment is protected by strict access controls and security groups, with no outbound internet connectivity to prevent data exfiltration and block C2 connections. Forensics investigators can safely use specialized tools to examine the compromised system without risking further infection, data loss, or attacker interference. Figure 11-4 is an example of the snapshot operation.

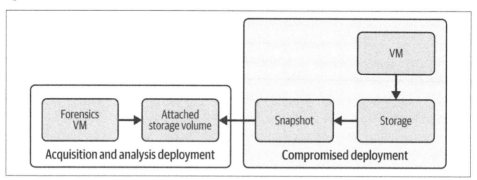

Figure 11-4. Copying forensic data to an isolated blast zone

Additionally, logs and other forensic artifacts from the compromised VM should be collected and correlated to re-create the attack timeline. This allows forensics teams to determine when the breach occurred, how the attacker gained access, and what actions were taken within the environment.

By following a structured forensics workflow, including isolated investigation environments, nondisruptive snapshot-based acquisition, and comprehensive log analysis, organizations can minimize risk, preserve evidence integrity, and improve the accuracy of their forensic investigations in the cloud.

Cloud Forensics: Container and Serverless Considerations

Given the ephemeral nature of containers and serverless workloads, forensics performed in the cloud will change dramatically compared to forensics performed on VMs.

The following subsections describe key container and serverless considerations.

Containers

Containers often exist for short durations before being terminated or replaced. This ephemeral nature creates significant challenges for forensics data collection and analysis, as traditional forensics methods may not apply. To address this, forensics strategies should focus on capturing container logs, retaining snapshots of container states, and monitoring network activity to reconstruct events. You should redirect logs—including container logs, VM logs, and service logs—to external storage for persistence and future analysis.

Serverless computing

Serverless architectures introduce additional forensics complexities by further abstracting the execution environment from the user. In serverless models, CSPs fully manage the underlying infrastructure, limiting access to traditional forensic artifacts such as disk and memory snapshots. As a result, forensic investigations in serverless environments rely heavily on logs generated by serverless functions, including execution logs, access logs, and application logs. Understanding invocation patterns, execution timing, and API interactions is essential for reconstructing events and detecting anomalies in a serverless security incident.

Support contracts

In real life, don't forget the importance of having the appropriate CSP support contract in place for assistance with forensics. These support contracts will play a crucial role in ensuring that organizations have the necessary tools, extended log retention, and expert assistance to conduct thorough forensic investigations.

Standard cloud logging and security services often retain data for limited periods, making it challenging to reconstruct events after an incident. Higher-tier CSP support contracts can provide extended access to logs, forensic snapshots, and detailed network activity data that may not be available to standard users.

Ultimately, investing in a CSP support contract enhances forensics capabilities, accelerates incident response, and provides access to critical forensic tools and expertise, making it an essential component of an appropriate cloud security strategy.

Containment, Eradication, and Recovery

Containment, eradication, and recovery is arguably the area impacted the most by the new offerings that the cloud brings, such as IaC, auto-scaling, microservices, identity federation, and others. Although the virtual nature of the cloud requires new processes and new tools, these bring new opportunities for incident containment, eradication, and recovery, unlike those available in traditional IT.

Containment

IAM and management plane containment should be the top priorities in any security incident. To know the access levels of entities that should be in an environment, you need to engage the application owner as well as the cloud owner. These individuals may prove to be valuable in the creation and even the implementation of a containment plan.

IAM containment

Effective IAM containment can be challenging in cloud environments, especially due to the widespread use of FIMs, where authentication and authorization are separated and often handled on different platforms. This separation requires coordinated containment measures on both the identity provider (IdP) and the relying party (RP) to effectively respond to security incidents and limit unauthorized access.

On the IdP side, containment can be done by revoking active sessions, rotating access keys, or invalidating access tokens. However, federated models can allow previously issued tokens to remain valid until their expiration, even if the user's session is terminated or their account is disabled. Therefore, on the RP side, a critical containment strategy is to accept only tokens issued after a specific cutoff time. By configuring the RP to reject any tokens issued before a defined cutoff time, organizations can prevent token replay attacks and contain the breach without disrupting unaffected users.

Another area of concern regarding IAM containment is the compromise of service account credentials. Service accounts often have overly permissioned access to cloud resources, making them valuable targets for attackers. Effective containment of these service accounts requires investigation to determine if the attacker used the compromised credentials to escalate privileges or pivot to other identities, similar to how attackers navigate through a traditional network during lateral movement. This investigation involves tracking the attacker's activities within the IAM system, including API calls, role assumptions, and access token usage. This may require tight coordination between an analyst and a responder if those are separate roles.

Network containment

Network containment is fairly straightforward thanks to software-defined networking (SDN) functionality such as stateful virtual firewalls (security groups) and network access control lists (NACLs), where rules can be quickly changed through both APIs and web consoles. For example, applying a deny-all rule on the virtual firewall attached to a resource will immediately restrict all network traffic. Applying the same to an NACL will restrict all traffic to a subnet.

Containment efforts should focus on securing resources that have been publicly exposed or shared with unknown entities, such as unrecognized cloud accounts, subscriptions, or projects within the same CSP. When critical data is at risk, containment measures may outweigh application functionality. In these situations, incident responders must have a clear and rapid escalation path to reach a decision-making authority who can approve containment actions without delay. This escalation path should have been identified in the planning phase covered earlier. This approach ensures that, during highly critical incidents, the protection of sensitive assets takes precedence over operational continuity.

Eradication

The primary focus of eradication activities in a cloud environment takes place at the management plane. This involves IAM activities such as credential rotation, revoking all active sessions and invalidating all tokens, policy conditions such as a deny-all statement on all accounts except the incident response user account, implementation of MFA or digital certificates, and other techniques to remove an attacker's access to the management plane.

These global restrictions can only be relaxed once the compromised account can be identified. As the attacker may have had the ability to move laterally between accounts, the actions performed by all accounts need to be continuously monitored to identify unexpected actions after eradication.

After the compromised account(s) has/have been identified and locked down, the incident response team can start creating new resources (e.g., images, serverless code, and IaC). New resources should be built and implemented. This is because, if the original version has an unknown vulnerability that the attacker used to gain access in the first place, reusing these items will simply lead to another successful compromise.

Recovery

Recovery in a cloud environment can be performed quickly. This is possible through automated tools such as IaC and auto-scaling services. These can be used to deploy new, clean infrastructure and resources. As covered in the previous section, these should be new resources. At the very least, the images, resources, and templates used should be analyzed to ensure that any vulnerabilities have been eliminated and no backdoors exist.

For images, these should be immutable as a standard practice by major CSPs. This means any modification to an image will result in a new image with a new unique identifier being created. Steps must be taken to ensure that only approved images are deployed during recovery in case they have had malicious code injected by an attacker. This requires that the customer know the unique identifiers of approved images. Large CSPs will often have some form of image registry to store only approved and signed images in a centralized image repository. If a CI/CD pipeline is available, this can be used to inspect images prior to deployment.

You can also use policies to ensure that your teams only deploy approved images. This, however, takes additional maintenance to update policies every time new images are created.

Post-Incident Analysis

Learning from mistakes is a way to achieve personal growth. It is also the way to improve your incident response capability. People don't wake up in the morning and say, "How can I mess up today?" Take this to heart when it comes to post-incident analysis. This requires a *just culture*, which is a culture that emphasizes learning over punishment. Let's use an example of just culture with a developer who commits insecure code into a version control repository (which does often happen unintentionally). Instead of rushing to a decision to fire the developer, the team would investigate introducing code review, better automated security tools, and training so that it hopefully doesn't happen again. The goal is not to punish people for mistakes, nor should this be used as a game of "gotcha." This isn't to say that there shouldn't be accountability for actions, but the primary goal is determining the root cause of the incident and then identifying how processes that people follow can be improved.

> ### From the Trenches: Standing Up for Just Culture
>
> I am extremely passionate about the just culture approach in post-incident analysis. This stems from an incident response process in which my director told me they wanted me to note everything a coworker did wrong during an incident and discussion with the client. They wanted to build a case so that they could pin the blame for the incident on the actions of my coworker, fire them, and tell the client the root

problem had been addressed by terminating the employee. I refused to do this and quickly came to learn that I would be punished for not following directions. I wasn't fired; I was just limited in advancement. I left that organization a few months after this occurred. I just couldn't work for an organization that was so quick to throw its own team members under the bus.

The goal is to understand areas of improvement to reduce the likelihood or impact (a.k.a. risk) of future events requiring incident response. To this end, the CSA calls out the following cloud-specific best practices:

- Teams that manage the impacted cloud deployments should be included in any post-incident analysis.
- Responders should update or create new runbooks/playbooks for any new incident types they encountered during the response.
- Identify what misconfigurations led to the incident. For example, if an IAM account had excessive privileges assigned, action should be taken to scan all IAM accounts for such a misconfiguration. This may lead an organization to add a new capability such as implementation of MFA, just-in-time entitlements, or other improvements to address the root cause of the incident.

Summary

In this chapter, you learned about incident response and forensics for both traditional and cloud environments. For the CCSK exam, you should be prepared to:

- Know the incident response lifecycle stages.
- Know in general the activities that happen in each phase of the lifecycle.
- Remember that knowing what a CSP offers in support of incident response is important.
- Remember the need for training of incident response staff on cloud-specific elements of incident response.
- Know that responders will need continuous read-only access to the cloud environment and just-in-time elevation of privileges in the event of an incident.
- Remember that incident response needs people, processes, and tools, and that they all need to be adjusted for cloud incident response.
- Remember that the development environment is a key target for attackers. Incident response staff need to understand tools used in development as well.
- Know the key aspects of cloud forensics.

- Remember the need for forensics to be performed in a separate, hard security boundary (the forensics blast zone).
- Remember the key considerations for incident response with containers and serverless workloads.
- Know IAM and network containment approaches.
- Remember what a just culture is for post-incident analysis.

This concludes our coverage of incident response in cloud environments. In the next chapter, we'll look at related technologies of cloud services such as zero trust and the role of AI in cloud services.

CHAPTER 12

Deep Dive into Zero Trust and AI

New technology demands new ways of thinking.
—Jeff Bezos

In this chapter, we look at two technologies the CSA refers to as "related technologies." While both zero trust and AI are not exclusive to the cloud, these technologies are often related to cloud services. Let's start with zero trust, then make our way to AI.

Zero Trust

Let's get one thing out of the way when it comes to zero trust (commonly abbreviated as *ZT*): it is not a buzzword. Marketers do their best to make it seem like a single product will amount to a "zero trust network." This is false. ZT is a strategy, not a tool.

The ZT approach does what it sounds like. Nothing is trusted. Not users, not devices, not networks. Nothing...not even that WiFi-enabled thermostat that nobody considers a computing device. This is very much unlike networks today. For decades, networks have been built with the concept of trusted versus untrusted users and devices and are usually created using a zoning approach. An organization may have an operational zone that is separate from a restricted zone, for example. When network traffic goes from the operational zone to the restricted zone, an inline network device usually inspects it. This is referred to as *north–south traffic*. Network traffic within a zone is referred to as *east–west traffic* and isn't inspected as it goes from one system to another in the same zone.

This unfettered traffic flow in a zone is what allows for phishing and ransomware campaigns to be so effective. I don't mean the initial compromise. I mean lateral movement to other systems after the initial compromise. It's the lateral movement that causes a single compromise to become a full-blown breach. This is where the concepts of microsegmentation and microperimeters come into play.

Microsegmentation involves dividing the network into smaller, more granular segments, each with its own security policies. This segmentation helps limit lateral movement by ensuring that even if one segment is compromised, the attacker cannot easily access other segments. Microperimeters are the security boundaries around these segments, enforcing strict access controls and monitoring traffic to protect the resources within each microsegment. You can think of microsegmentation as the design of the different segments and microperimeters as the tools to secure the different segments. Figure 12-1 shows the difference between a traditional zoning approach and a microsegmentation network approach.

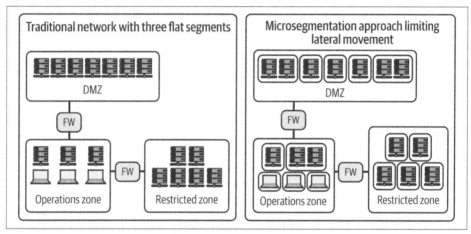

Figure 12-1. Traditional network versus microsegmentation

On the lefthand side of Figure 12-1, you see a traditional network zoning approach with three flat segments. Between the DMZ and the Operations zone, there is network inspection via a firewall (labeled FW). However, once in the zone, all machines can access each other (unfettered east–west traffic). On the righthand side of the figure, you see a microsegmentation approach. With this segmented approach, only servers and workstations that need to communicate are grouped together in the same zone (as denoted by the boxes around the systems). This is what is meant by limiting lateral movement. There is restricted east–west traffic in this network architecture.

Although the concepts of microsegmentation and microperimeters are an essential part of ZT, ZT involves much more than just networking principles. It addresses all facets of cybersecurity. The strategy can be implemented to secure assets in both cloud and traditional networks. The goals of a ZT strategy are plentiful from both a technical and business viewpoint. You'll see what I mean in the following sections.

Let's also clarify the difference between zero trust and zero trust architecture, because you're going to see both terms in the sections that follow. They aren't quite interchangeable terms. Zero trust (ZT) is the strategy and zero trust architecture (ZTA) is the implementation of the ZT strategy.

Zero Trust Principles

The principles of ZT are foundational guidelines that shape how security is designed and enforced in ZT environments. These principles shift security from a perimeter-based model to one based on continuous verification, least privilege, and explicit trust decisions. In its paper titled "Zero Trust Architecture" (Special Publication 800-207), NIST outlines the following tenets (principles) of ZT:

- All data sources and computing services are considered resources.
- All communication is secured regardless of network location.
- Access to individual enterprise resources is granted on a per-session basis.
- Access is determined by dynamic policy—including the observable state of the user, device, service, and context.
- The enterprise monitors and measures the integrity and security posture of all owned and associated assets.
- All resource authentication and authorization is dynamic and strictly enforced before access is allowed.
- The enterprise collects as much information as possible about the current state of assets, network infrastructure, and communications for decision making.

By adhering to these principles, organizations can move beyond implicit trust models and build a security architecture that is resilient, adaptive, and aligned with the realities of modern threats. These NIST tenets serve as a practical and strategic foundation for designing, assessing, and evolving a ZTA across any environment.

Zero Trust Technical Objectives

Let's dive into the technical objectives of ZT. By technical objectives, I mean the security benefits of creating a protective framework, improved user experience, reduced attack surface, reduction in complexity, and other technical benefits.

Protective Framework

ZT establishes a strong protective framework and introduces a new (yet old) approach to cybersecurity. It's all based on the core principle of ZT that no entity (entities are anything, including users and devices), whether inside or outside an organization, should be inherently trusted. Why did I say old? Well, as an example, network access control (NAC) was implemented back in the early 2000s by Cisco to assess the security posture of devices before they would be allowed on the network. Even though it is an "old" technology, NAC can play a role in a mature ZT implementation.

This framework allows organizations to align their security measures with business goals, focusing on the value of their data and specific protection needs. It requires that an organization know what its critical assets are. Traditional security procedures and strategies (we have a firewall!), once effective, are increasingly inadequate in today's threat landscape. Consequently, investments in older cybersecurity techniques and technologies are yielding limited results and insufficient protection.

Relying on traditional approaches and frameworks, such as those based on physical hardware or code signatures (SolarWinds being a significant example), is no longer feasible. With the rise in the number and scale of cyberattacks and the interconnected nature of today's world, implementing more dynamic and comprehensive security strategies like ZT is essential to effectively mitigate modern threats.

Simplified User Experience

ZT enhances security while maintaining a seamless user experience by implementing a consistent access model across the entire environment, including both network and applications, be they internal or cloud resources. This model improves the user experience by using intelligent authentication mechanisms, such as Single Sign-On (SSO), FIM, and MFA, which operate in the background. Every access request is evaluated based on identity, context, and other attributes, such as: Who are you? What is your role? Do you have the right permissions? Is this access request happening at an appropriate time?

If your access request passes muster, you get access to the resource seamlessly for a defined period. This ensures security without constant interruptions, making access to resources smoother and more efficient. As you can probably tell, this improves both user experience and security.

Here are some of the benefits of a simplified user experience:

Eliminates complex nested group structures
    Legacy access control lists (ACLs) and nested groups, which can lead to unexpected results, are removed.

Removes outdated group management layers
    Groups are no longer overseen by decision-makers who may have changed roles or left the company.

Avoids orphaned groups and inconsistent authorization
Groups without current owners and with inconsistent authorization mechanisms are prevented.

Decreases delays in provisioning or deprovisioning
Policy decision points (PDPs) handle access provisioning, deprovisioning, and revocation consistently and in real time. I will discuss both PDPs and policy enforcement points (PEPs) later in this chapter. For now, just know that the PDP makes the access decision based on enhanced knowledge of the identity and device status, and the PEP enforces the decision by blocking or allowing access.

How is this simplified user experience implemented? It often involves a new IAM system that supports ZT capabilities such as dynamic groups, SSO, FIM, and other ZT capabilities.

For example, in a traditional Active Directory (AD) environment, when a user is created, they are added to static groups manually (e.g., managers, corporate users, all users). In contrast, in Azure AD with ZT capabilities, users are dynamically assigned to groups based on an attribute of their account that designates their role. So a user isn't added to a group manually; instead, their role attribute determines their group membership automatically.

For instance, if a user is promoted from manager to director at 2:10 p.m., their access changes dynamically at 2:10 p.m., when their new role is assigned via the role attribute being changed by the administrator. There is no need for the administrator to sift through different groups the user is a member of. More importantly, changing the role attribute updates the user's permissions automatically—not the next day, when they log in again. This is where the "real-time" aspect comes into play. Since their privileges are assessed at every access attempt, they now get access to the resources meant for directors and are automatically removed from access intended for managers.

Real-time authorization checks your access rights each time you request access to ensure it's appropriate, whereas just-in-time authorization grants you temporary access only when needed, such as for performing critical administrative tasks or accessing sensitive classified information, and for a specific duration, and then automatically revokes it.

Reduced Attack Surface

ZTA implements strict access controls, continuous authentication, and least-privilege principles across the entire network and infrastructure. This approach assumes that threats and attackers may already exist within the network and adopts a "never trust, always verify" approach to access and permissions.

The key benefit here is that an attacker's lateral movement (east–west traffic) can be restricted. This can dramatically limit the potential impact of a security breach. For example, if an employee who works in HR is successfully compromised, their network access will be limited to only the HR resources by default. Add behavior analysis to the mix and that will quickly challenge the attacker with step-up authentication (requesting the user enter a new MFA code, for example) and/or restrict the account and the device from accessing other systems. This also aids in incident response, as there are fewer systems that may need to be triaged because of the breach being contained.

Reduced Complexity

Companies are ever expanding their computing footprint to include multicloud implementations, hybrid clouds, and use of edge computing. With a ZT approach, your main goal is to create secure individual resources and users rather than relying on traditional network perimeters.

With ZT, you apply consistent security principles—such as least privilege, strong identity verification, and microsegmentation—regardless of where the resource resides. This means you don't need to build and maintain separate architectures for on-premises and cloud environments. Instead of building and maintaining multiple, perimeter-based security models, you build security around resources and access policies. Of course, organizations still need people knowledgeable about the platforms to secure the resources with platform-specific tools, but when the CSA states ZT reduces complexity, this is what it means.

Continuous Authentication

Unlike traditional models, where authentication is only checked when a user logs in, continuous authentication means that user and device credentials are continuously checked throughout the session through a variety of means. This ensures that access is valid throughout the session, not just at the time of initial logon. Continuous authentication can be performed in many ways, including the following:

User and entity behavior analytics (UEBA)
UEBA (a.k.a. behavioral analysis) monitors user and entity behavior patterns such as the access time versus normal access times, access to applications and data, network activity, and typical usage habits. Any significant deviation from normal behavior can trigger a reauthentication challenge, access denial, or other security measures.

Adaptive authentication
This adjusts the level of authentication based on the perceived risk level. For example, a user accessing sensitive data from a different device may be prompted

for MFA. In fact, you may have seen this on some websites already. Take, for example, an airline site that doesn't recognize your device and makes you answer challenge questions, or a banking site that makes you enter a code texted to your phone.

Contextual authentication
This involves evaluating contextual factors like location, device health, time of day, and network used to continuously verify access permissions based on the current context.

Session monitoring
This is really a subset of UEBA. This monitors user activities within a session to detect and respond to suspicious behaviors in real time, potentially terminating sessions if significant risks are detected.

Device trust
This involves continuously checking the health and compliance status of devices accessing the network and ensuring that devices maintain the required security posture throughout the session.

By continuously verifying the identity and security posture of users, devices, and applications, ZT limits the potential impact of security breaches by limiting lateral movement of attackers. Continuous authentication ensures that if an attacker gains initial access by compromising a user account, even if they use the user's device, they face ongoing barriers to moving laterally within the network, because they will most likely act differently than the user who has been compromised. This leads to a reduced attack surface and enhanced overall security.

Improved Incident Containment and Management

Microsegmentation and continuous authorization for network access reduce the blast radius of a potential breach by limiting an attacker's ability to move from system to system (lateral movement). When a breach occurs, the organization can limit the event's impact through more effective containment and easier eradication and remediation, limiting the scope of the incident. Additionally, the continuous monitoring capabilities in ZTA allow for more effective identification of anomalies and incidents. Incident-related information can be used to update the PDP, enabling dynamic policy definition and enforcement.

Principle of Least Privilege

The principle of least privilege allows people to do what they need to do and nothing more. ZT embraces new technologies to augment this principle, such as UEBA, privileged access management, and identity access governance.

Zero Trust Business Objectives

Beyond the technical benefits of ZT, businesses benefit from reduced risk, improved compliance, and demonstrating a commitment to security for partners and customers. Let's look at these now.

Reduce Risk

We already know that ZT aims to reduce risk by adopting the concept that assumes the network is already breached. This is very different from traditional security models that have invested millions into their perimeter, assuming everything inside the network is trusted. However, with the increasing number and sophistication of attacks and the rise of remote work and cloud computing, this perimeter-centric approach is no longer sufficient. The traditional perimeter isn't dead; rather, ZT moves the perimeter to the resources being protected, be they internal or external.

Improve Compliance

Compliance with regulatory requirements and industry standards is a top concern for executives in regulated sectors such as finance, healthcare, and government. Regulations like GDPR and HIPAA require organizations to implement strong access controls and data protection measures. ZT aids in achieving this.

Let's look at PCI DSS as an example of compliance with standards, since ZT shares some of the same concepts as PCI. In PCI, there's the concept of a cardholder data environment (CDE) that stores and processes credit card data. This area must be strongly protected. PCI assessments will ensure that the CDE network and systems are secured. In ZT, this can be thought of as the *protect surface*. PCI also requires that anything that interacts with the CDE is secured. This is similar to the concept of the *attack surface* in ZT, where any access point with access to the protect surface must be secured as well. I'll cover protect and attack surfaces in greater depth later in this chapter.

Demonstrate Commitment to Cybersecurity

This aspect can be easily dismissed, but it's really important. Adopting ZT requires buy-in from all levels of the organization—mainly executives, because it's not a cheap journey. If the executives buy into ZT, this will naturally implement a culture of security awareness, accountability, and continuous improvement. By embracing ZT principles, organizations demonstrate their commitment to cybersecurity and resilience, which can enhance trust and confidence among customers, partners, and stakeholders.

Core Logical Zero Trust Components

At the heart of a ZT implementation are the PDP and the PEP. The names are indicative of their roles. The PDP determines what access level (if any) a user and device should have to a resource, and the PEP enforces that decision by acting as a gatekeeper or gateway. You may remember these components from Chapter 7. As a reminder, Figure 12-2 shows the NIST 800-207 diagram of the PDP and PEP, as well as policy information points (PIPs).

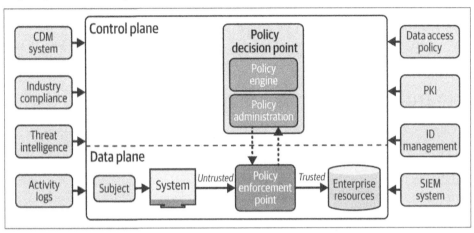

Figure 12-2. Core logical components of ZT

A network will have many PDP systems. Take the AD IAM system as an example. This is a PDP. What about a NAC system? This too is a PDP. Anything that decides whether a user or a device should have access to a resource is a PDP.

The key to the accuracy of decisions made by the PDP is the information it receives from the PIPs. Figure 12-2 also shows some examples of PIPs that are leveraged by the PDP to make better access decisions. (Note that, even though the NIST diagram has the PIP arrows pointing to both the PDP and PEP, you can rest assured that this information is used by the policy engine that is part of the PDP.)

It's important to note that the word *policy* in the ZT world does not necessarily refer to a document, like some kind of static security policy document that is reviewed and approved yearly. In a ZT context, policies are technical documented rules that are enforced (or conditions that must be met for access). An example of a potential documented policy would be: "Employees accessing financial data must authenticate using MFA." From a ZT perspective, this would be enforced with a dynamic policy. This is done by the PDP querying access logs to confirm the user did authenticate with MFA. The PEP protecting the requesting resource enforces this decision by restricting access until the PDP determines the rule has been met.

As the figure shows, the PEP acts as a gateway that protects the resource(s) behind it. The PEP could be an inline network device, or it could be installed on the server itself. Essentially, the flow is as follows:

- The client requests access to the resource.
- The PEP checks with the PDP in real time.
- The PEP accepts or rejects the access request based on the response from the PDP.

Even after initial access, every action repeats the process of the PEP consulting the PDP to accept/reject in real time (decisions can be cached, if desired, for a short period of time; think seconds to address latency) to offer continuous security.

Zero Trust Security Frameworks

In Chapter 7, you learned that there are two primary implementation models in the software-defined perimeter (SDP) and Zero Trust Network Access (ZTNA) frameworks. In both frameworks, a secure tunnel is created between the authorized client and the resource once the user and device are authenticated and authorized as being permitted to access a resource. Although they both do authentication and authorization, and they both create secure tunnels once resource access is approved, there are some differences we need to cover and some additional information for each. Let's start with SDP.

Software-Defined Perimeter

SDP is a security framework developed by the CSA in 2013. Its goal is to create secure, trusted connections (using mTLS) between users and resources by hiding resources from public view and making them accessible only through authenticated and authorized sessions. It's this hiding of resources (called *dark* or *invisible networks*) that really differentiates SDP from ZTNA. If a person or a device is not authorized to access a device, it doesn't even know of the device's existence. It's pretty hard for an attacker to gain unauthorized access to a system they can't even see, right?

In reality, SDP is implemented when protecting very high-value targets; think critical government and financial systems. Companies will likely use the ZTNA framework to protect average, run-of-the-mill internal resources and cloud systems.

Zero Trust Network Access

Like SDP, ZTNA is a security framework that aligns with the principles of ZT, focusing on verifying every access request as though it originates from an open network. SDP's strength and differentiating factor lies in creating dark networks and enforces the use of mTLS. ZTNA, on the other hand, relies on controlling access based on user identity and device security posture.

For data in transit, ZTNA does force TLS, but unlike SDP, mTLS is optional. This isn't meant to imply ZTNA is less secure than SDP. It's just that, because of the complex nature of SDP, it is often used to protect highly sensitive systems, and ZTNA is used to protect general systems. Access is granted based on continuous authentication and authorization processes, as required to uphold ZT principles. As mentioned, ZTNA is often used by a wide range of organizations as part of a ZTA. There are many more vendors that offer ZTNA solutions compared to those offering SDP solutions. These are often cloud-based solutions offered by security vendors as part of a Secure Access Service Edge (SASE) solution.

Zero Trust Pillars

Although there are several ZT documents out there, the CSA leverages the Cybersecurity and Infrastructure Security Agency (CISA) Zero Trust Maturity Model documentation as its reference for both ZT pillars and maturity models. The CISA states that there are a total of five unique pillars of a ZTA and three cross-cutting pillars to protect what it calls Data, Applications, Assets, and Services (DAAS). The five unique pillars of a ZTA are as follows:

Identity
An identity refers to an attribute or a set of attributes that uniquely describes a user or entity, including nonperson entities.

Devices
A device is any asset (including hardware, software, firmware, etc.) that can connect to a network, including servers, desktop and laptop machines, printers, mobile phones, IoT devices, networking equipment, and more.

Networks
A network is an open communications medium such as internal networks, wireless networks, and the internet as well as other potential channels such as cellular and application-level channels used to transport messages.

Applications and Workloads
Applications and workloads include systems, computer programs, and services that execute on premises, on mobile devices, and in cloud environments.

Data
Data includes all structured and unstructured files and fragments that reside or have resided in systems, devices, networks, applications, databases, infrastructure, and backups (including on-premises and virtual environments) as well as the associated metadata.

I have spoken with numerous government agencies and financial institutions, and they find the Data pillar is the hardest to address. Discovering and classifying data in multiple locations is a substantial challenge for large organizations. So don't find yourself falling into the trap of spending time and money perfecting the "easy" pillars (like Identity, for example) while ignoring the challenging ones. You need to work on all the pillars to achieve effective ZTA.

The three cross-cutting aspects of a ZTA are underlying capabilities that support these pillars. Quite simply, without these, you can't implement a ZTA. They are as follows:

Visibility and Analytics
Visibility refers to the observable artifacts that result from the characteristics of and events within enterprise-wide environments. The focus on cyber-related data analysis can help inform policy decisions, facilitate response activities, and build a risk profile to develop proactive security measures before an incident occurs.

Automation and Orchestration
ZT makes full use of automated tools and workflows that support security response functions across products and services while maintaining oversight, security, and interaction of the development process for such functions, products, and services.

Governance
Governance refers to the definition and associated enforcement of cybersecurity policies, procedures, and processes, within and across pillars, to manage an enterprise and mitigate security risks in support of ZT principles and fulfillment of requirements.

Zero Trust Maturity Model Levels

In the CISA Maturity Model document, there are four levels of maturity for each pillar. Let's look at each level, along with some examples:

Traditional
The Traditional maturity level represents the starting point for organizations on their ZT journey. At this stage, security practices are typically perimeter focused, with implicit trust in internal network traffic.
Authentication capability example: Organization authenticates identity using either passwords or MFA with static access for entity identity.

Initial
> Organizations adopt foundational ZT principles and technologies in the Initial maturity level to enhance their security posture.
> Authentication capability example: Organization authenticates identity using MFA, which may include passwords as one factor and requires validation of multiple entity attributes (e.g., locale or activity).

Advanced
> At the Advanced maturity level, organizations have significantly progressed in implementing ZT practices and technologies across multiple domains.
> Authentication capability example: Organization begins to authenticate all identity using phishing-resistant MFA and attributes, including initial implementation of passwordless MFA via FIDO2 or PIV.

Optimal
> The Optimal maturity level represents the highest level of ZT maturity, where organizations have fully integrated ZT principles into their security strategy and operations.
> Authentication capability example: Organization continuously validates identity with phishing-resistant MFA, not just when access is initially granted.

> Personal Identity Verification (PIV) is a US government smart-card–based authentication mechanism.

As you can likely tell, the cost and effort associated with each level increase, sometimes dramatically. For example, at the Optimal level, you are implementing a means to analyze user behavior. These tools do exist, but is the technology mature enough for your organization currently?

In reality, attempting to achieve the Optimal level for all pillars in the maturity model is likely an unrealistic goal for your organization. Like many things in life, you must pick your battles. ZT is likely to be a yearslong journey.

You don't need to memorize all the details for every level of every pillar for the CCSK exam. Your goal is to remember there is a well-regarded maturity model that contains eight pillars (five functional areas and three cross-cutting ones), each with defined levels of maturity. For a much deeper view of the CISA maturity model, consult the latest version of the document from the CISA website directly.

Zero Trust Design and Implementation

The CISA maturity model paints part of the picture what I like to refer to as the macro (big-picture) view. When considering the tactical aspects of adopting ZT, there are four key design principles for building a resilient architecture, and a repeatable, five-step implementation process for interactive and incremental execution to secure organizational assets with risk-based prioritization. This is the micro view of ZT. Focus on protecting resources one at a time. Start with simple systems (low-hanging fruit) to get some quick wins and demonstrate traction to the business owners paying for the ZT initiative. Then, once you get your footing, you can focus on the critical systems.

Here are the four ZT design principles:

Focus on business outcomes
    Understand how ZT aligns with and supports the organization's primary business goals. This is a key step, as technology serves the business, not vice versa.

Design from the inside out
    Build a security strategy that focuses on protecting the organization's most critical assets—whether internal or cloud based—before expanding security measures across the entire environment. This doesn't contradict my previous statement about starting small. Protecting your critical assets is the goal. You may just decide to start small and then move on to larger systems.

Determine who or what needs access
    Identify which users and devices require access to specific resources.

Inspect and log key traffic
    Aim to monitor and record critical activity for potential threats as a targeted approach.

Now that you understand the general principles at work, let's talk about how to implement them. I discuss each of the five steps in detail in the following sections.

Step 1: Define the Protect Surface

The protect surface refers to the narrowly defined set of critical assets that require ZT protections. The protect surface focuses on what truly matters to the business. There are four key steps in defining the protect surface:

1. Begin by identifying and evaluating the critical business information systems, which include the DAAS elements mentioned earlier. This step involves cataloging these components and understanding their role within the organization.

2. Assess the business risk level of each DAAS element based on factors like data sensitivity, compliance requirements, and business impact in case of a breach. This classification will help prioritize which systems need immediate ZT protections.
3. Evaluate the current security posture and maturity of each identified system. This includes understanding existing controls and vulnerabilities and how these systems are currently secured.
4. Use the gathered information to prioritize the implementation of ZT measures based on the risk and maturity levels of the DAAS elements.

Step 2: Map the Transaction Flows

Once critical assets have been identified as part of the protect surface, the next step is to map the transaction flows associated with those assets. This involves identifying and documenting how data moves between users, devices, applications, and services when interacting with each protected resource. This step can be extremely challenging if you are trying to map transaction flows for legacy systems that are poorly documented.

Mapping transaction flows provides a clear understanding of who or what is accessing the protect surface, how they access it, and what dependencies exist. Mapping involves the following steps:

1. Map the flow of data, applications, and interactions both within the internal network and between external entities. This mapping should include all data exchanges, user interactions, and system communications.
2. Assess the sensitivity and importance of each flow, considering the type of data being transmitted and the potential impact of unauthorized access or data breaches.
3. Use this mapping to identify the attack surface—the points where unauthorized access could occur. Understanding this helps in designing the ZTA by pinpointing where security controls need to be applied.
4. Identify dependencies between systems and how they interact with the protect surface. This will help in ensuring that all relevant pathways are secured.

Step 3: Build a Zero Trust Architecture

With critical assets identified and transaction flows mapped, the next phase is to design and implement the ZTA itself. This step involves deploying the necessary security infrastructure, controls, and integrations to protect the defined protect surface. Following are the steps to construct a resilient and scalable ZTA:

1. Develop the necessary infrastructure, capabilities, and controls to protect the identified protect surface. This may include microsegmentation, microperimeters, encryption, access control mechanisms, IAM, and continuous monitoring tools.
2. Apply security layers such as firewalls, IdPs, MFA, and NACs to enforce ZT principles.
3. Ensure that the ZTA integrates seamlessly with existing IT infrastructure, including on-premises systems, cloud services, and hybrid environments.
4. Where possible, implement automation and orchestration to manage and enforce security policies, monitor compliance, and respond to security incidents in real time.

Step 4: Create a Zero Trust Policy

After designing and deploying the foundational architecture, the next step is to define and enforce access policies that reflect the ZT principles we have covered in this chapter. The goal of creating this technical policy is to establish a framework that reflects business objectives and is enforceable, transparent, and adaptable to evolving threats and business needs:

- Develop access control policies based on the principle of least privilege, ensuring that users and devices only have access to the resources they need for their role. These policies should be dynamic and context aware.
- Establish enforcement points, such as PDPs and PEPs, to ensure that access policies are applied consistently across the network.
- Create detailed guidelines and rules for network, system, and data access. Ensure that these are documented and communicated clearly to all stakeholders.
- Ensure that policies align with regulatory requirements and organizational governance standards.

Step 5: Monitor and Maintain the Environment

Now that the ZTA is deployed and access policies are in place, the final step is to continuously monitor and maintain the environment to ensure its long-term effectiveness. This phase involves real-time monitoring for anomalies and threats, maintaining a strong security posture, preparing for incident response and forensic analysis, and regularly reviewing and refining policies. The goal is to create a resilient security framework that evolves to address new threats and continues to align with business objectives:

- Implement continuous monitoring of the network and systems to detect anomalies, suspicious activities, and potential breaches. Use tools like SIEM systems, UBA/UEBA, and threat intelligence platforms.
- Regularly assess and update the security posture based on new threats, vulnerabilities, and changes in the IT environment. This includes adjusting access policies, updating software, and applying patches.
- Develop and maintain an incident response plan to quickly address security breaches. Regularly review and analyze security incidents to improve the ZTA.
- Periodically review the ZT implementation, policies, and controls to ensure that they remain effective and aligned with business goals. Incorporate feedback and lessons learned to continually refine the security posture.

These elements are vital in shaping and executing an effective ZT security strategy that aligns with an organization's objectives and risks.

Zero Trust and Cloud Security

Table 12-1 shows how CCSK domains map to the practices associated with implementation of a ZTA.

Table 12-1. Mapping CCSK domains to ZT

CCSK security domain	ZT practices
Organizational Management	Implementing ZT as an enterprise security and connectivity strategy; best implemented with a ZT culture
Identity and Access Management	Implementing continuous, phishing-resistant MFA with context-based authorization of users, devices, and access requests
Security Monitoring	Monitoring everything; presuming breaches, detecting suspicious activity early, and dynamically adjusting access
Network	Implementing microsegmentation, a ZT network architecture, and SDP
Workload	Verifying ZT device and workload security and integrity, monitoring malware and data exfiltration with ZT workload access controls
Application	Conducting fine-grained, least-privilege access authorization with separation of duties; limiting user permissions to the minimum required data and functionality
Data	Classifying, protecting, and monitoring data at rest, in transit, and in use with strict ZT data access controls

Artificial Intelligence

The second "related technology" the CSA lists as part of its CCSK material is AI. As mentioned at the beginning of this chapter, AI is not dependent on a cloud service, but there is a substantial leveraging of cloud services for both AI as a service (AIaaS) and AI platforms leveraged by organizations building their own AI systems. While AI services are commonly deployed in the cloud, on-premises hosting options are always possible for specific use cases. From a security perspective, the major issue is that AI plays a dual role in cloud security in that it can be used as a tool by both the attacker and the defender.

For the defender, it can be used to strengthen security measures by detecting threats and, more importantly, automating responses, but it is also being used by attackers. AI-driven algorithms can identify vulnerabilities, develop exploits, and conduct advanced attacks, underscoring the need to integrate AI into security tools as quickly as possible.

Characteristics of AI Workloads

Currently, the most popular AI technologies are based on neural networks, which are inspired by the structure and functioning of the human brain. These networks can require hundreds of gigabytes of data or more, depending on their complexity. AI workloads are generally divided into two categories: training and inference. Training involves feeding the network massive amounts of data and using substantial computational resources—often costing millions of dollars—to develop models that can then be used for inference. In essence, training builds the models, while inference applies them to new data to make predictions or decisions.

Models created through training are used for tasks such as recognizing and classifying images and sounds, but they can also be generative, capable of creating new images, sounds, and text. A particularly popular and advanced class of models is large language models (LLMs), which encode language and world knowledge. These are considered foundational models because they can be adapted to a wide variety of tasks, ranging from natural language processing to complex problem-solving.

How AI Intersects with Cloud Security

AI workloads are workloads like any other, although often bigger. They also ingest and store large amounts of data, which has its own security implications. Furthermore, they can be consumed as services, as applications, or as components of applications. AI workloads related to cloud security can be categorized into four areas, which I'll discuss in the following sections.

AI as a service for consumption (full SaaS)

This model is likely what the average person thinks of when they hear "AI" today. In this model, the provider offers AI as a complete, ready-to-use service. Offerings like chatbots (e.g., ChatGPT, Claude) allow organizations to leverage AI capabilities without the need to build, train, or manage their own models. This approach is ideal for organizations that want to quickly adopt AI solutions without requiring deep technical expertise or significant investment in infrastructure and data science resources.

Security control recommendations for this model include:

- Only allow approved services.
- Upgrade for data privacy.
- Only allow approved data.
- Track prompts and results.

AI as a service (PaaS/foundation model hosting)

In this model, the cloud provider offers the underlying infrastructure, tools, and pre-trained foundation models to host and run AI applications, but the customer is responsible for developing, fine-tuning, and deploying their own models and applications. AWS Bedrock is an example of this approach—it provides access to foundation models and a hosting environment, allowing customers to build their own solutions on top of these models. This model offers organizations more control, flexibility, and customization compared to full SaaS solutions, as they can tailor the AI models and applications to better meet their specific needs.

Security control recommendations for this model include:

- Secure training data.
- Secure the application's integration.
- Secure the deployment environment.
- Secure users and access.
- Defend against adversarial attacks (e.g., injection, jailbreak).

Cloud as workload host for AI (bring your own model)

Since we've addressed SaaS and PaaS models, you can think of this model as an IaaS scenario. In this scenario, organizations develop their own AI models from scratch or deploy off-the-shelf models (code) using the cloud solely as the hosting environment. They are responsible for the entire AI lifecycle, including data preparation, model training, deployment, and ongoing management.

In this model, the cloud provides the raw compute resources, such as processing power, storage, and networking, without offering additional AI-specific services. This approach offers the greatest flexibility and customization but requires significant in-house AI expertise and resources. It also carries the same responsibilities and complexities as building and managing an in-house application.

As for security controls, I'm sure you imagine that, because this model is likely run in IaaS, the customer has the most responsibility to secure the workloads. All the security controls we have covered in the book (compute, network, data, IAM, etc.) apply for protecting AI systems running in an IaaS service model.

AI-enhanced security tools

In addition to hosting options, AI is increasingly being integrated into various cloud security products to enhance their intelligence and effectiveness. Examples include AI-powered threat detection, smart access control, and automated policy enforcement. As AI technology continues to evolve, it is expected to further improve and augment traditional security solutions such as SIEM, EDR, and DLP, as well as be the foundation for yet unknown technologies.

Summary

For this chapter, you should be comfortable with the following:

- Know the technical objectives of ZT.
- Know the business objectives of ZT.
- Remember the pillars of the CISA Zero Trust Maturity Model.
- Know how ZT practices map to CSA CCSK security domains.
- Remember the categories of AI workloads and security recommendations for each.
- Know how AI enhances security tools.

This concludes all the material (and more) you will need to not only pass the CCSK exam, but also hopefully make you a well-rounded cloud security professional. In the final chapter, we will cover some exam preparation tips and how to use AI as a study tool.

CHAPTER 13
Preparing for Your CCSK Exam

Victorious warriors win first and then go to war.
—Sun Tzu

Congratulations! Now that we have covered the content of the CCSK v5 exam, let's focus on the test itself. This chapter reviews key logistics and shares test-taking tips that have helped many of my former students succeed. I also talk about generative AI as an incredible study tool, specifically ChatGPT.

Studying for the CCSK Exam

This book has covered everything from the CCSK study guide, and more. I believe the knowledge provided in this book will prepare you to take the CCSK exam. That said, there are two other documents that you will need for your exam. Both documents are in the CCSK prep kit that is available free of charge on the CSA website, but you do need to create a free account on the website to access them:

- The exam is based on the "Certificate of Cloud Security Knowledge Official Study Guide." I strongly suggest you have this PDF document open on a second monitor during your exam.
- "Cloud Security Alliance Guidance for Critical Areas of Focus in Cloud Computing v5" is a larger version of the study guide that goes well beyond the exam. Have this document open as well, just as a backup. You shouldn't get any questions that are answered only in this document.

> ### From the Trenches: A Study Guide Is Born
>
> To explain why I'm listing both documents, let me give you a bit of background on them. Initially, the CSA developed the v5 guidance document as it did for the previous version (v4). Once it was complete, the CSA determined that it went too deep into many subjects for the target audience of CCSK certification (someone with two years of IT experience).
>
> To address this, the CSA created a small team (which I was part of) to identify the core material that a cloud security professional needs in order to work with security in a cloud environment. This resulted in the creation of the CCSK study guide. All exam questions are based on the study guide, not the guidance. Here's a quotation from the CCSK FAQ:
>
>> The CCSK Study Guide is a more condensed version of the Security Guidance v5 and only includes the information covered in the exam. The Security Guidance for Critical Areas of Focus in Cloud Computing v5 is a more comprehensive, deep dive into the 12 domains of the CCSK v5 and provides readers with a greater body of knowledge on each of those topics. It is not required to pass the CCSK v5 exam.
>
> The bottom line is that the guidance is great for reference if you want to take a deeper dive into particular subjects after you pass your exam.

Exam Details

The CCSK v5 exam consists of 60 multiple-choice questions with a time limit of 120 minutes. It is an open-book exam that is done online from wherever you want, whenever you want. You do not need to take the exam at a test center, nor do you have to schedule your test in advance. The score required to pass the exam is 80%. This means you need to correctly answer 48 out of 60 questions to pass the exam.

Your exam will be generated based on a set number of questions drawn from a larger pool of questions. See Figure 13-1 for the domain weightings from the CCSK FAQ available from the CSA.

Domains	# of Questions
1. Cloud Computing Concepts & Architectures	5
2. Cloud Governance	5
3. Risk, Audit & Compliance	5
4. Organization Management	5
5. Identity & Access Management	4
6. Security Monitoring	4
7. Infrastructure & Networking	6
8. Cloud Workload Security	7
9. Data Security	5
10. Application Security	6
11. Incident Response & Resilience	5
12. Related Technologies & Strategies	3

Figure 13-1. CCSK domain weightings

Signing Up for the CCSK Exam

To take the CCSK v5 exam, you'll need to sign in to your account and register for the exam on the CSA website. The fee for the exam at the time of writing is $445 US. This will grant you an exam token for the CCSK exam. This token is also good for two test attempts. If you don't pass the first time, the second attempt is automatically available. Although there is no mandatory wait time between taking exams, I discourage you from immediately taking the exam a second time.

At the end of the exam, you will immediately be told your score and how you did in each domain. You won't know which questions you got right or wrong, but you will know how you did in each domain (e.g., "Domain 10: 6/6"). Know your strengths and work on your weaknesses. If you struggled with three domains but got 100% on the others, then focus your studying on the three domains and just do a refresher of the other domains. I'll cover how to do this shortly.

Exam Tips

Following are my top exam tips that I share with students at the end of every CCSK training session. These come from years of experience. I strongly suggest you follow these when taking your CCSK exam:

- As with all multiple-choice exams, be certain to go through a process of elimination before choosing what you believe is the correct answer. You may find there is only one possible correct answer because all other possible choices are obviously wrong.

- You can mark questions and return to them if needed. Refrain from changing answers; trust your gut!
- You have lots of time (two hours) to answer the 60 questions. You'll have to answer some easy questions quickly to give yourself time to research the tougher questions. Time management is very important with this exam.
- Since the test is open book, you can select keywords from a question or from the potential answers to find the answer. It is unlikely that you will find exact phrases in the study guide.
- Although the exam is based on the study guide, make sure you have both the study guide and the guidance open so that you can search both if required. You may find the guidance has a clearer answer to the question, whereas the study guide makes reference to the subject but doesn't contain the keywords the guidance has.
- You may encounter answers to questions that are not directly addressed in either reference document. In this case, it's likely not the correct answer.
- You have two attempts to pass the test. This isn't heart surgery. Nobody's going to die if you don't pass the test. Don't forget to breathe. Tests can be anxiety inducing. Back to tip 3, you have more than enough time to relax, focus, and pause if needed.
- Don't overthink a question, or invent a new question in your mind because the wording is weird. Weird wording shouldn't happen often, but it can. Take the question at face value, not at what you think the question means. If you see a question that is poorly worded, jot down the question number and you'll have an opportunity to speak your mind at the end of the exam via a feedback form.
- Things change quickly in IT, especially the cloud. If the CSA guidance says one thing and you know it changed in real life very recently, go with the official CSA answer. The exam owner just hasn't yet removed questions related to the subject.
- The CSA only cares that you know what it has to say on a subject. Do not open Google, ChatGPT, or other GenAI products (like CSA's Orb, for example) to answer questions. There's nothing stopping you from doing so, but you risk going down a rabbit hole and wasting a lot of time chasing dead ends or having an AI hallucination make you answer a question incorrectly.
- Absolutes are rarely correct. Potential answers that give a specified duration or guarantee of something are often wrong, especially in a field like cloud security! Durations, or how often something should be done, usually come down to the risk associated with the asset.

Using ChatGPT as a Study Tool

Although the CSA does offer its own chatbot, called Orb, it says it is trained on both the study guide and the guidance documents. That said, I want to share with you a couple of tricks I have learned using ChatGPT to prepare for the CCSK exam.

As a bonus, this is a lifelong skill that is very much in demand by employers. I recently read a story that stated that nearly 25% of IT job postings included the ability to use tools like ChatGPT. I see no reason why this won't increase in the future. Knowledge + prompt engineering = success both today and in the future.

Before we start discussing ChatGPT, I want to mention that there is a substantial difference between the free and paid versions of ChatGPT. You'll want to sign up for the paid version for your exam preparation. The model used in the paid version is better, the limits are higher, file uploads are allowed, and other benefits with the paid version merit subscribing to the $20/month (US) package. Everything I'm going to cover regarding exam preparation with ChatGPT is based on the paid ChatGPT Plus version.

About Generative AI Large Language Models

Before getting into using ChatGPT or other GenAI tools, there are two key elements you need to understand about the inner workings of GenAI and how it works at a high level. In the following sections, I explain this tool in more detail and why prompt engineering is important when working with it to prepare for your exam.

Inference

Inference in ChatGPT refers to its ability to analyze input, recognize patterns, and generate meaningful responses based on contextual understanding. Unlike simple keyword-based retrieval systems, ChatGPT uses deep learning models to infer intent, relationships between concepts, and logical connections within a conversation. This allows it to provide coherent answers, summarize complex topics, and even predict what information might be useful next. Effective inference is crucial when handling ambiguous queries, where ChatGPT must interpret missing details, draw logical conclusions, and adapt responses dynamically. For example, if a user asks, "What are the risks of multicloud?" ChatGPT can infer that the question pertains to cloud security and may provide insights on compliance challenges, inconsistent security policies, and vendor lock-in risks—even if those specific terms were not explicitly mentioned. By refining prompts and guiding the conversation, users can harness inference more effectively to obtain precise, relevant, and insightful responses tailored to their needs.

Training

Training in ChatGPT involves a multistage process in which the model learns from vast datasets to generate humanlike responses. It is initially trained using supervised learning, where it analyzes large volumes of text from books, articles, and online sources to understand grammar, context, and knowledge across various domains. This is followed by reinforcement learning with human feedback (RLHF), where human trainers fine-tune the model by ranking its responses to improve accuracy, coherence, and relevance. Unlike traditional rule-based systems, ChatGPT does not store direct knowledge but instead predicts the most probable next words based on input and learned patterns. Continuous training updates help refine its reasoning, reduce biases, and improve contextual understanding.

Tokens

A token in GenAI is roughly equal to four English language characters. This includes spaces and punctuation. This is a rough average, as there are all kinds of outliers (like a % or ?) that may be a token on their own. But the main takeaway here is that the more concise your prompts are, the fewer tokens are consumed. Skip the pleasantries. If you want to know who the CEO of Microsoft is, ask it directly: "who is Microsoft CEO". You'll get the same response as if you wrote "can you please tell me who the CEO of Microsoft is?" Through inference, the system knows both prompts mean the same thing: who is the CEO of Microsoft? The big difference is in token usage. The first example is 4 tokens; the latter is 12. This is important for the next topic: context windows.

Context windows

The context window is simply a maximum of what ChatGPT (and other GenAI tools) can remember. In the case of the free version, it can remember about 3,000 words (or about five to eight pages). The Plus version has a context window of approximately 100,000 words, or roughly 300 pages of text. It is this memory that allows you to continue a conversation without repeating the original subject.

Using the previous Microsoft CEO example, if you want to know where he was born, you can just follow up your question by asking "where was he born" instead of having to repeat yourself by asking "where was the CEO of Microsoft born". The bigger the context window, the more questions on the original subject you can ask.

I have seen that ChatGPT Plus can get confused when you ask it to work with long documents that are within the context window size. In my experience, the less data you upload to it, the better your results will be. For example, you may get better results on incident response if you just send it relevant documentation on the subject via a copy and paste of relevant text, rather than uploading the entire study guide and asking it questions about incident response. I don't think this will impact your exam preparation, but it's a good thing to remember when working with ChatGPT in other situations.

The Importance of Projects

The Plus version of ChatGPT allows for the creation of projects. When you use a project, it will remember files that are uploaded. More importantly, it will also remember the format of output that you want based on previous prompts (to a degree).

For your exam preparation, you want to ensure that you create a project. If you have questions about anything outside of your exam preparation, ask it in a different chat so that you don't pollute the memory ChatGPT stores about your conversations that are exam related.

I mentioned that projects will remember conversations in a project. This is true, but to a degree. I have found that most of the time, if you ask it to create output in a certain format, it will remember the desired output, but every so often, it may still change a bit from a project that you started several days earlier. I don't think this will impact you for exam preparation purposes, but if you are relying on a certain output format, you may find yourself having to repeat the exact same prompt you used at the beginning of the project—a friendly reminder, if you will.

Uploading Files

To generate questions and other study tools for the CCSK v5 exam, you're going to want to upload the CSA study guide PDF to ChatGPT. Stick with the study guide so that the AI doesn't ask questions on subjects that are in the guidance document that are irrelevant for the exam. Start a new chat to clear any memory it may have of previous conversations, and upload the whole study guide PDF. It will be able to understand the domains in the document. I tried to be cute and generated a PDF for domain 11 by printing it to a file. I think the system couldn't properly read the file and it defaulted to the v4 guidance it was trained on, even though it said it was using the document I uploaded. Remember what I was saying about hallucinations? This is a perfect example, and it took me about an hour to figure out what was going on.

Downloading Files

ChatGPT can also create files in a variety of formats (e.g., PDF, PPT, CSV) that you can download. Simply add to your prompt that you want it in a certain file type and it will generate a link for you to download the file. Please note that your download file is ephemeral. I'm not sure exactly what the timeout is, but you should download it right away.

Introduction to Prompt Engineering

Good prompt engineering is a crucial skill for effectively leveraging ChatGPT to prepare for your exam, as the quality of responses depends heavily on how questions and instructions are created. Unlike a simple search engine that everyone knows how to use, ChatGPT is highly dependent on how you prompt it for your needs. Well-crafted prompts deliver accurate, relevant, and insightful answers, making interactions more productive and tailored to individual learning or problem-solving needs.

The trick to success with GenAI products like ChatGPT is to imagine you are speaking with a 12-year-old genius who has a very short attention span and takes everything you say literally. This person also has a huge ego and will never say they don't know something. Instead of saying "I don't know," they will make up a best guess (based on inference) but will say it with such authority that you believe it. In GenAI, this is called a *hallucination*.

Creating good prompts requires you to keep in mind that the system doesn't think or know information. It does a great job assuming what you want based on inference, but to make the most of it you need to understand that the more direct the questions and the more direct the information you want to work with, the better the responses will be. Remember the KISS principle: Keep It Simple, Stupid. Tell the system what you want. Again, don't ask it politely. Rather than appreciating your manners, it just puts empty words into a prompt that may confuse the system.

Unlike a traditional search engine, ChatGPT can work with PDFs and many more file types. By uploading the CCSK study guide and basing prompts on that document, you ensure that you are working with what the CSA has to say about cloud security, not some random website that was used to train the LLM. This is where you can benefit from asking it for references to the documents you upload. When you upload a document, that will be used as its primary source of information in that specific chat session or project.

ChatGPT can remember your previous questions and commands, but this is limited to individual chats, for the most part. As a best practice, before you start your CCSK exam preparation, you should start a new project to begin with, and upload the CCSK study guide to start with a clean slate. Only ask CCSK exam prep–related questions in this session. If you want to ask a completely unrelated question on a different topic, you should open a new chat session, then return to your exam prep project. Of note, document uploads only work in a single chat, and the documents will have to be uploaded again if you leave the chat session. If you use a project, it remembers the document—or at least it says it does.

One of the key advantages of prompt engineering is its ability to guide ChatGPT in delivering structured, detailed, and nuanced explanations. For example, asking "Explain zero trust in cloud security" may yield a general overview, but refining it to

"Explain zero trust in cloud security with an example of microsegmentation implementation" results in a more specific and actionable response. This ability to refine and iterate on prompts enables users to dive deeper into complex topics and obtain information that aligns precisely with their needs.

To make the most of ChatGPT (or any generative AI LLM product), proper prompt engineering is needed. This also applies to using these products to make the most of exam preparation. A generic request like "Give me CCSK practice questions" might produce a broad set of questions, but a more precise request, "Generate five expert-level multiple-choice questions on cloud identity and access management based on the attached document, with detailed explanations for each correct answer", yields a much more valuable study resource. Of course, the document referenced would be the CCSK study guide.

Furthermore, iterative refinement of prompts helps uncover deeper insights. The ability to improve prompts enables a better output that adapts to different levels of expertise and areas of focus.

Ultimately, mastering prompt engineering is essential to unlocking ChatGPT's full potential. By learning how to craft precise, context-aware, and goal-oriented prompts, you can transform your interactions from simple question-answer exchanges into powerful learning and problem-solving sessions. Whether for exam preparation, technical research, or brainstorming, the right prompts ensure that ChatGPT becomes a go-to tool for knowledge enhancement and skill development.

Components of a Good Prompt

A well-structured prompt significantly improves the quality and relevance of ChatGPT's responses. A good prompt should include the following key components.

Clarity and specificity

The prompt should be clear and unambiguous. Avoid vague language, and be as precise as possible.

> Example (Vague): "Tell me about cloud security."
>
> Example (Clear): "Explain the shared responsibility model in cloud security with an example of IaaS."

Context

Providing relevant background information helps ChatGPT tailor responses to your needs.

> Example: "I am preparing for the CCSP exam. Explain cloud governance principles as they relate to risk management."

Desired format

Specify the structure or format you want the response in, such as bullet points, a step-by-step guide, a summary, or a detailed explanation.

> Example: "List the top 5 cloud security threats and provide a one-sentence description for each."

Role or perspective

Asking ChatGPT to take on a specific role can improve responses.

> Example: "Act as a cybersecurity consultant and explain how a financial company can implement zero trust in a multicloud environment."

Constraints and parameters

Define scope, word limits, or focus areas to make responses more precise.

> Example: "Summarize GDPR's impact on cloud service providers in less than 100 words."

Examples for guidance

If applicable, providing an example can help refine the response.

> Example: "Explain infrastructure as code (IaC) using a real-world example, like Terraform or AWS CloudFormation."

Iterative refinement

This is a big one. If the response isn't perfect, refining the prompt with additional details or follow-up questions can yield better results. You don't need to issue the same prompt again. Just tell it what you also want as part of its response.

> Example (Refinement): "Expand on your last response by adding challenges companies face when implementing zero trust in cloud environments."

Asking ChatGPT for a prompt

After iterating through a series of prompts and getting the answer in the format and level of detail you want, ask ChatGPT for the prompt it used. Save this prompt for future use.

Example: My initial prompt was "I want you to act as an exam writer. Generate 5 interactive, expert-level, multiple-choice exam questions based on domain 11 of the attached PDF document. Give detailed answers for why answers are correct or incorrect."

The results here are OK, but I had some issues. It wasn't interactive. Some of the answers came back with the correct answer in bold when being presented. It also assigned answer A as the correct answer. The great news is that you can ask what it inferred from your prompt!

Here's ChatGPT's inference of my prompt:

> Act as a professional exam writer specializing in cloud security certification exams. Based on the CCSK v5 Study Guide, Domain 11: Incident Response & Resilience, create 5 interactive expert-level multiple-choice questions. Each question should:
>
> Be complex enough for experienced cloud security professionals
>
> Include real-world cloud-specific scenarios
>
> Have four answer choices (A, B, C, D) with only one correct answer
>
> Provide a detailed explanation of why the correct answer is right and why the incorrect answers are wrong
>
> Address different aspects of incident response, such as classification, detection, containment, forensic analysis, and resilience best practices

Notice what it's doing? It's using the following structure:

<Role it plays> <Subject> <Action> <Details>

I can take this prompt and modify it as I please. Once I get a great prompt, I'll save it in my notes so that I can repeat the same questions, alter the domain, or do whatever I want.

Creating Study Tools

The rest of this chapter focuses on using ChatGPT to create study tools you can use to prepare for an exam.

Generating Pretest Questions

As you just read in the previous section, you can generate pretest questions for your CCSK exam studies. We just covered prompt engineering and an example prompt to generate test questions. Following are some prompts to get you started with generating different types of questions.

Multiple-choice question prompt

One note before I get to the specific prompt you can use to generate pretest questions: make sure you state you want expert-level questions. These will properly prepare you for the level of difficulty you should expect in the real CCSK exam.

> Act as a professional exam writer specializing in cloud security certification exams. Based on the CCSK v5 Study Guide, Domain 11, create five non-scenario-based multiple-choice questions that meet the following criteria:
>
> Designed for cloud security professionals with at least 2 years of experience
>
> Each question has four answer choices (A, B, C, D) with only one correct answer
>
> Randomize correct answers across A, B, C, and D to avoid patterns
>
> Provide a detailed explanation of why the correct answer is right and why the incorrect answers are wrong
>
> Avoid scenario-based wording—focus on conceptual or technical knowledge questions

Adjust as necessary by changing the domain and the number of questions. You don't need to alter the prompt; you can do this by just telling it to change domains and the number of questions (e.g., "repeat using 3 questions from domain 4").

Unlike the real exam, you can contest a question and answer. While testing this prompt, I came across a hallucination. I asked it for the reference section of the document and then told it there was no reference to what it said. It corrected itself and reposed the question with the correct answer.

If you want to really enhance your studies, adjust the prompt to include the reference section as part of the answer! This way, you can combine the fun of taking a pretest with the study material for reinforcement.

Scenario-based multiple-choice question prompt

Generating real-world scenario questions can greatly assist with reinforcing your understanding and improving retention. I should note here that although the CCSK exam questions will be more direct than a scenario-based question, scenario-based questions are an excellent study tool as they can be more nuanced than a short and direct multiple-choice question. Maximize your exam preparation by taking the time to understand the rationale for both the correct and incorrect answers.

> Using the attached document, act as a CCSK version 5 exam proctor. Create 5 expert level scenario-based questions for domain 3: cloud risk management. Provide feedback for both correct and incorrect answers. Ensure there is only 1 correct answer. Wait for answer before proceeding to next question

Creating Flashcards

I'm not a big flashcard user myself, but they are very popular and very easy to create. You simply prompt "make flashcards for domain 11 of the document I uploaded". What is interesting is that you can generate these in different formats, including your own HTML page to create interactive flashcards you can use locally. You can preview and use the results within ChatGPT by clicking Preview once the code is generated.

Or you can save the HTML code itself, but the cards themselves won't change. Figure 13-2 is the result of previewing the code in ChatGPT.

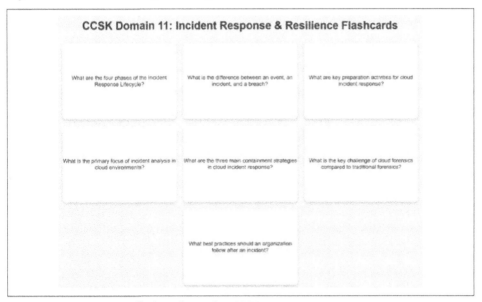

Figure 13-2. Interactive flashcards in ChatGPT

Here is the prompt according to ChatGPT:

> Act as a web developer specializing in interactive learning tools. Create an interactive HTML flashcard set that allows users to click each card to flip it and reveal the answer. The flashcards should be based on CCSK Domain 11: Incident Response & Resilience from the CCSK v5 Study Guide. The file should include:
>
> A modern, user-friendly design with clean formatting.
>
> A set of at least 7 flashcards, each containing:
>
> A front side (question or concept).
>
> A back side (detailed answer or explanation).
>
> A flip animation effect when users click a card.
>
> Mobile responsiveness, ensuring cards display well on all screen sizes.
>
> Minimal JavaScript to toggle the flip effect for usability.
>
> CSS styling for a professional appearance (e.g., shadow effects, rounded corners).
>
> No external dependencies, so the file runs standalone in a browser without additional libraries.
>
> Ensure that the flashcards cover key concepts such as: the cloud incident response lifecycle, forensic challenges in cloud security, containment strategies, and post-incident best practices.

Playing Games

As a kid, I loved a series of books called *Choose Your Own Adventure* (CYOA). When you started the book on page 1, it would lay out a scenario and then would present options to choose from. You could choose which path you wanted to take. Based on your response, it would send you to a certain page of the book that would tell you the results of your decision.

I was very excited when I experimented with ChatGPT to re-create this type of learning tool. Not only does it know of these books, but it can even let me choose my own adventure based on any domain or subject of the course material. Let's try a prompt to create an incident response based on domain 11.

I initially used the following prompt:

> I want to play a Choose Your Own Adventure-style game based on domain 11 of the CCSK study guide I uploaded. Each step should have multiple options, including a bad idea that leads to a negative outcome, and the results should unfold naturally without explicitly stating if the outcome is positive, neutral, or negative.

The scenario it generated for me was very logical, was based on the study guide material, and better yet, was fun to play. Seriously, you must try this. Do your best with a couple of run-throughs, and then do a scenario where you intentionally do everything wrong to see what happens. Make sure you take the time to read the scenarios, because they're great learning tools. You can even tell it to make the scenarios more challenging to choose the best answer at each step.

Study Plans

ChatGPT can make study plans that are completely customized for you. You can have it ask you questions to create the plan.

> Create a study plan for me to prepare for the CCSK v5 exam. Ask me interactive questions to determine how many hours a day I should study

The system asked me how soon I wanted to take the exam and how much time per day I could study. It then created a three-week study plan for me.

ChatGPT Annoyances

I love ChatGPT, but it has its own issues that you're likely to run into. I'm not sure why, but it seems that when it comes to the output it generates, it can be a little hit or miss. My theory is that when you start a session, you are put into a pool of servers that display output a certain way. It could also be that we're all guinea pigs being subjected to A-B testing. I have found, though, that if you keep working, the output format remains the same. However, if you finish for the evening and then come back the next day, you might find yourself being assigned to a different group of servers. The new group may not generate the output in the same way. I can't see this interfering with exam preparation, but just be aware that this will likely happen. For example, you might have detailed answers for prep test question generation one day, and then no rationale generated the next day. The bottom line is that OpenAI appears to be "tweaking" the system all the time.

This is where reissuing the original prompt and giving it an example of the output format based on a previous output may help. To aid this, when you get the prompt and resulting output to what you want, save the prompt you used and the resulting output as an example. That should make subsequent sessions more productive.

Final Exam-Day Thoughts

If you didn't have time to read the entire chapter, here are the most important things to take away for the day of your exam. When you're ready to take the exam, you will want to have two monitors available. Have the exam open on one monitor and the following documents open on the second monitor:

- CCSK v5 study guide PDF
- CCSK v5 guidance PDF
- Latest version (4.x) of the Cloud Controls Matrix Excel file (covered in Chapter 2)

As I mentioned previously, you should be fine with just the study guide (the CSA's words, not just mine). As you'll likely get a few questions on the Cloud Controls Matrix and/or Consensus Assessments Initiative Questionnaire, having that document open isn't a bad thing, just in case.

The exam questions themselves are multiple choice, and several exam questions will not include overly complex scenarios as the basis. The exam is also not an adaptive exam that will stop once the test engine determines a pass or fail grade. You will get all 60 questions in a two-hour time limit.

Remember from the exam tips that I listed earlier that time management for the exam is critical. You have two minutes per question. Don't fall into the trap of thinking you need to research every question just to be sure you're right because it's an open-book exam. If you are confident you know the answer, answer the question and move on. The time saved can be used on the more difficult questions.

Remember also that the test is based on what the CSA says about cloud security. As an open-book exam, there's nothing stopping you from using Google or ChatGPT, but please do not do this. The CSA has perspectives that may not align with what other people or organizations think of cloud security. You also risk blowing your time management by going down rabbit holes. Everything you need to know is in the CCSK study guide.

It is also critical to remember that this is not a vendor exam. You will not get questions on how to configure a particular vendor cloud offering. You will also not get questions that refer to a particular vendor service name (e.g., Azure VNet versus AWS VPC). If you've worked with cloud offerings before, just try to ignore what you know about how a particular vendor implements things. Vendors don't necessarily follow CSA best practices.

Finally, I'm going to go back to my exam tips and remind you of tip 7. Taking the CCSK v5 exam isn't a life-or-death scenario. I know I get anxiety when taking an exam, but remember to breathe and don't get too worked up about the test. Even if you don't pass the first time, you get a second attempt. Also, if you don't pass the first time, please don't get down on yourself. I assure you, you're in good company. I have seen many people with incredible backgrounds fail the first time. Just take note of the domains you did well on and the ones you need to focus on to pass the next time.

You got this. Now go get it.

All my best,

Graham

Index

Symbols
2FA (two-factor authentication), 99

A
ABAC (attribute-based access control), 101
abstraction, 4-5
    IaaS, virtualization of resources, 12
access controls, 98
access policies, data security, 186
account factories, 80
accounts
    definition, 76
    identity management, 81-84
adaptive authentication, 244
AES (Advanced Encryption Standard-256), 191
AI (artificial intelligence), 256
    cloud as workload host, 257-258
    cloud computing, 170
    enhanced tools, 258
    infrastructure security, 174
    LLMs, 256
        assets, 170-171
    model security, 174
    neural networks, 256
    PaaS, 257
    prompt engineering, 266-267
        prompt structure, 267-269
    risk mitigation, 173
    SaaS, 257-257
    security monitoring, 130
    supply chain security, 175
ALE (annual loss expectancy), 56
annual rate of occurrence (ARO), 56
API gateway, logs, 120

APIs (application programming interfaces)
    data encryption, 190
    gateways, security controls, 93-94
    role in IaaS, 13
application plane, 140
application programming interfaces (APIs) (see APIs (application programming interfaces))
application security
    challenges and issues, 199-200
    development lifecycle, 200-201
        stages, 201-204
    post deployment testing, 209-210
    pre-deployment testing, 207-209
    risk assessment matrix, 206-207
    threat modeling, 204-205
        STRIDE model, 205
application security posture management (ASPM), 123
application-based hierarchies, 80
applications, encryption, 191
applistructure (cloud logical model), 6
architecture
    compared to design, 210
    resilience, 211
    security, 134, 211
ARO (annual rate of occurrence), 56
artifact repositories, container images, 161
ASPM (application security posture management), 123
assertion (IAM), 104
asset classification, 45
asset value (AV), 56
assets, 51
asymmetric encryption, 193-194

275

attack surface, 243-244
attack vectors, 51
attackers, 51
attestation engagement report, 63
attribute-based access control (ABAC), 101
attributes (IAM), 100
audit logs, 68
auditing, resource logs, 121
audits, CSPs, 61
authentication, 111-111
    adaptive, 244
    contextual, 245
    continuous, 244-245
    device trust, 245
    IAM, 99
    session monitoring, 245
    UEBA, 244
authoritative sources (IAM), 103
authorization, 110
    hard tokens, 111
    IAM, 99
    out-of-band tokens, 112
    real-time, 243
    soft tokens, 111
auto-scaling, 154
automated security code review, 208
automation, 5
    IaC (infrastructure as code), 147-148
AV (asset value), 56
AWS
    accounts, 76
    policy example, 101-102

B

backups, snap, 159
bare metal servers, 14
bastion hosts, 88
bastion networks, hybrid multicloud model, 87-89
bastions, 88
benchmarks, secure deployment and configuration, 134
blast radius, 77-79
blast zones, digital forensics, 232-233
block storage, 181
blue-green deployment model, 154
broad network access, 10
brute-force attacks, 192
bug bounty programs, 210

buildfiles, container images, 161
business unit hierarchies, 80

C

CAIQ (Consensus Assessments Initiative Questionnaire), 22
    provider assessment, 47-47, 61
CASBs (cloud access and security brokers), 92
cascading log architectures, 85, 129-130
CCM (Cloud Controls Matrix), 22
    cloud governance, 46-47
    control objective example, 40
    policy example, control specification, 38-39
CCoE (Cloud Center of Excellence), 31, 34
    benefits, 36-36
    components and responsibilities, 35-35
CCSK (Certificate of Cloud Security Knowledge)
    ChatGPT as study aid, 263
    description, 260
    domains, mapping to zero trust architecture, 255
    exam -taking advice, 273-274
    registration and cost, 261
    study resources, 259
    test-taking advice, 261-262
CDR (cloud detection and response), 124
Center for Internet Security (CIS), 134
certifications, CSPs, 61
chain of custody, digital forensics, 231
change management
    PaaS, 16
    records of details, 68
    rollback plans, 148
ChatGPT
    context windows, 264
    as exam study aid, 263
    files, uploading and downloading, 265
    flashcards, generating, 270-271
    games as learning tool, 272
    inference, 263
    issues with, 272-273
    pretest questions, generating, 269-270
    projects, 265
    prompt engineering, 266-267
        prompt structure, 267-269
    study plans, 272
    tokens, 264
    training, 264

CI server, 216
CI/CD pipelines, 215-217
    incident analysis, 228
CIEM (cloud infrastructure entitlement management), 123
CIS (Center for Internet Security), 134
classification process, 38, 41
classification techniques, 184
client-side encryption, 188
cloud
    deployment models, 17
        community cloud, 18
        hybrid cloud, 18-19
        multicloud, 19
        private cloud, 18
        public cloud, 18
    host for AI, 257-258
    IAM, 97-98
    infrastructure, CSP security responsibilities, 135
    logical model, 6
        applistructure, 6
        infostructure, 6
    logical structure
        infrastructure, 8
        metastructure, 7-8
    security monitoring, 115-117
    security process model, 23
    security services, compared to traditional environments, 87
    security, frameworks, 37
    storage types, 178-182
cloud access and security brokers (CASBs), 92
cloud breaches, 2-3
cloud bursting, 19, 86
Cloud Center of Excellence (CCoE) (see CCoE (Cloud Center of Excellence))
cloud computing
    AI, 170
    capabilities, 1
    definitions
        ISO/IEC 17788, 5
        ISO/IEC 22123, 5-6
        NIST 800-145, 5-6
    essential characteristics, 9
        broad network access, 10
        measured service, 11
        multitenancy, 11
        on-demand self-service, 10
        rapid elasticity, 10
        resource pooling, 10
    resource pools, 4
    tools, 4-5
cloud connectivity, CSP resources, 144
cloud controller, role in IaaS, 12
Cloud Controls Matrix (CCM) (see CCM (Cloud Controls Matrix))
cloud detection and response (CDR), 124
cloud governance
    CCM (Cloud Controls Matrix), 46-47
    challenges and issues, 29-30
    Cloud Center of Excellence, 31
    cloud registry maintenance, 32-34
    control objectives and specifications, 31
    data and asset classification, 32
    governance hierarchy, 30
    regulatory and legal compliance, 32
    requirements and information gathering, 31
    risk management, 32
    roles and responsibilities, 31
    security frameworks, 30
    security policies, 31
cloud infrastructure entitlement management (CIEM), 123
cloud management plane, 13
    CSP security responsibilities, 136
    digital forensics, 231
    logs, 119
    security monitoring, 116
cloud native applications
    application security posture management, 123
    CIEM, 123
    cloud detection and response, 124
    cloud security posture management, 122
    cloud workload protection platform, 122
    data security posture management, 123
    SaaS security posture management, 122
    security tools, 121
Cloud Security Alliance (CSA) (see CSA (Cloud Security Alliance))
cloud security alliance tools, 46-48
cloud security posture management (CSPM), 122
cloud service customer (CSC), 1
cloud service models, 11
    IaaS, 12-13
    PaaS, 15-16

SaaS, 16-17
cloud service providers (CSPs) (see CSPs (cloud service providers))
cloud sprawl, 75
  security considerations, 116-117
cloud telemetry, 119
  API gateway logs, 120
  management plane logs, 119
  resource logs, 121
  service logs, 120
cloud threat intelligence reports, 54
cloud web application firewalls, 120
cloud workload protection platforms (CWPPs), 122, 157
clusters, 165
COBIT (Control Objectives for Information and Related Technologies), corporate governance definition, 26
collection architecture, 121, 128-130
  cascading log architecture, 129-130
  log storage and retention, 128-129
Common Criteria, 62
community cloud, 18
Complementary User Entity Controls (CUECs), 63
compliance
  AI threats, 172
  artifacts of compliance, 68
    activity reporting, 68
    audit logs, 68
    change management details, 68
    system configuration details, 68
  due care, 73
  due diligence, 73
  jurisdiction considerations, 68-70
  requirements, sources, 67
  resource log retention, 121
configuration
  cloud infrastructure, benchmarks and standards, 134
  management tools, 157
Consensus Assessments Initiative Questionnaire (CAIQ) (see CAIQ (Consensus Assessments Initiative Questionnaire))
consolidated IAM, 84
containers
  container networking, 162-163
  forensics, 233

orchestration and management systems, 163-165
orchestration security, 166
runtime protection, 167-168
secure artifact repositories, 166-167
security, 160
  image creation, 160-162
contextual authentication, 245
continuous authentication, 244-245
continuous integration server, 216
continuous monitoring, 134
Control Objectives for Information and Related Technologies (COBIT), 26
control objectives, governance, 40
control plane, 140
control specifications and implementation, 40-44
controls
  access controls, 98
  normalizing, 87
  types and categories, 52-53
corporate governance, domains, responsibilities, 27
correlation and detection, SIEM, 125
countermeasures, 52
CSA (Cloud Security Alliance)
  documentation, 46-47
  standards, 3
  STAR registry, 48
CSA Large Language Model (LLM) Threats Taxonomy, 171-172
CSC (cloud service customer), 1
CSPM (cloud security posture management), 122
CSPs (cloud service providers)
  advanced security services, 85
  assessment considerations, 44, 58
    compliance requirements, 64-65
    data classification requirements, 65
    documentation, 59-64
    external reviews and recommendations, 64
    final approval, 66
    needs assessment, 59
    required controls, 66
  CAIQ, 22
  DNS logs, 146
  firewalls, 145
  flow logs, 146

hypervisors, 13
incident response, 225-226
infrastructure
    multiprovider resilience, 138-139
    multiregion resilience, 138
    resilience, 136-137
    security responsibilities, 135-136
    single-region resilience, 137
    single-region resilience case study, 137
IP addresses, 4
migrating applications, 2
multicloud deployments, 89
object storage, 180
organizational capabilities, 79-80
organizational hierarchies, 76
policy categories, applying, 82-83
security breaches, 29
security groups, 7
security pillar, 145
    detective controls, 146
    preventative controls, 145
shared responsibility, 17, 20
software-defined networking, 139-142
    connectivity resources, 144
    internet gateways, 144
    load balancers, 144
    NACLs, 143
    private endpoints, 144
    route tables, 143
    security groups, 143
    subnets, 142
    virtual networks, 142
STAR registry, 48
virtual appliances, 145
web application firewalls, 146
CUECs (Complementary User Entity Controls), 63
customer-managed encryption keys, 188
customer-provided encryption keys, 188
CWPPs (cloud workload protection platforms), 122, 157

D

DAAS (Data, Applications, Assets, and Services), 249
DAST (dynamic application security testing), 209
data
    categorization, 178
    classification, 45-45, 178, 183-184
        approaches, 185
        techniques, 184
    encryption, 189
        APIs, 190
        applications, 191
        asymmetric, 193-194
        data at rest, 186
        databases, 190
        files, 190
        hardware security modules, 187
        key generation and management options, 188
        key management, 187
        recommendations, 195-196
        symmetric, 191
        volume storage, 189
    localization laws, 72-74
    ownership, 29
    ownership, SLAs, 60
    security
        access policies, 186
        DSPM, 196
        IAM, 185
        loss prevention, 186
    structures, 177-178
data exfiltration, policies, 83
data loss prevention (DLP), 186
data security posture management (DSPM), 123, 196
Data, Applications, Assets, and Services (DAAS), 249
data/forwarding plane, 139
databases
    encryption, 190
    storage, 181-182
DDoS (distributed denial-of-service) attacks, STRIDE model, 206
dedicated hosts, 14
dedicated private links, hybrid clouds, security considerations, 87
dedicated server instances, 14
dedicated workloads compared to shared workloads, 14
denial-of-service (DoS) attacks (see DoS (denial-of-service) attacks)
deployment
    blue-green model, 154
    CI/CD pipeline, 217

CSA definition, 76
multiple, managing, 76-79
post deployment application testing, 209-210
pre-deployment application testing, 207-209
secure, benchmarks and standards, 134
deployment accounts, 76
deployment models, 85-86
    cloud, 17
        community cloud, 18
        hybrid cloud, 18-19
        multicloud, 19
        private cloud, 18
        public cloud, 18
deployment-level policies, 83-83
design, compared to architecture, 210
detective controls, CSP security pillar, 146
detective guardrails, 134
development environment, security, 166
device trust, 245
DevOps, 213-214
    CI/CD pipeline, 215-217
    lifecycle, 214-215
DevSecOps, 213-214
    CI/CD pipeline, 215-217
    lifecycle, 214-215
Diffie-Hellman key exchange, 193
digital forensics
    blast zones, 232-233
    containers, 233
    legal considerations, 229
    serverless computing, 233
    support contracts, 233-234
    volatile memory, 231-231
    workflow, 230-231
DLP (data loss prevention), data security, 186
DNS logs, 120, 146
DoS (denial-of-service) attacks
    AI threats, 172
DoS (denial-of-service) attacks, STRIDE model, 206
DSPM (data security posture management), 123, 196
due care, 73
due diligence, 73
dynamic application security testing (DAST), 209

E

east-west traffic, networks, 239
EDR (endpoint detection and response), 157
elevation of privilege (EoP) attacks, 206
employees, CSP security responsibilities, 135
encapsulation, network packets, 140
encryption
    APIs, 190
    applications, 191
    asymmetric, 193-194
    data at rest, 186
    databases, 190
    files, 190
    hardware security modules, 187
    key generation and management options, 188
    key management, 187
    object storage, 180, 189
    quantum computing, 195
    recommendations, 195-196
    symmetric, 191
    volume storage, 189
endpoint detection and response (EDR), 157
endpoints, private, 144
entities (IAM), 98
entitlement (IAM), 100
entitlement matrix (IAM), 100
environment-based hierarchies, 80
EoP (elevation of privilege) attacks, STRIDE model, 206
EV (exposure factor), 56
event-driven security, 118
events
    data sources, SOAR, 127-128
    security considerations, 117-118
exposure factor (EV), 56

F

FaaS (function as a service), 168-169
    security issues, 169
facilities, CSP security responsibilities, 135
FAIR (Factor Analysis for Information Risk), 44
Fast Identity Online 2 (FIDO2), 111
feature parity, 75
federated IAM, hybrid cloud security, 87
federated identity brokers, 92
federated identity management, 84
federated identity management (FIM) (see FIM (federated identity management))

FedRAMP, 65
FIDO2 (Fast Identity Online 2), 111
FIM (federated identity management)
    IAM, 103
    OIDC workflow, 105-106
    SAML workflow, 107-108
    standards, 104-105
firewalls, 145
flow logs, 146
forensics (see digital forensics)
forensics support, SIEM, 126
forklifting migration, 2
frameworks
    cloud security, 37
    risk management, 54-58
    security, 21-23
    selection considerations, 46
    zero trust, 248-249
freeform model, 110
full-read access, incident responders, 227
function as a service (FaaS) (see FaaS (function as a service))
function logs, 120
fuzzing, 179

G

gap analysis for the cloud, 44
GDPR, 70-72
geography-based hierarchies, 80
governance, 26, 27
    (see also corporate governance)
    AI threats, 172
    definition, 25
    frameworks, selection considerations, 46
    risk tolerance, 44-45
governance, risk management, compliance (GRC), 66
GRC (governance, risk management, compliance), 66
    compliance, 67-74
group, CSA definition, 76
group-level policies, 82
guardrails, 134-135
guests, 4

H

hard security boundaries, 77
    monitoring considerations, 116
hardware security modules (HSMs), 187

hardware, infrastructure, 12
HKOK (hold your own key), 188
HMAC (hash-based message authentication), 206
host machines, 4
HSMs (hardware security modules), 187
hub-and-spoke model, 109
hybrid clouds, 18-19
    definition, 86
    features, 85
    security, organizational management, 86-89
hybrid multicloud model, bastion networks, 87-89
hypervisors, 4, 13

I

IaaS (infrastructure as a service), 12-13
IaC (infrastructure as code)
    provisioning and managing infrastructure, 147-148
    scanning templates, 208
IAM (identity access management), 16
IAM (identity and access management), 97
    cloud considerations, 97-98
    data security, 185
    federated, hybrid cloud security, 87
    incident response, containment, 234-235
    relaying party, 103
    secrets management, 212
        workflow, 213
    serverless computing, 169
    terminology, 98-104
IAST (interactive application security testing), 209
identifier (IAM), 99
identity (IAM), 99
identity access management (IAM), 16
identity brokers
    cloud access and security brokers, 92
    federated, 92
identity management, 81, 108
    (see also IAM (identity and access management))
    account access, 81-84
    architectural patterns, 109-110
    overview, 108
IdP (identity provider)
    IAM, 103
    incident response, 234

IEC (International Electrotechnical Commission), definition of cloud computing, 6
IGWs (internet gateways), 144
image factories, secure images, 155-156
images
    containers, creating, 160-162
    VMs, 153
        creating secure, 155-156
immutable servers, 154
impact likelihood matrix, 44
incident detection and analysis, 228
incident response, 222
    containment and management, 245
    CSP support contracts, 226
    data classification, 183
    digital forensics
        legal considerations, 229
        workflow, 230-231
    eradication of activities, 235
    IAM containment, 234-235
    lifecycle phases, 222-225
    network containment, 235
    post-incident analysis, 236-237
    preparation, 225-226
    recovery, 236
    SIEM, 126
    staff training, 226-227
information disclosure
    security issues, 178
    STRIDE model, 206
Information Systems Audit and Control Association (ISACA), 26
infostructure (cloud logical model), 6
infrastructure
    AI, security, 174
    cloud logical model, 8
    multiprovider resilience, 138-139
    multiregion resilience, 138
    provisioning and managing, 147-148
    resilience, 136-137
    security responsibilities, CSPs, 135-136
    single-region resilience, 137
        case study, 137
infrastructure as a service (IaaS), 12
initialization vector (IV), 192
instances, VMs, 4, 153
interactive application security testing (IAST), 209

International Electrotechnical Commission (IEC), 6
International Organization for Standardization (ISO), 5
internet gateways (IGWs), 144
IP addresses, network pools, 4
ISACA (Information Systems Audit and Control Association), corporate governance definition, 26
ISO (International Organization for Standardization), cloud computing definition, 5
ISO/IEC 17788, 5, 6, 11
ISO/IEC 22123, 5-6, 11
ISO/IEC 27001, 22, 61, 63
ISO/IEC 27002, 22, 64
ISO/IEC 27017, 23, 61
ISO/IEC 27018, 23, 64
isolated servers, types, 14
isolation, VM security, 14
IT governance (ITG) (see ITG (IT governance))
IT security governance, structure, 36
    frameworks, 37
    policies, 37-39
    security control objectives, 40
    specifications and implementation guidance, 40-44
IT, traditional compared to cloud computing, 1
ITG (IT governance), 27-28
    (see also corporate governance)
    domains, 27-28
IV (initialization vector), 192

J

jumpboxes, 88
jurisdictions
    compliance, 68-70
    data localization laws, 72
just culture, 236-237

K

KMSs (key management services), 187
Kubernetes, 163-165

L

landing zones, 80
large language models (LLMs) (see LLMs (large language models))
least privilege, 98, 245

legal requirements, framework selection considerations, 46
LGPD (General Personal Data Protection Law), 72
liability, cloud governance issues, 29
libraries, container images, 161
lift-and-shift migration, 2
LLMs (large language models), 256
    assets, 170-171
    threat, 171-172
    threat categories, 171-172
load balancers, 144
logs
    API gateway, 120
    audit, 68
    cascading architectures, 129-130
    cascading log architecture, 85
    digital forensics, management plane, 231
    DNS, 146
    flow, 146
    incident analysis, 228
    management plane, 119
    metastructure security, 8
    normalization, 124-125
    resource, 121
    security considerations, 117-118
    service, 120
    storage and retention, 128-129

M

management plane (see cloud management plane)
measured service, 11
Meltdown vulnerability, 14
metadata read access, incident responders, 227
metastructure (cloud logical model), 7-8
metrics, usefulness, 119
MFA (multifactor authentication), 111-112
    IAM, 99
microperimeters, network security, 240
microsegmentation, networks, 240
migration, without changes, 2
monitoring, 119
    (see also security monitoring)
    cloud telemetry, 119
        API gateway logs, 120
        management plane logs, 119
        resource logs, 121
        service logs, 120
    continuous, 134
    posture management, 119
    security, AI, 130
    session, 245
multiclouds, 19
    deployment, 86
    portability issues, 90
    security, organizational management, 89-90
multifactor authentication (MFA) (see MFA (multifactor authentication))
multiple deployments
    managing, 76-79
    policies, consistency across, 84-85
multiprovider resilience, 138-139
multiregion resilience, 138
multitenancy, 11
    risks, 14

N

NACLs (network access control lists), 143
National Institute of Standards and Technology (NIST), 5
network access control lists, 143
network fabric, 143
network logs, 120
network pool, IP addresses, 4
network security, hybrid clouds, 86
networking, CSPs
    connectivity resources, 144
    internet gateways, 144
    load balancers, 144
    NACLs, 143
    private endpoints, 144
    route tables, 143
    security groups, 143
    software-defined networking, 139-142
    subnets, 142
    virtual networks, 142
networks
    container networking, 162-163
    incident response, containment, 235
    isolation, packet encapsulation, 140
    overlays, 140-142
    SDN automation of operations, 140
    zoning, 239
neural networks, 256
NIST (National Institute of Standards and Technology), cloud computing definition, 5
NIST 800-145, 5-6, 10-11

NIST SP 800-53, 23
nonrelational databases, storage, 182
normalizing controls, 87
north-south traffic, networks, 239
NoSQL databases, storage, 182

O

OAuth 2.0, 105
object storage
    encryption, 189
    security, 180
    technical aspects, 179-180
    versioning, 180
OIDC (OpenID Connect), 105
    workflow, 105-106
on-demand self-service, 10
operational hierarchies, types, 80
orchestration, 5
    container management, 163-165
    container security, 166
organization, CSA definition, 76
organization-wide policies, 82
organizational hierarchies, 78
organizational structures, 76-79
    blast radius, 77-79
overlay networks, 140-142

P

PaaS (platform as a service), 15-16
    AI, 257
    CSP security responsibilities, 136
packet encapsulation, 140
PAM (privileged access management), 113
Pandemic 11, 54
pass-through assessments, 91
pass-through audits, 61-64
pay-as-you-go computing model, 11
PBAC (policy-based access control), 101-102
PCI DSS, requirements, 64-65
PDP (policy decision point), 148
    zero trust, 247-248
penetration testing, 209
PEP (policy enforcement point), 148
    zero trust, 247-248
performance, metrics, 119
permissions, object storage, 179
personas (IAM), 100
PIM (privileged identity management), 112
PIPs (policy information points), 148, 247

platform as a service (PaaS) (see PaaS (platform as a service))
playbooks, SOAR, 128
policies
    consistency across deployments, 84-85
    CSPs, categories, 82-83
    data exfiltration, 83
    data security, 186
    format and scope, 37-39
    guardrails, 134-135
    override capabilities, 84
    types, 101
    usage scenarios, 83
policy decision point (PDP) (see PDP (policy decision point))
policy enforcement point (PEP) (see PEP (policy enforcement point))
policy information points (PIPs), 148, 247
policy-based access control (PBAC), 101-102
post-deployment testing, application security, 209-210
posture management, monitoring, 119
pre-deployment testing, application security, 207-209
preshared keys, 193
preventative controls, CSP security pillar, 145
preventive guardrails, 134
privacy laws
    GDPR, 70-72
    jurisdiction considerations, 68-70
    LGPD, 72
privacy, governance considerations, 29
private cloud, 18
private endpoints, 144
private keys, 194
privileged access management (PAM), 113
privileged identity management (PIM), 112
processes, risk management, 54-58
prompt engineering, AI, 266-267
    prompt structure, 267-269
protect surface, 252-254
provisioning infrastructure, 147-148
public clouds, 18
    network security considerations, 87
public keys, 193

Q

qualitative assessments, 56
quantitative assessments, 56

quantum computing, encryption, 195

R

rapid elasticity, 10
RASP (runtime application self-protection), 203
RBAC (role-based access control), 100
reactive guardrails, 134
real-time authorization, 243
regulations
  data classification, 183
  frame selection considerations, 46
relational databases, storage, 181
relaying party (RP) (see RP (relaying party))
repudiation (STRIDE model), 206
residual risk, 53, 57
resource logs, 121
resource pools, 4, 10
resources
  provisioning, 10
  scalability, 10
risk appetite, 55
  (see also risk tolerance)
risk assessment, application security, 206-207
risk management, 32
  policies, consistency across deployments, 84-85
  process steps, 54-58
  terminology, 51-54
risk mitigation, 53, 56
  AI threats, 173
risk tolerance, governance considerations, 44-45
risk-based data classification approach, 183
RoEs (rules of engagement), 210
role-based access control (RBAC), 100
roles (IAM), 100
rollback plans, infrastructure change management, 148
route tables, 143
RP (relaying party)
  IAM, 103
  incident response, 234
rules of engagement (RoEs), 210
running instances, VMs, 153
runtime
  container images, 160
  protection for containers, 167-168

runtime application self-protection (RASP), 203

S

SaaS (software as a service), 16-17
  AI, 257-257
  cloud management challenges, 91
    API gateways, 93-94
    cloud access and security brokers, 92
    federated identity brokers, 92
  cloud storage options, 182
  CSP security responsibilities, 136
  security and compliance reviews, 91
SaaS security posture management (SSPM), 122
SAML, 104
  workflow, 107-108
SANs (storage area networks), 4
SASE (Secure Access Service Edge), zero trust architectures, 150-151
SAST (static application security testing), 208-208
SBOM, 208
SCA (software composition analysis), 208
SDLC (secure development lifecycle), 200-201
  stages, 201-204
SDN (software-defined networking), 139-142
  cloud connectivity resources, 144
  internet gateways, 144
  load balancers, 144
  NACLs, 143
  private endpoints, 144
  route tables, 143
  security groups, 143
  subnets, 142
  virtual networks, 142
SDN controller, 140
SDP (software-defined perimeter), 149-150, 248
secrets management, 212
  workflow, 213
Secure Access Service Edge (SASE), 150-151
secure artifact repositories, 166-167
secure development lifecycle (SDLC) (see SDLC (secure development lifecycle))
secure software development lifecycle (SSDLC), 200
security, 199
  (see also application security; data, security; IAM (identity and access management))

access controls, 98
API gateways, 93-94
architecture, 134
architecture-level, 211
authentication, 111-111
authorization, 110
    hard tokens, 111
    out-of-band tokens, 112
    soft tokens, 111
broad network access, 10
cascading log architecture, 85
cloud infostructure, 6
cloud metastructure, 8
cloud threat list, 54
control objectives, 40
data
    access policies, 186
    IAM, 185
    loss prevention, 186
data classification, 183-184
event escalation model, 222
frameworks, 21-23, 37
groups, 143
guardrails, 134-135
IAM
    importance, 85
    in the cloud, 97-98
    terminology, 98-104
infrastructure, CSP responsibilities, 135-136
isolated servers, 14
least privilege, 98
metrics, 119
monitoring, 115
    accounts and subscriptions, 116
    AI, 130
    cloud sprawl, 116-117
    events, 117-118
    logs, 117-118
    management plane, 116
    responding to resource changes, 116
    responsibilities, 117
multitenancy, risks, 14
PaaS considerations, 16
PAM, 113
policies, 31
    general format and scope, 37-39
privileged identity management, 112
process model, 23
risk tolerance assessment, 44

SaaS considerations, 16
SDP (software-defined perimeter), 149-150
serverless computing, 168-169
shared responsibility, 20
as shared responsibility model, 2
shifting left, 147
snapshots, 159
storage, 178
techniques, 134-135
tools
    cloud detection and response, 124
    cloud infrastructure entitlement management, 123
    cloud native applications, 121-122
    cloud security posture management, 122
    cloud workload protection platform, 122
    data security posture management, 123
    SaaS security posture management, 122
VM isolation, 14
zero trust, 148, 239
    business benefits, 246
    components, 247-248
    design implementation, 252-255
    design principles, 252
    pillar maturity levels, 250-251
    pillars, 249-250
    principles, 241
    security benefits, 241-246
    security frameworks, 248-249
    ZTNA (Zero Trust Network Access), 150-150
security data lakes, 85
security information and event management (SIEM) (see SIEM (security information and event management))
security orchestration, automation, and response (SOAR) (see SOAR (security orchestration, automation, and response))
security pillar, CSPs, 145
    detective controls, 146
    preventative controls, 145
security through obscurity, security issues, 179
Security, Trust, Assurance, and Risk (STAR), 48
semistructured data, 178
server-side encryption, 188
serverless computing
    forensics, 233
    IAM, 169
    security, 168-169

service credits, 60
service level agreements (SLAs), 60
service logs, 120
session keys, 194
session monitoring, 245
settings, container images, 161
Shadow IT, 10
    SaaS, 17
shared responsibility models
    example scenario, 2
    governance issues, 29-30
    incident response, 225
    security considerations, 20
shared security responsibility model (SSRM), 20
shared services, consolidated IAM, 84
shared workloads compared to dedicated workloads, 14
shift left (security), 147
SIEM (security information and event management), 124, 157
    correlation and detection, 125
    incident response and forensics support, 126
    log normalization, 124-125
    threat intelligence, 125
    user and entity behavior analytics, 126-127
Simple Notification Service (SNS), 118
single loss expectancy (SLE), 56
Single Sign-On (SSO), 103
single-region resilience, 137
    case study, 137
SLAs (service level agreements), 60
SLE (single loss expectancy), 56
SMEs (subject matter experts), hybrid cloud environments, 89
    staffing levels, 91
snapshots, 159
    digital forensics, 230
SNS (Simple Notification Service), security notifications, 118
SOAR (security orchestration, automation, and response), 127, 157
    event data sources, 127-128
    playbooks, 128
SOC reports, 62-63
soft security boundaries, 77
software as a service (SaaS) (see SaaS (software as a service))

software composition analysis (SCA), 208
software-defined infrastructure, 13
software-defined networking (SDN), 139
software-defined perimeter (SDP), 149
Spectre vulnerability, 14
SPI stack (cloud service models), 11
spoofing (STRIDE model), 205
SSDLC (secure software development lifecycle), 200
SSO (Single Sign-On), 103
SSPM (SaaS security posture management), 122
SSRM (shared security responsibility model), 20
standards
    federated identity management, 104-105
    secure deployment and configuration, 134
STAR (Security, Trust, Assurance, and Risk), 48
    STAR Attestation, 48
    STAR Certification, 48
STAR registry
    CSP assessments, 61
Statements on Standards for Attestation Engagements (SSAE) 18, 62
static application security testing (SAST), 208
storage
    block storage, 181
    data encryption, 189
    database storage, 181-182
    digital forensics, 230
    location considerations, 182
    logs, 128-129
    SaaS, 182
    security, 178
    snapshots, 159
    types, 178-182
    volume storage, 181
storage area networks (SANs), 4
storage logs, 120
storage pools, 4
STRIDE (threat modeling), 205-206
structured data, 177
study resources, CCSK exam, 259
subnets, 142
support contracts
    CSPs, 226
    role in forensics, 233-234
symmetric encryption, 191

Index | 287

T

tampering (STRIDE model), 205
targets, 51
terms of service (ToS), 61
third-party audits, 61-64
threat intelligence, incident analysis, 229
threat modeling, 204-205
    STRIDE model, 205-206
threats, 52
    intelligence, SIEM, 125
    list of, 54
Time-based One-Time Password (TOTP), 111
TLS handshakes, 194
tokens, authentication, 111-112
ToS (terms of service), 61
TOTP (Time-based One-Time Password), 111
traditional IT compared to cloud computing, 1
transaction flows, 253
transit networks, 88
Trust Services Criteria, 62
two-factor authentication (2FA), 99
Type 1 hypervisors, 13
Type 2 hypervisors, 13

U

UEBA (user and entity behavior analytics), 244
    SIEM, 126-127
unstructured data, 177
user agent, 108
user and entity behavior analytics (UEBA) (see UEBA (user and entity behavior analytics))
user authentication, multiple cloud services, 85

V

version control repository, 216
virtual appliances, 145
Virtual Extensible LAN (VXLAN), 140
virtual machine monitors (VMMs), 13
virtual machines (VMs) (see VMs)
virtual private clouds, 142
virtualization, 13
    infrastructure, CSP security responsibilities, 135
VMMs (virtual machine monitors), 13
VMs (virtual machines), 4, 13, 153-154

images, creating secure, 155-156
security challenges, 155
volume storage, 181
volume storage encryption, 189
vulnerabilities, 52
    management lifecycle, 158
    mitigation, 159
VXLAN (Virtual Extensible LAN)
    compared to VLANs, 140-141

W

WAFs (web application firewalls), 120, 146, 217
    deployment models, 217-219
Well-Architected Framework, 23
work factor, 192
workloads
    containers, 160
        image creation, 160-162
    shared compared to dedicated, 14

X

XaaS, 11

Z

zero trust (see ZT (zero trust))
zero trust architecture (ZTA) (see ZTA (zero trust architecture))
Zero Trust Network Access (ZTNA), 150
zoning, networks, 239
ZT (zero trust), 148, 239
    business benefits, 246
    components, 247-248
    design implementation, 252-255
    design principles, 252
    pillar maturity levels, 250-251
    pillars, 249-250
    principles, 241
    SASE (Secure Access Service Edge), 150-151
    security benefits, 241-246
    security frameworks, 248-249
ZTA (zero trust architecture), 241
    pillars, 249-250
ZTNA (Zero Trust Network Access), 150-150, 248-249

About the Author

Graham Thompson is an information security professional with over 25 years of enterprise experience across engineering, architecture, assessment, and training disciplines. He is the author of the *CCSK Certificate of Cloud Security Knowledge All-in-One Exam Guide* (McGraw-Hill) and is a principal trainer for the Cloud Security Alliance.

Colophon

The animal on the cover of *Certificate of Cloud Security Knowledge (CCSK v5) Official Study Guide* is an Old English sheepdog. It is a large, thickset breed of dog known for its long, shaggy coat of gray and white fur, which often covers its eyes. Its shoulders are lower than its hips, leading to a distinctive bear-like shuffle as it walks.

As the name suggests, they were originally bred for herding work, though the breed is not actually old, having been developed in the 18th century. Full-grown Old English sheepdogs can reach 22 to 24 inches high at the withers and between 60 and 100 pounds, with males slightly larger and heavier than females. They are known to be intelligent and even-tempered and have been popular as show dogs for many years.

Many of the animals on O'Reilly covers are endangered; all of them are important to the world.

The cover illustration is by Karen Montgomery, based on an antique line engraving. The series design is by Edie Freedman, Ellie Volckhausen, and Karen Montgomery. The cover fonts are Gilroy Semibold and Guardian Sans. The text font is Adobe Minion Pro; the heading font is Adobe Myriad Condensed; and the code font is Dalton Maag's Ubuntu Mono.

O'REILLY®

Learn from experts.
Become one yourself.

60,000+ titles | Live events with experts | Role-based courses
Interactive learning | Certification preparation

 Try the O'Reilly learning platform free for 10 days.